THE

THE EVERYTHING® AMERICAN HISTORY BOOK

People, places, and events that shaped our nation

Loriann Hoff Oberlin

Adams Media Corporation
Avon, Massachusetts

An Everything® Series Book.
Everything® is a registered trademark of Adams Media Corporation.

Published by Adams Media Corporation
57 Littlefield Street, Avon, MA 02322
www.adamsmedia.com

ISBN: 1-58062-531-2
Printed in the United States of America.

J I H G F E D C B A

Library of Congress Cataloging-in-Publication Data
Hoff Oberlin, Loriann
The everything American history book / by Loriann Hoff Oberlin.
p. cm.
Includes index.
ISBN 1-58062-531-2
1. United States–History. 2. United States–History–Miscellanea. I. Title.
E178 .H723 2001
973–dc21 2001022610

Cover illustrations by Barry Littmann.
Interior illustrations by Roberta Collier Morales, Barry Littmann, and Kurt Dolber.

To my father,
Elmer Hoff, the avid historian.

CONTENTS

☆ Chapter 5 ☆

Shaping a New Nation and Government / 57

☆ Chapter 6 ☆

Early American Struggles / 75

☆ Chapter 7 ☆

A Country Unraveling / 91

☆ Chapter 8 ☆

The Civil War / 105

☆ Chapter 9 ☆

Mending America / 125

☆ Chapter 10 ☆

The Age of Industry, Invention, and Discovery / 139

☆ Chapter 11 ☆

The World War I Era / 153

☆ Chapter 12 ☆

The Great Depression / 169

☆ Chapter 13 ☆

The World War II Era / 181

Acknowledgments

History has always been a favorite subject of mine. Researching it was quite another story. I'd forgotten just how complex our national heritage was, and still is–the 2000 presidential election certainly convinced me of that. Nonetheless, after months of reading and research, this book came to print with the help of the following generous (and patriotic, if you please) souls:

Pam Liflander continues to be a wonderful editor to work with, and I thank her for the project. My two sons, Andy and Alex, sat through hours of history videos and helped me in my role as adventurous tourist so that I could encourage your family to do the same. They'll thank *me* when they're older! Bob Laurenzano showed me the intricacies of New York City and Washington, D.C., and ventured to Williamsburg to help me learn about these fascinating cities where history overflows. Special thanks goes to Kevin Gaydosh and Kingsmill Resort–a great place to unwind near Colonial Williamsburg. And my father, Elmer Hoff, always the historian, always the proud World War II veteran, put his extensive library to excellent use. Here's to this book I feel certain dad would like, for with terms like Eisenhower, Patton, and "the Bulge," how could he not!

–Loriann Hoff Oberlin

Introduction

How is it that a country barely out of its infancy, compared with its European counterparts, can be so respected, awed, and revered? In some respects, it's amazing. In others, it comes as no surprise.

People are proud to be associated with the United States of America. It's so respected that hardly anyone renounces U.S. citizenship, and indeed many risk their lives to obtain it. America is a country so creative that it overflows with achievement in virtually every arena of life, and its heritage is so enduring that it makes for fascinating stories and study.

Just look at what Americans have accomplished in the short span of 225 years. And the amazing part is, we're all contributing in some way to the next stages in history. Yes, ordinary citizens, like you and me, make a difference in large and small ways. With scientific and technological breakthroughs, cures for ailments and diseases, intellectual insights and artistic expressions, faith, fads, and fancy outfits, votes, obsessions, and foibles—the list never seems quite complete.

Chances are, your place in history is still evolving in a personal and collective sense. What better way to make a mark on American culture and move forward in a new millennium than by reading, learning, and visiting the highlights of what got us as a country and as a people to this point in time!

Of the subjects I studied in elementary school, American history stands out for the rich texture of stories and fascinating facts woven into legends. It's no wonder I spent an entire summer in high school with a bicentennial book in hand, or why history became my favorite category when playing Trivial Pursuit. It's why some citizens can recite certain passages of important speeches or documents, or follow a particular event with pride, as my father has with World War II. Indeed history is a subject that comes alive with each unique retelling. It's a heritage and a legacy.

If you're still wondering whether American history can come alive for you, this book should convince you that it can. In the pages ahead, you'll read interesting facts and explanations, revisit material you may not have encountered since grade school, and be challenged to explore many historical settings as they exist today. That's the unique component of this book–your ability to step back in time by visiting living history museums, cities our founding fathers built, and monuments erected for the sole purpose of our reflection, reminding us of other circumstances.

Maybe you've never thought about visiting modern-day sights such as Williamsburg, Virginia, flying off to walk the Freedom Trail in Boston, Massachusetts, or stepping aboard the USS *Arizona* Memorial in Hawaii. I hope that this book will inspire you. Who knows, you might even plan your next vacation around some of these destinations and sights. For families with children, this book may make a real difference in turning those children on to the richness of American history.

That's because our country's history, as defined in *The Everything® American History Book*, is more than Christopher Columbus and his ships, General George Washington and his militia, or even the dedicated troops of Desert Storm. It's people like Mister Rogers, Walt Disney, and Oprah Winfrey–all legends of their time, all contributing to what we have today. Here, history is also a visit to Plymouth, Massachusetts, a boat ride to the Statue of Liberty and Ellis Island, or a stroll through the Smithsonian. Learning sinks in so much better when you can see, hear, and reflect on what happened years ago. Time travel was never so much fun!

The goal of this book is to make American history enjoyable, with interesting glimpses into the people and places that brought us to the present. This book probably won't make the recommended or your reading list of college history majors, but if it gets you or your children to turn off the PlayStation and turn on the History Channel, if it incites the idea of a new and different vacation, if you find just the right book or video for that curious soul on your gift-giving list, or if it makes you just a little more comfortable with a vast and sometimes intimidating subject, then it's been successful. Ultimately, if it boosts your score in Trivial Pursuit, I'll be happy!

–Loriann Hoff Oberlin

1

DISCOVERING THE NEW WORLD

To the Ends of the Earth

It's often believed that Columbus had to work hard to convince the king and queen, as well as his crew, that the Earth was spherical rather than flat. However, at the end of the fifteenth century, the idea of a round world was not a new concept. Even some ancient Greeks such as Aristotle believed in the Earth's roundness. So Columbus was hardly alone in this notion.

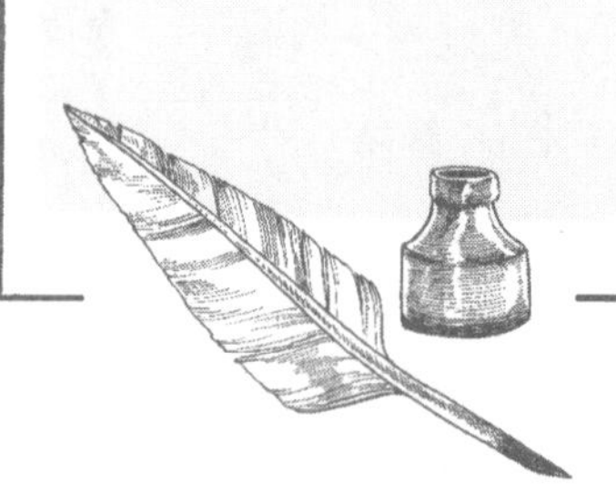

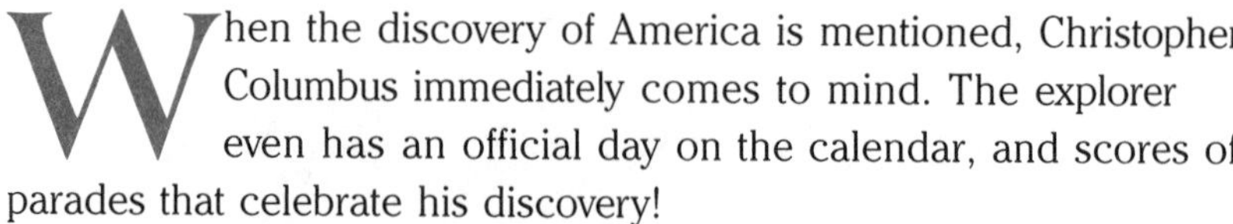

When the discovery of America is mentioned, Christopher Columbus immediately comes to mind. The explorer even has an official day on the calendar, and scores of parades that celebrate his discovery!

Christopher Columbus was born near Genoa, in northern Italy, in 1451. Young Columbus began his seafaring career shortly after Portuguese navigators reached the Cape Verde Islands off the coast of West Africa in 1460. A few years later, he sailed commercial routes between Genoa and other Mediterranean ports before voyages to the Aegean island of Khios (near what is now Turkey), England, the Portuguese island of Madeira, and Guinea (on Africa's west coast). In between these journeys, he married and became a father.

Columbus Had a Hunch

Around 1483, Columbus went to King John II of Portugal for endorsement of his plan to discover a new route to Asia by sailing west. Asia had what everyone wanted back then—spices. These aren't simply the mildly aromatic pleasures that enhanced the taste of food. This was long before Whirlpool refrigerators! Spices were essential for preserving food. But Columbus met rejection. By 1485 and now a widower, Columbus moved with his son to Spain. Persistent as ever, he presented a plan the following year to Isabella of Castile and Ferdinand of Aragon, the queen and king of Spain. Again, Columbus was refused. However, in 1489 Queen Isabella listened to Columbus again. He left their meeting with hopes of organizing a future expedition, once Spain's war with the Moors was over.

Ready, Set, Sail

Two years passed with no developments. Columbus grew frustrated with the delays and even prepared to leave Spain, but was summoned by Queen Isabella, who gave him the assurances he needed. Sure enough, the Moors surrendered in 1492, and the Spanish sovereigns approved Columbus's expedition to find a western route to Asia on behalf of Spain. Preparations in the Spanish port of Palos began in May with the requisitioning of three ships, and by August the *Niña*, *Pinta*, and *Santa María* set sail. The expedition was financed in part by royal money granted by the king and queen as well as Columbus's own private funding. What was in it for Columbus? The seafarer was commissioned with the promise that he would receive one-tenth of the profits from the expeditions, and he was granted several titles, including "Admiral of the Ocean Sea," viceroy, and governor of whatever lands he discovered.

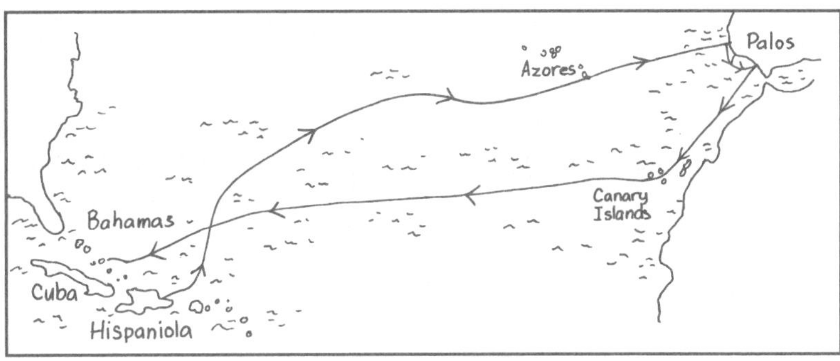

MAP OF COLUMBUS'S VOYAGE IN 1492

And over the horizon they went. After taking on supplies in the Canary Islands and sailing over the vast sea, on October 12, 1492, crew members of the *Santa María* sighted land. The natives they encountered called the land Guanahani, which Columbus later dubbed San Salvador. Historians still argue about the precise landing spot, but we know it was somewhere in the Bahamas.

Oops

Columbus believed he had found Asia, but actually he'd miscalculated the distance, and a few other minor details. In fact, to say he misjudged would be an understatement. Some believe he underestimated the Earth's size by 25 percent. Many people, including Columbus, thought the oceans were far smaller than they really are, and that the land masses were much larger. His crew wasn't the least bit pleased that their journey took as long as it did. There were rumblings of mutiny.

Believing he'd landed in Asia, or the Indies, Columbus called the natives he encountered "Indians." Since he hadn't found the spices he was looking for, he kept sailing, discovering Cuba and Hispaniola (modern-day Haiti and the Dominican Republic). In a Christmas Day storm, the *Santa María* struck a coral reef, split open, and sank. The exact location of the wreck is unknown, but it's thought to be in the vicinity of today's Cap-Haitien in Haiti.

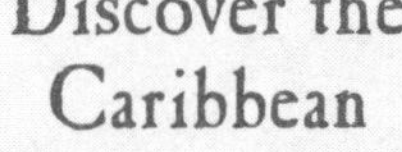

To learn more about the development of these islands, read *A Brief History of the Caribbean: From the Arawak and the Carib to the Present* by Jan Rogozinski. Travel guides covering the Bahamas and Caribbean are plentiful. Magazines such as *Caribbean Travel & Life* and *Islands* devote themselves to the region.

THE FIRST COLONY

Columbus didn't know what to do with the survivors of the *Santa María*. The *Pinta* wasn't nearby, and the *Niña,* the smallest of the fleet, could not make room for the *Santa María's* crew. So in the end, Columbus decided to leave behind thirty-nine of his men to establish a colony he named La Navidad, the first attempt at European settlement since the Vikings. Some actually volunteered to stay behind in the Caribbean outpost. (Imagine the beauty of the Caribbean back then—this was probably a no-brainer!) Among them were a surgeon, a barrel-maker, an artillery man, and a tailor, in addition to the many seamen who made up the crew.

These European settlers discovered not only a new land, but new ways of living and eating. For instance, the Arawak Indians slept in hand-woven *hamacas*, or hammocks, as we know them today. Columbus's men discovered a new diet of corn (maize), sweet potatoes, and red chili pepper, and they learned to grow squash, pumpkins, and beans. Then there was the botanical novelty these Indians smoked—tobacco. In turn, the Arawaks learned how to farm with cattle, pigs, and horses that the Europeans later brought with them. However, with the novel comes the dreaded. The Native Americans had no resistance to European diseases, and many succumbed to smallpox, whooping cough, and measles.

COLUMBUS HAILED BY SPANISH COURT

Columbus sailed home triumphantly. He took several Native Americans as proof of his successful expedition. In fact, Columbus made his way to the Portuguese king—the same monarch who once refused to support the admiral's voyage—before heading back to Spain. While in Lisbon, he wrote a soon-to-be-famous letter describing his Caribbean discoveries, and shortly thereafter appeared before Queen Isabella and King Ferdinand. This was his moment of glory!

They're Back

After an absence of six and a half years, the *Pinta* reappeared in Hispaniola. When Columbus had departed years before, he'd left La Navidad unfortified, for he assumed the relations between his settlers and the Indians were amicable. Little did he suspect that the Spaniards would take to pillaging and plundering, and that the once-friendly Indians would retaliate in defense. No doubt some colonists also succumbed to illness and perhaps were unaccustomed to the tropical climate. On his return voyage in 1493, Columbus found no survivors at the settlement. There would be no reunion.

Fourteen caravels sailed as part of Columbus's second expedition. That second crossing was fairly uneventful, with another stop at the Canary Islands to take on provisions along with sheep, mares, goats, and pigs. Columbus set a more southerly course this time, aiming for unexplored islands he'd learned about. These included Dominica, Guadalupe (now Guadeloupe), Puerto Rico, and Jamaica.

Unhappy that his first settlement site had been dictated by the shipwreck, Columbus chose to sail east to establish another new colony. But this time weather was a deterring factor. With trade winds so strong he could not safely continue sailing, he chose another site for his new settlement (still on Hispaniola), which he named La Isabela. Surprisingly, perhaps, this great explorer still believed that Cuba was a part of the Asian mainland and that he wasn't far off his original course. No doubt he was impressed by the verdant splendor of the Caribbean, but he was discouraged to find none of the golden treasures that Marco Polo had described from his journeys in Asia.

Did Vikings Discover America?

Some believe that around the year 1000, the Norse explorer Leif Eriksson, the second son of Erik the Red, found the North American shore, which he called Vinland for its profusion of wild grapes.

Other experts think Leif came after the Norseman Bjarni Heriulfsson, who first came to North America around 986. Some believe he settled in Newfoundland, while others favor Nova Scotia, or even New England.

In 1963, archaeologists found ruins of a Viking settlement in northern Newfoundland—a settlement that corresponds to Eriksson's description of Vinland. Leif's brother Thorvald established a colony, but relations with the natives were poor. The Vikings were forced to flee.

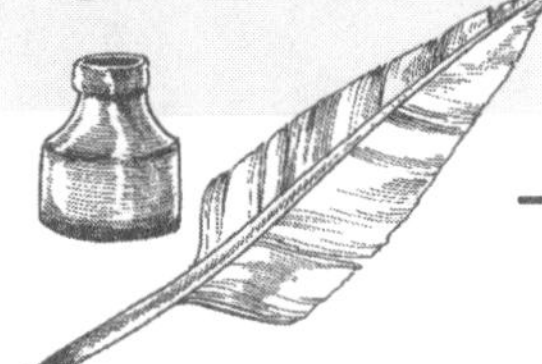

Poor Management

During his life, Columbus held the titles of admiral, viceroy, and governor. But how was he at administering these new lands? Well, in all honesty, his leadership was lacking.

Columbus made a series of blunders, including leaving his brother in command of La Isabela. It's said he also adopted harsh measures against the natives and had a heavy hand when it came to disciplining his own men. Rather than sending gold back to the Spanish court, Columbus captured natives, sending them home to be sold as slaves. The natives revolted, skirmishes ensued at the colony, and Queen Isabella objected to the slaves, sending a royal commission to investigate things. Because of the criticism he received, Columbus established a new capital, calling it Santo Domingo. He then retreated to Spain to plan yet a third voyage.

Hollywood Heralds Columbus

Commemorating the 500th anniversary of Columbus's discovery, moviegoers were able to watch *1492: Conquest of Paradise* on the big screen back in 1992. The film starred Armand Assante, Sigourney Weaver, and Gerard Depardieu as Christopher Columbus.

Dividing and Conquering

Not long before this time, a decree called the Treaty of Toledo, signed in 1480, had divided Portuguese and Spanish territories. This gave Portugal territorial rights to Morocco and other areas, and prohibited Spain from sailing beyond the Canary Islands.

It is thought that Columbus may have intentionally reported the latitude of his discoveries incorrectly, knowing full well these islands belonged to Portugal by the terms of the treaty. Remember, there was no love lost between Columbus and the Portuguese, who had rejected his voyage plans years before. Politics wasn't pretty even back then!

But in 1493, Pope Alexander VI issued a papal bull (decree) that a line be drawn from north to south dividing the Atlantic Ocean. He decreed that all lands discovered to the east of that line would belong to Portugal. Everything to the west would be property of Spain. It was quite convenient for Columbus that the new pope was Spanish!

Third Time the Charm?

Competition among the explorers was growing intense. Portugal had sent Vasco da Gama on an expedition in 1497. He reached

Visit the Bahamas and Caribbean Today

If you'd like to explore the lush, flowered, and forested islands Columbus visited, you have many options. The Bahamas and Caribbean islands include British colonies, French departments, U.S. territories, and independent islands ready for you and your family to discover.

Strewn over 100,000 square miles, the Bahamas consist of a vast archipelago. New Providence Island, where Nassau is nestled, is the most populated, and a frequent cruise port of call with its famous Straw Market and casinos. Grand Bahama Island boasts resort centers Freeport and Lucaya. The Out Islands are known among serious scuba divers, yachtsmen, and cruise lines, which often feature their own private islands. These islands treat visitors to steel bands and the calypso beat, duty-free shopping, and a laid-back lifestyle. Rainforests can be found on some islands while white sand beaches are prevalent throughout.

Savor West Indian cuisine with spicy dishes such as fish stew, fungi (a grit-like mixture of cornmeal, okra, and butter), and plantains. Of course, there's rum, a product of the thriving sugar cane crop. For French flair, visit Guadeloupe or Martinique, home of Napoleon's beloved Josephine. The French influence is also prevalent on St. Bart's as well as half of Saint Martin where the other half is Dutch (Sint Maarten). In the Western Caribbean, visit Cozumel (Mexican) and Grand Cayman.

Jamaica's rich heritage includes the reggae sounds of Bob Marley. Today's Hispaniola comprises Haiti and the Dominican Republic, providing a beach stop for some cruise lines.

Although you might use American currency in the U.S. Virgin Islands, do expect to get acquainted with the Danish influences such as the architecture on St. Croix. Indeed, the Danish, Dutch, Spanish, French, English, and even the Knights of Malta possessed these islands before the United States bought them.

On the ABC islands of Aruba, Bonaire, and Curaçao, you'll think you're visiting Arizona more than the tropics. Snap a picture of the indigenous divi-divi tree, bent by the gusty trade winds. On these islands, part of the Netherlands Antilles, the Dutch influence permeates. Trinidad, an independent nation within the British Commonwealth, and Tobago are nearby.

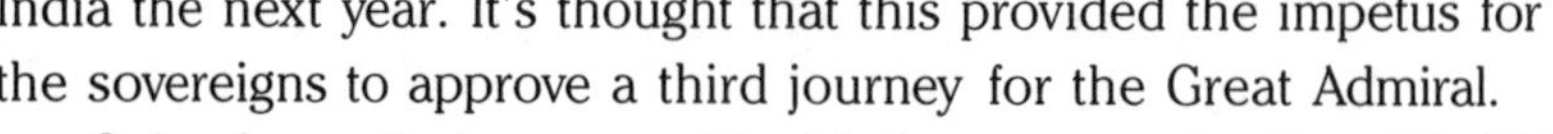

India the next year. It's thought that this provided the impetus for the sovereigns to approve a third journey for the Great Admiral.

Columbus sailed away on his third voyage to the New World in 1498. On this journey, he discovered Venezuela and the islands of Trinidad and Margarita, and again visited Hispaniola, only to find revolts against his brother's rule. In 1500, in an effort to restore order and peace, Queen Isabella and King Ferdinand sent another governor to Hispaniola. Columbus was arrested and sent back to Spain. Somehow he managed to finagle another chance and got authorization to undertake a fourth voyage.

Did You Know?

The United States purchased what we know as the U.S. Virgin Islands during World War I to protect passage to the Panama Canal.

LAST CHANCES

This trip in 1502 was the fastest Columbus ever sailed. He organized the entire fleet in roughly four weeks with the goal of circumnavigating the world. He left on May 9, 1502, only three months after the new "Governor of the Indies" had been sent off, but he was forbidden to return to Hispaniola.

Columbus explored the Central American coast for nearly six months in search of the westward passage that remained elusive. He attempted to establish a gold-mining camp in Panama. The natives thwarted these plans, however. He and his men explored Martinique briefly and were shipwrecked off Jamaica, where they remained for a year awaiting rescue.

Finally a ship sent from Hispaniola rescued them. Columbus then set sail for Spain, where he arrived in poor health. During his audience with King Ferdinand (the queen had passed on), he was rebuffed; the king revoked the admiral's rights and titles. On May 20, 1506, Christopher Columbus died, still hanging on to the notion that he'd reached Asia.

Christopher Columbus

2

English, French, and Dutch Influences

Other explorers and expeditions established further colonies in the New World. French explorers led some of these expeditions, and the English some others. In fact, some of their explorations occurred almost concurrently.

Sir Walter Raleigh, an English adventurer, writer, and explorer, was a prominent member of English society and, for a while, the favorite of Queen Elizabeth I. In 1584, Raleigh obtained approval from the Queen to colonize America. He wasted no time sending out a reconnaissance voyage led by Philip Amadas and Arthur Barlowe, who returned full of enthusiasm, citing abundant resources and friendly Indians.

The Roanoke Colony

Bolstered with confidence, Raleigh then financed another sailing where he sent out 100 colonists in seven ships to establish a colony on Roanoke Island, off what we know today as North Carolina. Sir Richard Grenville and Sir Ralph Lane led this expedition.

They built a fort, constructed houses, planted crops, and searched for gold. But within a year, nature and the natives forced them back to England. The English settlers weren't used to hurricanes, and the Indians proved to be hostile neighbors. Even though they abandoned the area, this was the first Roanoke settlement, and the first English colony in America.

Undaunted, a British man named John White arrived in Roanoke in 1587 with more colonists, including his daughter Eleanor Dare, who was about to give birth. When she delivered a baby girl, she named the child (quite appropriately) Virginia Dare, the first English baby born in the New World. After a few weeks, White sailed back to England to gather more provisions. Fighting between England and Spain delayed his return, but when he did sail back in 1591, he found a deserted colony with the word "Croatoan" carved on a tree post. The fate of the colony, which became known as "The Lost Colony of Roanoke," is still a mystery, with some suggesting the settlers were attacked and killed by the natives or by the Spanish troops. Others believe that the colonists went to live with the Indians, or perhaps on nearby Croatoan Island.

There are Indians now living in North Carolina who call themselves Croatans, and they often have English names. Some believe this is proof that the lost colonists were their ancestors. But English ancestry cannot be substantiated. Fort Raleigh National Historic Site was established on Roanoke Island in 1941.

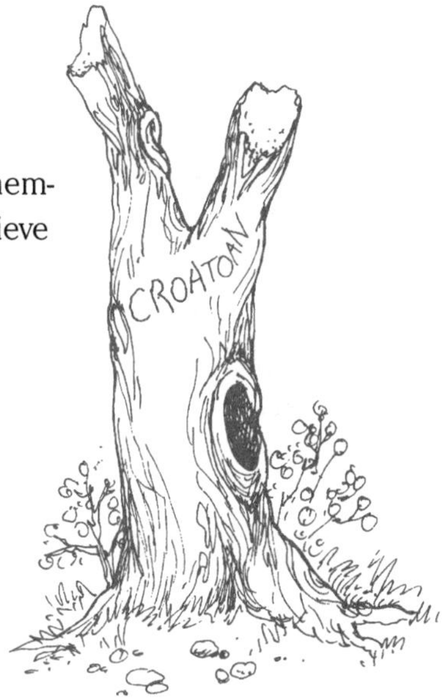

Jamestown Settlement

In 1605, two groups of London merchants who had combined the investments of many smaller investors petitioned King James I for a charter to establish another colony in Virginia. These two groups—prototypes of modern-day corporations—became the Virginia Company of London and the Plymouth Company.

After receiving its charter, the Virginia Company organized its expedition, providing free passage to America in exchange for a contract under which the settlers agreed to seven years of indentured servitude. This became a popular arrangement. In December 1606, those who signed on (a total of 120) boarded three vessels—the *Susan Constant*, the *Discovery*, and the *Godspeed*.

Under Way

By May 1607, the 104 remaining settlers commanded by Captain Christopher Newport sailed their three rather frail vessels through the Chesapeake Bay and thirty miles up the James River to reach a parcel of densely wooded, swampy land. There, the settlers built Jamestown, England's first permanent colony, and like many other explorers before, they set out to find treasure.

They arrived too late in the season to plant crops, and the swamps didn't help their chances of survival. Many of these genteel souls were not accustomed to manual labor, and neither were the valets who sailed with them. Everyone had to carve out homes in the wilderness. There was no choice but to adapt. And many did

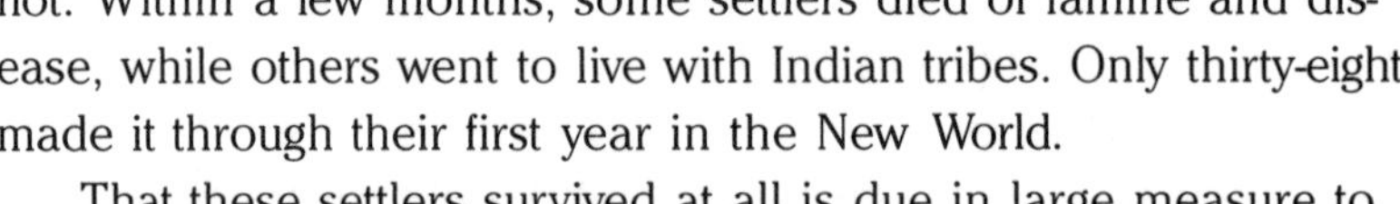

not. Within a few months, some settlers died of famine and disease, while others went to live with Indian tribes. Only thirty-eight made it through their first year in the New World.

That these settlers survived at all is due in large measure to Captain John Smith, a former crusader and pirate turned gentleman. Smith was chosen to lead the Jamestown Colony in 1608, but became a bit of a dictator, ruling with harsh orders such as "no work, no food." He turned the settlers into foragers and successful traders with the Native Americans, who taught the English how to plant corn and other crops.

> **Did You Know?**
>
> Pocahontas's real name was Matoaka. The Indian name "Pocahontas" means "playful one."

JOHN SMITH AND POCAHONTAS

Smith led expeditions to explore the regions surrounding Jamestown, and it was during one of these that the chief of the Powhatan Indians captured Smith. According to an account Smith published in 1624, he was going to be put to death until the chief's daughter, Pocahontas, saved him. From this the legend of Pocahontas sprang forth, becoming part of American folklore, children's books, and videos. But did it really happen?

Some historians note that Smith did not mention this Native American woman and his release in any of the documents he wrote about the colony's first year—that the account published in 1624 came later. In fact, Smith's treatment of the Native Americans was at times harsh. This became an unfortunate pattern throughout American history where settlers forged friendly relations with the natives, only to repay the natives' kindness with hostility.

Evidence is scarce that Pocahontas actually helped John Smith, risking her life to save him. Nonetheless, the story is told to countless generations of children. An account that is probably more accurate states that Smith participated in an initiation ceremony making him an honorary Powhatan tribesman. The Jamestown settlers did capture a young Pocahontas around 1612, returning her to their colony. In captivity, she caught the eye of John Rolfe, an Englishman, who later married her with the blessing of her father and the English governor. This established a peace with the

Powhatans that lasted eight years. Pocahontas converted to Christianity and took the name Rebecca. In 1615, she gave birth to her first child, Thomas.

With his bride and new son, Rolfe returned to England. Soon, Pocahontas captured the people's hearts. Just as she was preparing to return to Virginia in 1617, Pocahontas died of smallpox and was buried in the chapel of the parish church in Gravesend, England. After completing his English education, her son Thomas returned to Virginia.

The Top Crop

Although Pocahontas won the hearts of the English, tobacco also captured their attention. In 1612, colonists began growing tobacco, and it was a primary reason behind the Jamestown settlement's success. In fact, Jamestown became the capital of Virginia.

Moreover, the tobacco crop attracted more settlers to the colonies, where they planted it in every available inch of fertile soil. But once indentured servitude ended, settlers were hard pressed to maintain their tobacco and other crops. So they began purchasing laborers from Dutch traders who kidnapped black Africans in their homelands, transported them against their will across the ocean, and sold them to plantation owners—the start of slavery in America.

Relations with the Native Americans began to sour, for the natives frequently attacked Jamestown. In 1622, 350 colonists were killed. By 1644, a total of 500 had perished. In 1676, the colonists rebelled against the rule of Governor William Berkeley in what's known as Bacon's Rebellion. A group of former indentured servants, led by plantation owner Nathaniel Bacon, didn't think Berkeley was protecting them from Native American raids. When Bacon and his men formed a small army to punish the Indians, Berkeley denounced them as rebels. Marching against Jamestown in 1676, Bacon captured the town and burned it.

Middle Plantation, in what is now Williamsburg, became the seat of colonial government in 1699, and Jamestown was left deserted.

What Happened to John Smith?

In 1614, he had returned to America, exploring and mapping the New England coast. Following an injury from a fire in his powder bag, he sailed back to England with valuable furs and fish. He became a prolific writer and supporter of American colonization. It's during this period in his life that Smith penned *The Generall Historie of Virginia, New-England, and the Summer Isles* (1624) as well as *The True Travels, Adventures, and Observations of Captaine John Smith* (1630). Smith died in 1631.

Visit Jamestown Today

Imagine walking over land and looking out at the sea where early settlers sailed. You can do just that and see history re-enacted before your own eyes. We'll start in Jamestown, Virginia, along the Colonial Parkway.

At Jamestown Island, the National Park Service collects your admission fee. You can view an orientation film and join scheduled tours led by park rangers (or use the self-guided tour leaflets). While on the walking tour, explore the 1639 Church Tower, the sole seventeenth-century structure still standing, as well as the ruins of the original settlement. The Jamestown Archaeological Laboratory contains relics unearthed by National Park Service excavations. If you drive the suggested auto tour through the pine wilderness and swamps, you will see country similar to what the early colonists found when they came in 1607. There's also the reconstructed Glasshouse, where costumed craftspeople demonstrate the 400-year-old techniques of making glassware much like those the early settlers used.

Jamestown Settlement is minutes away and consists of an indoor theater showing a twenty-minute film, "Jamestown: The Beginning," as well as museum exhibits and the outdoor living history program that recreates the experiences and customs of the early colonists and Native Americans. Historical interpreters make tools from bone and prepare a meal at the Powhatan Indian Village. Walk a few paces more and board the ships the English settlers sailed on—well, not the real ones, but replicas of the *Susan Constant*, *Godspeed*, and *Discovery*. Finally, at James Fort you can smell the smoke of the fire used to heat and cook, see the thatched roof huts people lived in, try on armor, or help a colonist tend a garden. Mark your calendars for 2007 when the historic area will celebrate its 400th birthday. Contact the Jamestown–Yorktown Foundation at (888) 593-4682. Try their Web site at *www.historyisfun.org*.

The Dutch Arrive

Hired by the Dutch to find the northwest passage to the Orient, English explorer Henry Hudson sailed into the wonderfully sheltered bay at Manhattan Island, one of the greatest natural harbors in the world, in September 1609. Spurred by Hudson's tales of a fur trading paradise, the Dutch West India Company colonized this new region in 1624, calling it New Netherlands. The following year, they established a Dutch trading post, named New Amsterdam, on Manhattan's southern tip. Soon, the Dutch began other settlements in the Bronx, Brooklyn, Queens, and Staten Island, building a fortification to protect the colony from potential English or Native American invasions. This wall encompassed the area we now know as Wall Street.

In 1664, Peter Stuyvesant, then the governor, had to deal with a struggling colony where the lure of trading in spices or slavery was more lucrative for many Dutch. Then the British invaded. At first, Stuyvesant vowed to fight them, but when the leading merchants petitioned him to give up and not ruin their city, he relented. The new English governor offered free passage back to Holland for those who didn't wish to stay, but reportedly no one left. Two days later, on August 29, 1664, New Amsterdam was renamed New York after the Duke of York, as a birthday present from his brother King Charles.

A New England

To fully understand this story, you need to understand its historical background. In mid-sixteenth century, King Henry VIII had broken away from Roman Catholicism to establish the Anglican Church, otherwise known as the Church of England. But by 1600, during the reign of Elizabeth I (his daughter), this church also had its detractors. These reformers felt that the Church of England still resembled the Catholic Church too closely for comfort. They disliked the church government along with what they perceived as showy rituals. Because this group wanted to purify the church, they became known as the Puritans.

Hard times had fallen on England, and these reformers suffered greatly from the ills of a bad economy with high unemployment and low wages. The Puritans blamed their lot on the Church of England, and they weren't shy about telling anyone so. King James I, who succeeded Elizabeth I, did not take well to this outspokenness, doing everything in his power to make the Puritans miserable.

Most Puritans believed they could change the church and still belong to it. Others didn't think the Church of England could change, and they chose to create a separate congregation outside of the established church. They became known as the Separatists and suffered harsh treatment—which included not being able to attend universities or worship openly. Separatists were imprisoned and sometimes put to death. The English clergyman Robert Browne was influential among the group, and some of his followers became known as Brownists.

A good many of these Separatists escaped to the Netherlands, where some became sailors aboard Dutch merchant ships. Others returned to England in 1620, but were still unhappy. The New World in America that people spoke of was simply too enticing to pass up. In a new land, the Separatists could worship as they pleased, create a truly religious society, and yet retain their English identity. It was this group that made up the core of the Pilgrims.

Strangers among Them

Planning their voyage, the Pilgrims recruited a number of others to join them. Approximately eighty "strangers," who weren't Separatists or Puritans, decided to sail also, but not for religious freedom. They sought better lives, adventure, shipboard jobs, and of course, great wealth. Among these men were Captain Miles Standish and John Alden.

The group, to set sail on two ships, had obtained a charter to settle in the Virginia Colony. These ships, the *Speedwell* and the *Mayflower*, were outfitted for their Atlantic crossings. Twice during the summer months they set sail, and twice they returned to England on account of the *Speedwell*. It wasn't exactly a seaworthy vessel. So the *Mayflower* headed out alone, sailing from Plymouth, England, in September 1620.

The *Mayflower* spent two months crossing an angry Atlantic Ocean. To make matters worse, the maps the Pilgrims used weren't all that trustworthy. Those maps, along with the strong winds, took the sailors well north of the Virginia Colony (though some have speculated that the Pilgrims bribed Captain Christopher Jones to alter the *Mayflower*'s course). On November 21, 1620, the Pilgrims reached Provincetown Harbor at the point of Cape Cod, Massachusetts.

Signing the Mayflower Compact

Although the *Mayflower*'s passengers seemed happy to reach dry land, they were also concerned because their charter from the London merchants had sent them to Virginia. Some of the Strangers aboard talked of breaking away from the group. Noting the dissension among them, the passengers drew up an agreement while anchored in the harbor. The Mayflower Compact was the first colonial agreement that formed a government by the consent of those governed, for the signers agreed to follow all "just and equal" laws that the settlers enacted. Furthermore, the majority would rule in matters where there was disagreement. That might seem simple today, but back then, this was a giant leap away from the tradition of royal and absolute rulers. The Mayflower Compact guided the colonists until they joined with the Massachusetts Bay Colony in 1691.

Indian Aid at Plymouth Colony

When the Pilgrims established Plymouth Colony, they chose this site for its farm fields, its supply of fresh drinking water, and the hill that enabled them to build a fort. But by early 1621, the Pilgrims were cold, hungry, and sick. They had arrived too late to plant crops, and with the snow, cold, and dwindling food supply, as many as half the colonists died.

The hope of spring kept them going. So did a surprise in the form of an Indian named Samoset, who entered their settlement,

Pretend You're a Pilgrim

Plimoth Plantation brings to life seventeenth century Plymouth, the land where the Wampanoag Indians lived and the Pilgrims later settled. You'll step into the 1627 Pilgrim Village houses and feel the heat from their fires. The *Mayflower II*, the full-scale reproduction of the Pilgrims' ship, includes costumed crewmen who will tell you about ship-building and show you how to rig a ship. In Hobbamock's Wampanoag Indian Homesite, those dressed as natives explain the Pilgrims' arrival and impact. Nye Exhibition Barn gives visitors an in-depth look at the museum's rare breed program. There are also shops to visit. For more information, call (508) 746-1622 or visit *www.plimoth.org*.

speaking English. Samoset said he'd heard them speaking and learned their language, and evidently he saw the Pilgrims' needs. Soon he brought Squanto, another Indian friend and part of the tribe that had lived at Plymouth before the colonists' arrival, to serve as their guide, teaching them how to survive with new methods of farming and fishing. The Pilgrims learned to plant corn, fertilize their fields, and prosper in other ways as well.

Squanto acted as the interpreter between the Pilgrims and the great Chief Massasoit of the Wampanoags in southeastern Massachusetts. The two sides pledged not to harm one another, and by the following autumn in 1621, the Pilgrims celebrated their first harvest with their Indian neighbors. Both brought provisions for that first Thanksgiving feast, which lasted three days.

Thanksgiving Day

Early New Englanders celebrated Thanksgiving only when there was a plentiful harvest. Gradually the custom prevailed annually. During the Revolution, the Continental Congress proposed a national day of thanksgiving, and in 1863, Abraham Lincoln issued the proclamation designating the fourth Thursday in November as Thanksgiving Day.

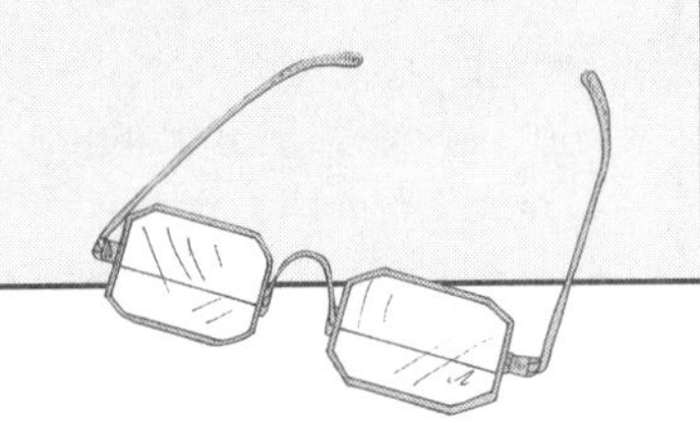

MASSACHUSETTS BAY COLONY

In 1623, the Council for New England issued a patent to the Dorchester Company, made up of English businessmen interested in trade, to settle in the American colonies. Cape Ann, along the Atlantic coast of Massachusetts, became a settlement, albeit one that didn't last longer than 1625. But the survivors, led by Roger Conant, founded Naumkeag (now Salem) in 1626.

This time period spurred further settlement around Massachusetts, including the towns of Mount Wollaston (now Quincy), Wessagusset (now Weymouth), and Nantasket.

In 1628, the Council for New England gave a group led by John Endecott a patent entitling them to land just south of the Merrimack River to just north of the Charles River, extending from sea to sea. This larger group of English Puritans settled on the shores of Massachusetts Bay. Between 1629 and 1640, more than 20,000 additional colonists made the crossing to settle in New England.

The Settlement at Salem

Endecott was soon sent to take over the settlement at Salem, and in 1629, King Charles I granted the charter for the Massachusetts Bay Colony. The first government was established in England, but in 1629, it moved to Massachusetts, and the government of the trading company soon became that of the colony. Men such as John Winthrop and John Cotton, along with other Puritan leaders, soon exercised absolute control, succeeding in their attempts to create a religious purpose for the colony they'd founded.

Putting the religious reforms of the Puritans aside, Puritanism valued hard work, a good business sense, and the need for education. Over time, these traits came to represent what America was all about. In a negative sense, people still use the term "puritanical" to describe rigid morality or narrowness of mind.

The Role of Religion in Colonial Life

Because their beliefs were based on independent congregations, free of the church hierarchy that existed back in England, the settlers became known as Congregationalists. Attendance at Sunday services was mandatory, and with the work required to thrive in the colonies, that left little leisure time. There was no dancing, no real recreation. Ironically, life was reminiscent of times past. The punishment for any crime committed was harsh, and those who spoke out against the puritanical dictates were persecuted. Indeed, the Puritans proved to be as intolerant as the king they had fled.

The Quakers were banished from the colony when they dared to disagree, and others fled for religious and economic reasons to establish other New England towns. Among them was Roger

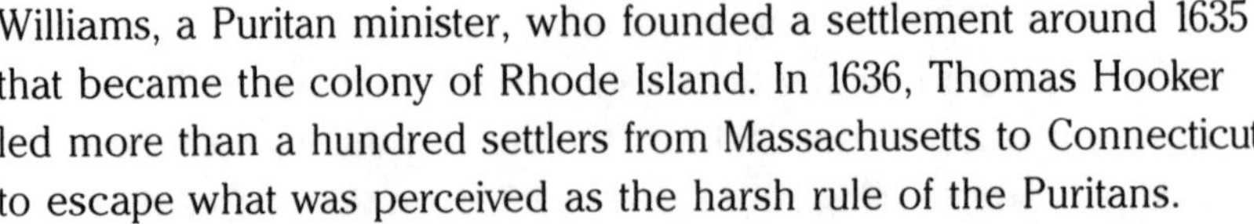

Williams, a Puritan minister, who founded a settlement around 1635 that became the colony of Rhode Island. In 1636, Thomas Hooker led more than a hundred settlers from Massachusetts to Connecticut to escape what was perceived as the harsh rule of the Puritans.

Salem Revisited

In 1953, playwright Arthur Miller retold the story of the Salem witch trials in *The Crucible*. This coincided with Senator Joseph McCarthy's own "witch hunt" for communists during the beginning of the Cold War.

From 1629 to 1660, the Massachusetts Bay colonists were pretty much independent of English control, because the English Parliament and the king had their own power struggles. Elder colonists used their financial muscle to influence adjacent settlements, and in turn the Massachusetts Bay Colony dominated proceedings of the New England Confederation, a military alliance the colonists had formed to stave off attacks by Native Americans and Dutch settlers. Members of this confederation—Connecticut, New Haven, Plymouth, as well as Massachusetts Bay—agreed to retain their independence while helping each other's militias. However, when the English monarchy prevailed in 1660, King Charles II tried to exert his influence over the American settlements, especially the Massachusetts Bay Colony.

The colonists were a persistent people, holding their own for many years. But after 1674, England tried once again to subdue the rebellious Massachusetts Bay colonists, charging that they had violated the Navigation Acts, among other misdeeds. In 1684, England revoked the Massachusetts Bay Colony's charter, and in 1691, the colony was granted a new royal charter that essentially ended the form of government the Puritans had created. The right to elect representatives was now based on property qualifications rather than church membership. The hysteria and wild accusations in Salem in 1692 further eroded the Puritanical influence.

Salem Witch Trials

To fully grasp the witchcraft scare, you have to remember that the 1690s had its share of religious, political, and social dissension. The last thing these Puritan leaders needed was the accusations made in 1692 by two girls—nine-year-old Betty Parris and her eleven-year-old cousin Abigail Williams. These girls caused quite a stir, not only in the home of the Reverend Samuel Parris, but in the town of Salem itself.

Betty and Abigail began acting quite strangely, running around the house, flapping their arms, screaming, and throwing themselves around the room. Local doctors were at a loss to explain their antics. Witchcraft became the diagnosis of their mysterious ailment.

In Puritan times, the term "witch" was applied to a poor, old person who was also contentious. During this time, people were encouraged to turn each other in, and that led accused witches down an unpleasant path.

Betty and Abigail identified the Parris family's West Indian slave, Tituba, as their tormentor, before adding other names such as Sarah Good and Sarah Osborne. As a black slave, Tituba already was at a disadvantage, and the two Sarahs suffered from financial woes and moral transgressions, respectively.

Many more of Salem's teenage girls began having fits, and the finger pointing continued. Thus it was what we call today a true witch hunt and persecution of the worst kind.

So-called witches reportedly had identifiable marks on their bodies—marks put there by the Devil himself—that professional witch finders could identify since the witches were insensitive to pain. The witch finders had monetary incentive to identify new subjects, for they were paid a fee for every witch conviction.

Nineteen people were executed in the wake of the Salem Witch Trials, until public opinion turned against the accusers and local judges. In 1696, the General Court adopted a resolution of repentance. Although the Puritan influence declined, the Congregational churches remained dominant in Massachusetts into the nineteenth century.

Life in New England

Even with a royal governor, colonists got an early taste of independence. The Puritans' belief that communities were formed by covenants led to the creation of town meetings, the first democratic

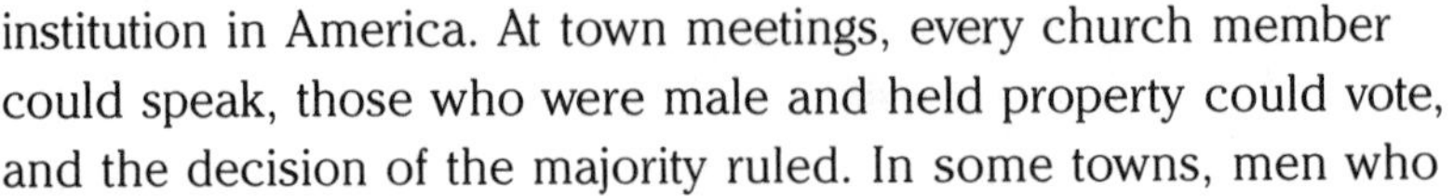

institution in America. At town meetings, every church member could speak, those who were male and held property could vote, and the decision of the majority ruled. In some towns, men who were not property holders could also vote. This democratic atmosphere later led to fewer restrictions regarding religious and personal freedoms.

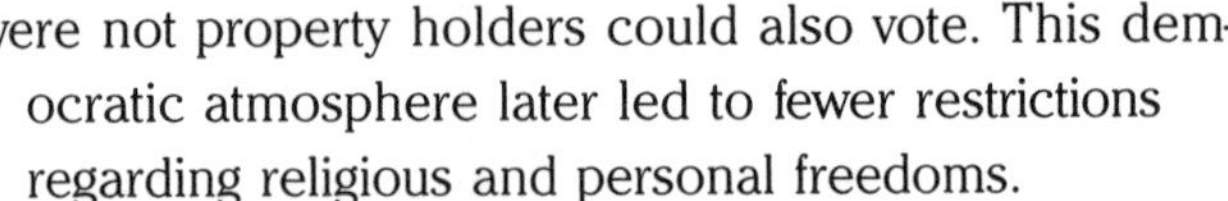

In the New England Puritan town, no one was more important than its minister. Ministers were expected to be well educated. Thus, Puritans laid the foundations of education in the colonies with America's first secondary school established in 1635. Harvard College (now Harvard University) began in 1636 as an institution to train ministers.

Indian Skirmishes

Most Native Americans were friendly to their colonist neighbors, some even welcoming the opportunity for trade and protection from other Indian tribes. But the Pequots were a more aggressive group, and soon the friction became intense enough that it escalated into the Pequot War of 1637, the first major war fought in New England. Connecticut declared war on the Pequots, and the colonists launched a surprise attack that included setting a Pequot village on fire. Few Pequot survived in the aftermath. Some may have been sold into slavery while others fled throughout New England.

The King Philip's War

Another conflict with the Native Americans resulted in King Philip's War in 1675. The problem was that the colonists had encroached on native land, and as might be expected, the tribe retaliated. Philip was the chief of the Wampanoag tribe, and sufficiently provoked, he joined together with other Native Americans to fight the colonists.

The colonies, as part of the military alliance called the New England Confederation, captured Native American women and children, destroyed crops, and defeated the southern New England tribes. The war continued throughout the winter of 1675, and by the following summer, Philip was killed. This ended the struggle, and peace ensued as colonists continued to expand their settlements.

Struggles with France

Between the years 1689 and 1763, England and France were entangled in a struggle for supremacy. During this period, Massachusetts played a role in the skirmishes between England and France over dominance in North America. Each side used Native Americans and attacked each other's settlements. Many Massachusetts towns were destroyed, and many ships sunk; thousands of colonists were captured and killed. Here's a summary of the four North American wars waged by the English and French from 1689 to 1697, all a part of this larger European conflict.

King Williams's War

King William's War broke out in 1689 after England's William III entered the War of the League of Augsburg against France. Indians, provoked by the French to attack, ravaged the English settlements in New England and New York. Retaliating, New Englanders gained control of Port Royal, a key French post in Nova Scotia. Bloody border skirmishes ensued for at least six years until the Treaty of Ryswick in 1697 halted both sides, restoring Port Royal to the French. However, this war accomplished nothing, for the treaty merely declared that the prewar positions would remain. As a result, the unresolved tensions led to further fighting.

Queen Anne's War

Queen Anne's War broke out in 1701. English colonists captured and burned St. Augustine, Florida (then Spanish territory). There were massacres at the hands of French troops and their Native American allies in the colonies, and troops also tried again to wrest away control of Port Royal. The British and colonists conquered Acadia in 1710, but failed to encroach on Quebec and Montreal. When the Treaty of Utrecht ended Queen Anne's War in 1713, it

Samuel de Champlain

Often referred to as the father of New France (the French colonial empire in North America), this French explorer made several discoveries. It was Champlain who produced the first accurate chart of the Atlantic coast, from Newfoundland to Cape Cod, as well as maps of the Saint Lawrence Valley and the Great Lakes, which he discovered. Champlain also created a trading post in what we know as the city of Quebec, and established the commercial and military alliances that endured to the end of the French regime in Canada.

ceded Acadia, as well as Newfoundland and the Hudson Bay territory, to the British. Cape Breton Island stayed French.

King George's War

King George's War broke out in 1744. The French captured and destroyed a British fort at Canso, Nova Scotia, and they took prisoners to their fortress at Cape Breton Island. Fearing the French, the governor of Massachusetts enlisted further colonial aid. Thus a militia of 4,000 sailed in British ships and fought under the command of Sir William Pepperell, a Maine merchant. They took Louisburg from the French, who reclaimed it the next year. This war ended in 1748 with the Treaty of Aix-la-Chapelle.

The French and Indian War

The French and Indian War finally decided the question of colonial control. It broke out in 1754 and lasted until 1763. In fact, all these early conflicts are sometimes collectively called the French and Indian Wars.

Both Britain and France had built new frontier fortresses in the Ohio Valley. During these other conflicts, English traders had forged relationships with the tribes that had previously traded solely with the French. It came to France's attention that they had better protect their own strategic interests with a series of forts from Lake Erie to present-day Pittsburgh.

It would appear that Britain had the clear advantage, with more resources and a greater supply of troops. However, France had powerful Indian allies.

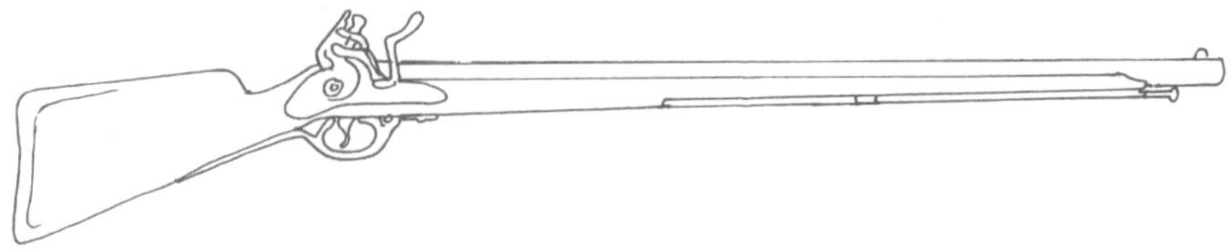

Virginia's governor tried unsuccessfully to warn the French to get out of British territory. To get the message across, he dispatched an armed force under the command of George Washington to drive the French away. But the French had a surprise for Washington. They defeated his troops at the Battle of Fort Necessity in 1754, sending them back to Virginia. This officially started the French and Indian War.

The following year, British General Edward Braddock with British regulars and colonial troops attempted to take Fort Duquesne (now Pittsburgh), but the French and Native Americans prevailed. There were some sporadic British victories. However, the French and Indians won battle after battle—at least until 1758, when British and colonial troops seized Louisburg as well as Forts Duquesne, Frontenac, and Ticonderoga. The British also claimed Fort Niagara, and that left French Canada open to attack.

The Treaty of Paris in 1763 ended more than a century and a half of French power in the New World. French control of Canada went to Britain, and France ceded all of its territories east of the Mississippi River to the British as well. Spain also gave Florida to the British.

In winning this war, though, Britain doubled its national debt and took on more territory than it could easily manage. The British tried to compel colonists to pay for these campaigns against French Canada. As you can imagine, this did not sit well with the American colonies.

Traipsing Through History

Turn the pages of history by joining the History Book Club, Camp Hill, Pennsylvania 17011-9526. To literally walk down the path of historical events, visit a living history museum that recreates life in an earlier time. Expect to find trained and costumed staff, painstaking research, and authentically recreated buildings and artifacts.

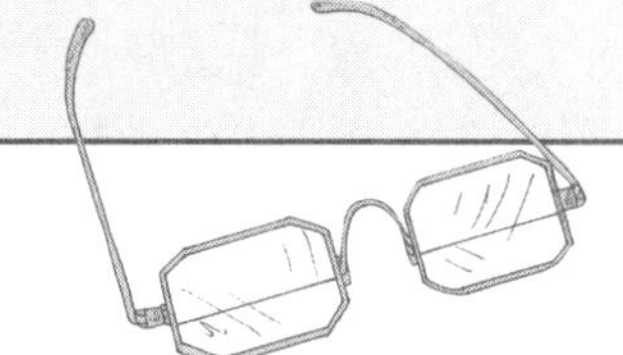

3

Foundations of Freedom

T he early French and English settlers disputed boundaries and territories throughout the vast Ohio Valley region between the Appalachian Mountains and the Mississippi River. In many respects, the French and Indian War set the stage for the American Revolution. The French suffered a humiliating defeat, and as a result, the French would do almost anything to act out against the British, even if the French monarchy could not afford public financial support of American causes. As we'll see, that support strengthened, and America was the beneficiary. Time would show, however, that France's support would only lead to the French fiscal crisis that climaxed in 1789 with the French Revolution.

The British Position

Britain had been engaged in the Seven Years' War in Europe, of which the American conflict had been only a part. The British treasury had to be replenished as the war efforts had nearly doubled the national debt. King George III, now sitting high as the monarch of all North American lands east of the Mississippi, tried to exert a little muscle and tighten his rein on the colonies. This vast kingdom would require not only further sources of revenue but additional administration, or so the king thought.

One of King George's edicts was the Proclamation of 1763, whereby the king established a boundary beyond which colonists could not settle. However, this did little to dampen the pioneer spirit. In fact, it spurred many adventurous souls to further exploration and trespassing.

No Taxation Without Representation

When Parliament tried to raise revenues at home, the British subjects rioted in protest of additional levies, and they succeeded in making their point. Still in need of money, the British government looked across the ocean.

Parliament levied high duties on various commodities needed in the colonies—everyday items such as molasses and sugar. Thus,

At the Newsstand

There are plenty of periodicals devoted to the pastime of history reading. You can even access many of these on the World Wide Web:

- *American Heritage, www.americanheritage.com*
- *Military Heritage, www.militaryheritage.com/magazine.htm*

Access the following magazines at *www.thehistorynet.com*:

- *American History*
- *America's Civil War*
- *Civil War Times Illustrated*
- *The Quarterly Journal of Military History*
- *Military History*
- *Wild West*
- *Vietnam*
- *World War II*

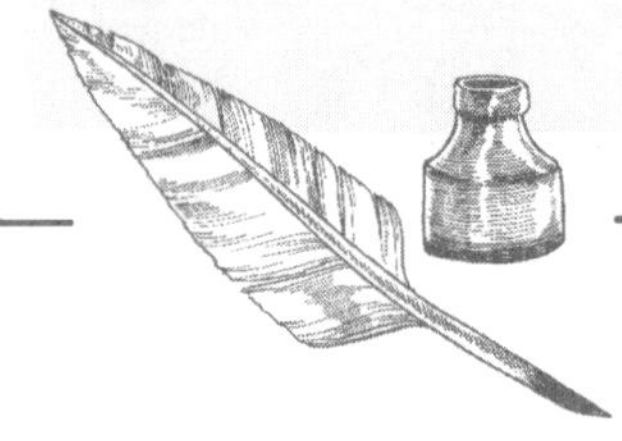

the Sugar Act, passed in 1764, became the first significant tax demanded of colonists. Furthermore, Parliament passed the Currency Act, whereby the colonies could not issue their own money. All transactions had to be made with gold. This angered the independent-minded colonists, who did not want to be financially dependent on England.

In addition, Parliament decided to enforce a previous law that had been passed in the 1650s but largely ignored. The Acts of Trade and Navigation, commonly known as Navigation Acts, were designed to protect commerce. The Navigation Act of 1651 stipulated that goods imported or exported by British colonies (including those in Africa, Asia, or America) had to be shipped on vessels constructed by British shipbuilders. The crews sailing these vessels also had to have 75 percent British crewmen. Goods from the colonies also had to arrive on British ships. The Act of 1660 stated that the colonists could ship particular items such as tobacco, rice, and indigo only to another British colony or to the mother country. That meant the colonists were not permitted to trade with other countries. Further acts prevented the manufacture of products such as hats and iron in the colonies, for it was thought industry in America would threaten its stability in England. The Navigation Acts weren't repealed until 1849.

New England town meetings were still common in the 1760s, and it was at one of these that the colonists bonded around the famous slogan "No taxation without representation." When the New Englanders protested peacefully with a boycott of English goods, Parliament took little notice. Shortly thereafter, the Quartering Act of 1765 declared that colonial citizens would have to provide food and housing for royal troops, a decree that understandably cast a financial hardship on the colonials as well as a blatant invasion of their personal privacy.

The Stamp Act

If the mother country hadn't already seemed tax happy, the worst was yet to come as even more products began being taxed.

This time the Stamp Act required colonists to pay extra for newspapers, land deeds, dice, and card games—even graduation diplomas, since every paper document would require a revenue stamp from a British agent. This further infuriated the colonists, who earnestly held to the belief that these taxes were the result of their lack of representation in the British Parliament.

The dissenters succeeded in getting the measure repealed, but the victory was bittersweet. The next edict—the Declaratory Act—stated that the British Parliament could create laws for the colonies however it saw fit. The Townshend Act levied tariffs on imports such as glass, lead, paint, and tea. The colonial protest was alive and well, and in April 1770, Parliament repealed the Townshend taxes, except for the levy on tea.

Rebels among Us

Opposing the Stamp Act, the Sons of Liberty soon organized with leaders such as Samuel Adams and Paul Revere. This secret, patriotic society kept meeting after the act was repealed in 1766, forming the Committees of Correspondence that fostered resistance to British economic control. The Sons of Liberty also defied the British dictates by helping American merchants who refused to import goods carried in British ships.

Educated at Harvard, Samuel Adams was a law student and merchant. But when his own ventures failed, he joined his father in a brewery business. With the now-famous Samuel Adams beer, you'd never guess that that business failed following his father's death! But Adams was known for his rebellious posture against many of the British acts. Active in Boston political circles, he was elected to the lower house of the General Court and promoted the Boston chapter of the Sons of Liberty.

Paul Revere, a silversmith and engraver, was also a patriot. His elegant silverware, bowls, pitchers, and tea sets were favorites of Boston aristocracy, but he also used his talents to make artificial teeth, surgical instruments, and engraved printing plates.

Patrick Henry was a self-educated statesman who rose to prominence in the colonies as a lawyer and later as a member of the Virginia legislature, the House of Burgesses, where he introduced resolutions against the Stamp Act.

John Hancock was another Harvard-educated patriot who became a colonial businessman, and a rather wealthy one, after inheriting his mercantile firm. Elected to the Massachusetts legislature, Hancock was soon at odds with the British government in 1768 when customs officials seized his sloop after he failed to pay import duties on his cargo. His zealous defense won him popularity among the factions of people opposed to British control of the colonies.

All of these famous rabble-rousers would play integral roles in the unfolding of the future political drama.

The Boston Massacre

On March 5, 1770, a group of colonists living in Boston were demonstrating in front of the not-too-popular Customs House, where British troops had been called to quell the American protests. The colonists felt beleaguered, and if you can imagine the scene, there were probably harsh words and bitter tensions. The squad of soldiers responded by firing shots into the crowd. Crispus Attucks, leader of this group of protesting colonists, became the first to die for American liberty, in addition to four others. Attucks was of mixed descent, most likely a man of black, white, and Native American heritage. The event became known as the Boston Massacre, depicted by Paul Revere in one of his most famous engravings. In 1888, a monument was erected in the Boston Common to honor Attucks and the others who gave their lives for liberty.

In retrospect, the Boston Massacre, though a tragic brawl, was probably not as heroic as the Patriots depicted it. Nonetheless, it stirred passions for personal liberty, justice, and independence. Following the assault, John Hancock joined others demanding the removal of British troops from Boston. Perhaps sensing that this was a no-win situation, the British acquiesced and indeed withdrew them.

TEA, ANYONE?

After the repeal of the Townshend Acts, the tea tax was the only remaining tariff. Again, to really understand the magnitude of this colonial dilemma, you have to envision yourself reared with the English tradition of sipping this favorite cup of brew. And even though Parliament awarded a monopoly on the sale of tea to Britain's primary tea producer, the East India Company, which sold tea directly at lower prices than those colonial middlemen could offer, the issue of taxation stung. Sipping a little less tea was indeed a small annoyance made into a mountain of resentment because of the tax. When half a million pounds of tea was sent to the four primary ports—Philadelphia, New York, Charleston, and Boston—anti-British sentiment rallied to the point that tea-laden ships turned back from Philadelphia and New York, unable to unload. In Charleston, although the tea was unloaded, it was stored rather than sold. That left Boston, where the Governor was adamant that colonists pay the levy. In December 1773, as the loaded ships sat at anchor, Samuel Adams, Paul Revere, and some fifty Patriots (some dressed as Native Americans) boarded the ships and dumped 343 chests of tea into Boston Harbor. This bold act, known as the Boston Tea Party, met with the king's wrath as he closed the port of Boston and imposed a military form of government. As the British army occupied Massachusetts, colonists had to house the troops, and they saw their civil liberties curtailed. The Quebec Act, extending the former French province of Quebec south to the Ohio River, further dashed any hopes of westward expansion. Indeed, these restrictions, known as Intolerable Acts, were meant to punish Massachusetts citizens for their rebellious attitude. It didn't take long for the other colonies to surmise that their liberty also might be at stake.

Visit Boston Today

There's no better way to learn about our country's path to freedom than to actually walk it today. Boston's Freedom Trail is a painted brick path connecting more than a dozen historic sites. It spans 2.5 miles through downtown Boston, the North End, and Charlestown. Visiting Boston, Massachusetts, is like having a history classroom come alive. What's more, many sites along the trail grant free admission.

Get the Boston Freedom Trail brochure, which starts you at Boston Common, the forty-eight–acre downtown park, before heading to the State House that Charles Bulfinch designed. It was erected in 1795, and Patriots such as Samuel Adams and Paul Revere laid the cornerstone. At the Granary Burying Ground dating back to 1660, see the final resting places of John Hancock, Samuel Adams, Paul Revere, and Benjamin Franklin's parents. The Boston Tea Party began at the Old South Meeting House, built in 1729. An award-winning exhibit lets you hear the fiery debates that led to this famous protest.

Boston's oldest public building, the Old State House, built in 1713, is along the trail with historical video and exhibits inside. Right across the street, a circle of cobblestones marks the site where five Americans lost their lives in the Boston Massacre. Faneuil Hall, once the site of town meetings, today gives visitors a variety of shops and food merchants, in addition to a public meeting room upstairs. The famous midnight ride began at Paul Revere House, where you can take a self-guided tour and see artifacts from the colonial era.

Nicknamed "Old Ironsides," the USS *Constitution* is the oldest commissioned warship afloat. Take a ferry out to the Charlestown Navy Yard. The obelisk at the Bunker Hill Monument commemorates the first major battle of the American Revolution. It also offers a great view of Boston.

The Greater Boston Convention and Visitors Bureau sells a tour booklet titled: "Kids Love Boston." Included is information about the sights explaining their significance. Don't miss the re-enacted town meeting at the Boston Tea Party Ship and Museum. Kids won't forget this history lesson, especially when they get to toss a bundle of tea into the harbor!

Finally, Boston offers many more attractions for learning and fun, including the Children's Museum, New England Aquarium, the Duck Tour splashing down into the Charles River, and the Swan Boats in the Public Garden, site of the famous children's tale *Make Way for Ducklings.* To plan your journey to Boston, contact the Visitors Bureau at (888) SEE BOSTON or visit *www.bostonusa.com.*

First Continental Congress

In September and October of 1774, colonial leaders met in Philadelphia's Carpenters Hall for the First Continental Congress. The Massachusetts House of Representatives had called for an intercolonial congress that would take any actions necessary to preserve or establish colonial rights. Only Georgia was not represented among the fifty-five delegates of the First Continental Congress.

Bringing even this small number of representatives together was no easy task. They bickered about who would give the opening prayer, and they disputed how many votes each colony would have until they settled on one vote for each colony, regardless of that colony's size. In fact, the British attempts to divide colonial support almost succeeded.

In a pamphlet titled "A Summary View of the Rights of British America," Thomas Jefferson of Virginia denounced all parliamentary legislation. Joseph Galloway of Pennsylvania proposed a much more conciliatory plan that would create a grand council overseeing matters of taxation and legislation in association with a royally approved governor-general. The delegates did away with Galloway's plan, but only by a narrow margin. They adopted the views of more radical Patriots, like those outlined in the Suffolk Resolves with which Paul Revere had galloped into Philadelphia as he rode from beleaguered Boston. This document enumerated many colonial grievances, demanded that the British back down over certain items, and gave the ultimatum that if the British did not acquiesce, they would face consequences.

Still hoping to reconcile their complaints with the British Crown, the delegates approved the Declaration of Rights and Grievances. Members of this First Continental Congress concluded their sessions by agreeing to meet again—in May 1775—where they would vote on stronger measures if their grievances had not been addressed by the British. They had taken the first steps towards freedom.

A Must-Have Resource

A handy guide to three historic areas is *The Insiders' Guide to Williamsburg, Jamestown and Yorktown*. It's a comprehensive guide to attractions, lodging, restaurants, shopping, and more. For more information, visit *www.insiders.com*.

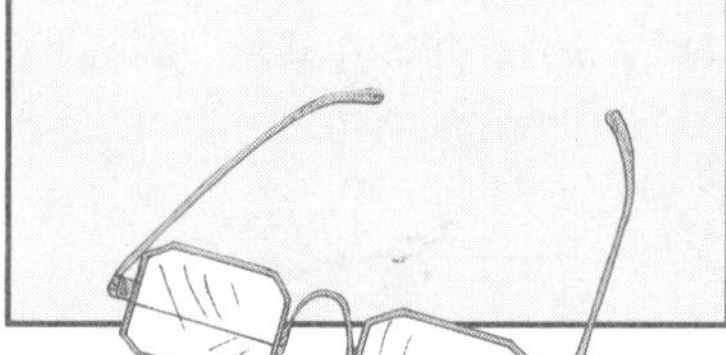

It Seemed Like Common Sense

In January 1776, political philosopher Thomas Paine wrote a fifty-page pamphlet titled *Common Sense.* Although it was published anonymously, it rallied the masses. Paine's rhetorical style was blunt, outlining the economic benefits of freedom and asking whether "a continent should continue to be ruled by an island." Even some loyalists, by now clearly in the minority, pondered the predicament Paine posed and agreed with his assertion that the British exploited the American colonies, and that establishing independence was only common sense. Paine continued writing a series of pamphlets between 1776 and 1783 called *The American Crisis*. In fact, General Washington ordered these read to his troops to inspire them to fight even harder for freedom.

The king and the British government remained steadfast in the face of colonial concerns. As relations worsened between Britain and the colonies, so did trade as the value of British exports to America fell. Merchants petitioned the king to settle the disputes quickly, for they feared financial ruin if the colonists could not pay the bills they'd accrued.

Lord North, the British prime minister, presented a number of proposals to Parliament, including one that would allow the colonies to tax themselves enough to pay for their own defense and administration of colonial government. Parliament did approve Lord North's proposition, but unfortunately, news did not reach the colonies until April 24, 1775.

Paul Revere's Ride

Earlier that same April, British orders had been sent to General Thomas Gage, then governor of Massachusetts, advising him to arrest dissidents and to capture their arms and munitions. On April 19, Gage ordered British troops to Concord, where he'd learned of a stockpiled arsenal. But the troops first met colonial resistance at Lexington, where on the evening of April 18, Paul Revere, William Dawes, and Samuel Prescott rode ahead to warn John Hancock and Samuel Adams, two Patriots whom Gage wanted to arrest. Revere's historic

midnight ride has become part of American folklore, though slightly exaggerated in Henry Wadsworth Longfellow's ballad "Paul Revere's Ride." In fact, Revere was detained by the British while en route with his message.

At Lexington, approximately fifty Minutemen (called this because they were ready at a minute's notice) met the British advance guard. When British Major John Pitcairn ordered the Patriots to disperse, a pistol shot rang out. Who fired this first shot is not entirely clear, but one thing was certain. British troops opened fire on the Minutemen even as the colonists retreated. By the time the firing stopped, eight Minutemen were killed and ten wounded.

As British troops reached Concord, they confiscated what few arms they found and suffered attack by colonists resulting in the death of three British soldiers and the wounding of eight more. This time, as the British made their way back to Lexington, an increasing number of colonists joined in the assault. Thus, by the time the Redcoats reached Boston, at least 270 British soldiers were dead, missing, or wounded in battle–a higher number than the colonial casualties.

Canadian Invasion

In the aftermath of Lexington and Concord, Americans occupied Fort Ticonderoga and Crown Point, both on Lake Champlain. Thinking they could convince the French-speaking Canadians to rally with their cause, a few rather gutsy Patriots–General Richard Montgomery and Colonel Benedict Arnold–invaded Quebec. Not only did they hope for allies, but they also wanted guns and gunpowder. However, the Canadians refused to join the Patriot cause. What's more, many of Arnold's men had met the requirements of their military service, and they left before the siege of Quebec.

Undeterred, Montgomery and Arnold attacked on New Year's Eve, but when Montgomery was killed and Arnold wounded, the British took hundreds of prisoners. The remaining American troops were forced back to Lake Champlain.

The Second Continental Congress

On May 10, 1775, the Second Continental Congress convened in Philadelphia to determine the fate of the Colonies' relationship with Britain. It took the delegates some time to gather, but by June sixty-five delegates had arrived, representing twelve colonies (Georgia wasn't represented until September). If you think this was a unified bunch, guess again. In past Congressional sessions, debate, fretting, and fuming took center stage, but the delegates hadn't confronted the ultimate decision—the push for independence. By now the time had come to confront the inevitable.

Many moderates, led by John Dickinson of Pennsylvania, held out hope that the American colonies could somehow remain British with Parliament recognizing particular rights. Radicals, however, held firm to their support for complete independence, advocated by the staunch Patriot Samuel Adams. Richard Henry Lee, representing Virginia, moved that the colonies absolve themselves of allegiance to the British crown. John Adams of Massachusetts seconded the motion, but action was deferred until July.

The Battle of Bunker Hill

In the night hours of June 16, 1775, colonial militia took up positions on Breed's Hill, adjacent to Bunker Hill overlooking Boston Harbor. This group, led by Colonel William Prescott, John Stark, and Israel Putnam, felt sure that they could seize control of the harbor, but British General Gage, eager to avenge his losses at Concord, was determined to take the hill. The next day, 3,000 Redcoats marched up Breed's Hill in close ranks, feeling pretty proud of themselves. It wasn't until they marched close enough (approximately forty paces from colonial forces) that American troops opened fire, forcing the British to suffer severe casualties and retreat. Remember, though—the British were determined, charging a second and third time until the Americans ran out of ammunition. Even though this battle occurred at Breed's Hill, it's been misnamed the Battle of Bunker Hill and is known as one of the bloodiest encounters in the Americans' struggle for freedom.

National History Day

Did you know there was a day devoted to our national history? Well, there isn't exactly. It's called that, but truthfully, it's a yearlong program for junior and senior high school students, begun in 1974. More than 8 million young people have participated, and each year, there is a special theme such as "Frontiers in History: People, Places, Ideas," the theme for 2000–2001. Students illustrate the theme in any of four categories—drama, research papers, tabletop exhibits, or multimedia documentaries. National winners earn $1,000 and perhaps special prizes at the finals held at the University of Maryland (College Park). To learn more about National History Day, visit *www.thehistorynet.com/nationalhistoryday*.

However, several positive outcomes resulted. For starters, America's part-time militia gained a renewed sense of confidence that helped effectively in recruiting enlisted, trained troops. Surrounding colonies not only came to the aid of New Englanders in ways that were comforting, but began establishing intercolonial ties that would prove unbreakable. The Second Continental Congress also commissioned Virginia's George Washington to take command of the American forces. Washington's Continental Army, a small, dependable regiment, arrived in Cambridge on July 3, 1775, where the new commander in chief took over. Washington refused any payment for his services, except for expenses.

Magna Carta

The Magna Carta was a thirteenth-century English legal document on which the United States based much of its original laws. England's powerful barons forced King John to grant a charter limiting his powers. The Magna Carta helped establish the principle that no one—not even a king—is above the law.

The Final Straws

After the Battle of Bunker Hill, there had been too much bloodshed to permit peace or compromise. The Second Continental Congress requested that Benjamin Franklin, Thomas Jefferson, John Adams, Roger Sherman, and Robert R. Livingston draft a formal protest against Britain, in line with Lee's resolution, declaring the colonies free of British rule. Not satisfied with the wording of this declaration, on July 6, Dickinson petitioned Congress for one more shot at the document. Thus, Congress approved a final "Olive Branch Petition" in July 1775. Once again, the king rejected it. In December, Parliament passed the Prohibitory Act outlawing trade with the rebellious colonies and establishing a naval blockade. Britain went one step further, sending additional troops and German mercenaries better known as the Hessians—acts undoubtedly meant to bring the patriots to their knees begging forgiveness. They didn't. Even the more moderate factions began contemplating all-out war against the mother country.

Committee members selected Thomas Jefferson, who had a reputation for being a stellar writer, to finish the drafts. The resulting document was the Declaration of Independence, which outlined the grievances against Britain and declared the colonies free and independent.

There's More to Williamsburg Than History

If you want to learn about Colonial America, there's no place like Williamsburg, Virginia, the state's capital from 1699 to 1780 (before the seat of government transferred to Richmond). Named in honor of William III of England, Williamsburg was the site of many notable debates preceding the Revolution.

Beginning in 1926, the historic area called Colonial Williamsburg was restored to its origins (or rebuilt) in a project principally financed by philanthropist John D. Rockefeller Jr. Among the 120 eighteenth-century buildings are Bruton Parish Church, still used for its original purpose; the Colonial Capitol (rebuilt to its 1705 appearance), home to the House of Burgesses; the Governor's Palace (reconstructed), site of many dances for the well-to-do and home to the royal and later state governors; the Raleigh Tavern (reconstructed), where Patrick Henry or Thomas Jefferson might have discussed politics; and the Public Gaol (pronounced "jail") built in 1704.

Stroll along and learn about trades such as bootmaking and silversmithing. Boys might have become blacksmiths, tanners, coopers, or wheelwrights. Many of the historic trade shops sell crafted items along Duke of Gloucester Street, the main drag, or at Merchants Square. At Williamsburg, re-enactments occur daily. Hear the wails of a woman whose husband has just been sold to another slave master, or participate in a witch trial.

Arrive early and buy a pass that includes admission to the Governor's Palace. Eat lunch early or late to avoid crowds. Nearby Busch Gardens and Water Country USA provide thrills in the warm-weather months. Accommodations range from budget motels and bed-and-breakfasts to the convenient Williamsburg Lodge (within the historical area) and the luxurious Kingsmill Resort, built on land that used to be Kingsmill Plantation, first settled in 1619.

Overlooking the James River, Kingsmill offers three eighteen-hole golf courses, multiroom suites with kitchenettes, children's programs, a marina, tennis, racquetball, billiards, swimming pools, restaurants, and a spa. To obtain information on Colonial Williamsburg, call (800) 447-8679 or visit their Web site at *www.colonialwilliamsburg.org*. To reach Kingsmill, call (800) 832-5665 or visit *www.kingsmill.com*.

After about eighty-four revisions, on July 4, 1776, Congress adopted the declaration by unanimous vote of the delegates of twelve colonies. Only New York abstained because representatives had not been authorized to vote (however, days later, the New York Provincial Congress endorsed the Declaration). John Hancock was the first to sign the document, which was considered an act of treason against King George III of England. It's rumored that he practiced writing his name prior to affixing his famous signature rather boldly to the historic document, spawning the expression about leaving one's "John Hancock" in subsequent generations.

The United States of America was born in Philadelphia's State House (now Independence Hall). This important document with its sharp yet poetic language finally convinced the British and the French that the American colonies had had enough and were determined to be an independent republic. No one, least of all King George, could ignore the situation.

The Declaration of Independence

Today, the Declaration of Independence is enshrined in the National Archives Exhibition Hall in Washington, D.C., where it is sealed in a glass and bronze case. Take a look at the following excerpts of this famous document.

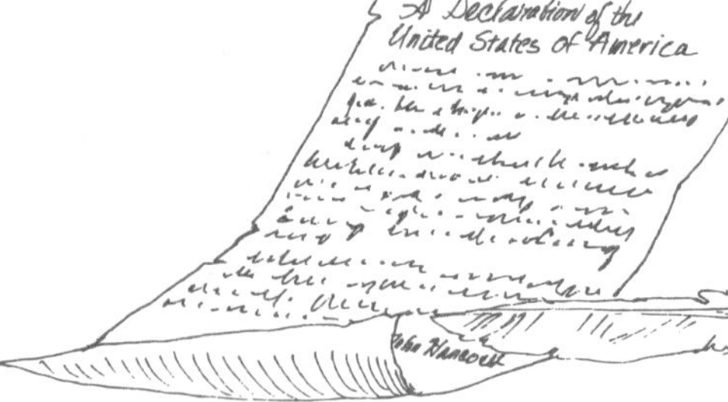

In Congress, July 4, 1776.
The unanimous declaration of the thirteen united states of america

. . . We hold these truths to be self-evident, that all men are created equal, that they are endowed by their Creator with certain unalienable Rights, that among these are Life, Liberty, and the pursuit of Happiness . . . Prudence, indeed, will dictate that Governments long established should not be changed for light and transient causes; and accordingly all experience hath shown that mankind are more disposed to suffer, while evils are sufferable, than to right themselves by abolishing the forms to which they are accustomed. But when a long train of abuses and usurpations pursuing invariably the same Object evinces a design to reduce them under absolute Despotism, it is their right, it is their duty, to throw off such Government, and to provide new Guards for their future security. Such has been the patient sufferance of these Colonies; and such is now the necessity which constrains them to alter their former Systems of Government. The history of the present King of Great Britain is a history of repeated injuries and usurpations, all having in direct object the establishment of an absolute Tyranny over these States. To prove this, let Facts be submitted to a candid world.

He has refused his Assent to Laws, the most wholesome and necessary for the public good . . .

. . . He has kept among us, in times of peace, Standing Armies without the Consent of our legislatures.

He has affected to render the military independent of and superior to the Civil Power.

He has combined with others to subject us to a jurisdiction foreign to our constitution, and unacknowledged by our laws; giving his Assent to their acts of pretended legislation:

For quartering large bodies of armed troops among us:

For protecting them, by a mock Trial, from Punishment for any Murders which they should commit on the Inhabitants of these States:

For cutting off our Trade with all parts of the world:

For imposing taxes on us without our Consent:

For depriving us in many cases, of the benefits of Trial by Jury:

For transporting us beyond Seas to be tried for pretended offenses:

For abolishing the free System of English Laws in a neighboring Province, establishing therein an Arbitrary government, and enlarging its Boundaries so as to render it at once an example and fit instrument for introducing the same absolute rule into these Colonies:

For taking away our Charters, abolishing our most valuable Laws, and altering fundamentally, the Forms of our Governments:

For suspending our own Legislatures, and declaring themselves invested with Power to legislate for us in all cases whatsoever.

He has abdicated Government here, by declaring us out of his Protection and waging War against us.

He has plundered our seas, ravaged our Coasts, burnt our towns, and destroyed the lives of our people.

He is at this time transporting large armies of foreign mercenaries to complete the works of death, desolation and tyranny, already begun with circumstances of Cruelty and perfidy scarcely paralleled in the most barbarous ages, and totally unworthy the Head of a civilized nation . . .

In every stage of these Oppressions We have Petitioned for Redress in the most humble terms: Our repeated Petitions have been answered only by repeated injury. A Prince, whose character is thus marked by every act which may define a Tyrant, is unfit to be the ruler of a free people . . . .

We, therefore, the Representatives of the United States of America, in General Congress, assembled, appealing to the Supreme Judge of the world for the rectitude of our intentions, do, in the name, and by authority of the good People of these Colonies, solemnly publish and declare, That these United Colonies are, and of Right ought to be Free and Independent States; that they are Absolved from all Allegiance to the British Crown, and that all political connection between them and the State of Great Britain, is and ought to be totally dissolved; and that as Free and Independent States, they have full power to levy War, conclude Peace, contract Alliances, establish Commerce, and to do all other Acts and Things which Independent States may of right do. And for the support of this Declaration, with a firm reliance on the Protection of Divine Providence, we mutually pledge to each other our Lives, our Fortunes and our sacred Honor.

4

Revolution Reigns

"The Revolution was in the hearts and minds of the people . . . long before a drop of blood was shed," said John Adams, Revolutionary leader and later president.

Many of the dictates set forth by Great Britain on the American colonies served as a prelude to war. Still, there's some debate as to which issues were more pressing. Certainly, the signers of the Declaration of Independence insisted it was about liberty and democracy, for it seemed the colonists had little choice in how they were governed. Yet some historians now argue that the Revolution was fought for money and trade because the British took everything for themselves. Indeed, all of these concerns probably had something to contribute to the revolt, which had most likely given King George more than a few sleepless nights. Moreover, the Patriots' call to arms spawned uprisings throughout Europe.

The Continental Army

General Washington had now organized militia companies upon his appointment as commander of the colonial forces. He was clearly the best choice in that he'd fought alongside the British in the French and Indian War. He knew the contempt the British military showed for colonial officers, and as tensions deepened, Washington's perspective broadened as a protestor. It didn't hurt that as a Virginian, he might bind the southern colonies to the New England Patriots. If there was to be victory, our forefathers knew it would take all thirteen colonies working together.

The Thirteen Colonies

Battles were already underway when Washington appeared at the Second Continental Congress in May 1775, dressed in his uniform of the Fairfax County militia. On June 25, 1775, Washington set out for Massachusetts to take command of the forces. Under much adversity, Washington took what many of us would term an armed mob and assembled them into the Continental Army with one goal—victory.

At first, Washington found his new army to be in good spirits, as it had inflicted heavy casualties among the British at Bunker Hill. However, the general was appalled at their lack of discipline. What's more, many of the men would end their military service soon, so Washington faced the triple challenge of recruitment, training, and impending battle.

Thus, Washington sought longer terms of enlistment from Congress as well as better pay for his troops. But a leery Congress, afraid of moving from one military dictatorship to another, was not easily convinced. Washington did what he could under the circumstances. When you factor in troop defection, insubordination, lack of discipline, and a shortage of gunpowder, it's understandable that Washington maintained order at times by flogging troops, or worse. Deserters and repeat offenders were often hanged.

When Washington first took command, there was much strategic planning. During that winter, the Americans dragged fifty heavy cannons by sled from Fort Ticonderoga in northern New York (which the Americans had captured from the British) to Boston. An astute Washington had the cannons mounted on Dorchester Heights, which commanded the city. Of course, British General Howe saw this and fled by sea to Halifax, Nova Scotia, where he awaited the reinforcement of German mercenaries from Europe. This brought a much-needed reprieve from the occupation of any British troops in the colonies.

Who Were the Big Whigs?

Those who supported the cries for colonial independence and the resulting revolution became known as Whigs.

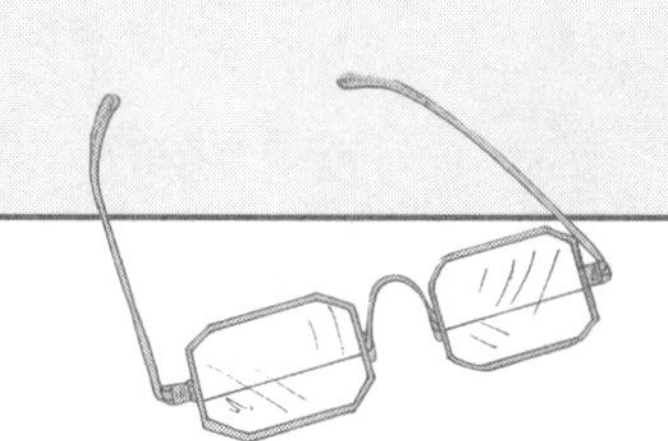

Battling for New York

Britain's clear advantage was its navy, for the Americans had none. Sensing the final break even before the Declaration of Independence was signed, in June of 1776, the British sent General William Howe to assemble his forces as well as a huge fleet. Howe landed on Long Island, pushing his way to New York City with an army of 30,000 soldiers—more than twice as many men as Washington had. Trying to cope with this mighty force, Washington committed a tactical blunder that nearly cost him the war. He split his troops between Brooklyn on Long Island and Manhattan Island. This weakened the overall American position. By the end of August, the Americans had to retreat to their Brooklyn Heights fortifications.

Thinking he had them cornered, Howe called off his Redcoats temporarily while he planned a potential siege. This proved to be a mistake. Surrender was not on Washington's mind. Though he had no navy to rely on, the undeterred general rounded up every seaworthy vessel he could find and obtained assistance from the experienced boatmen of Marblehead, Massachusetts. In the midst of a raging storm, he and his men rowed across the East River to safety in Manhattan, losing not one man in his command. But although this served as a brilliant escape, it also meant that an important American seaport had been lost to the British.

Mysterious Fire

A few days after Howe landed in Manhattan, a mysterious fire leveled much of the town. Was it mere coincidence? Some have attributed it to a Patriot arsonist, but whatever the fire's origin, it aided the American cause.

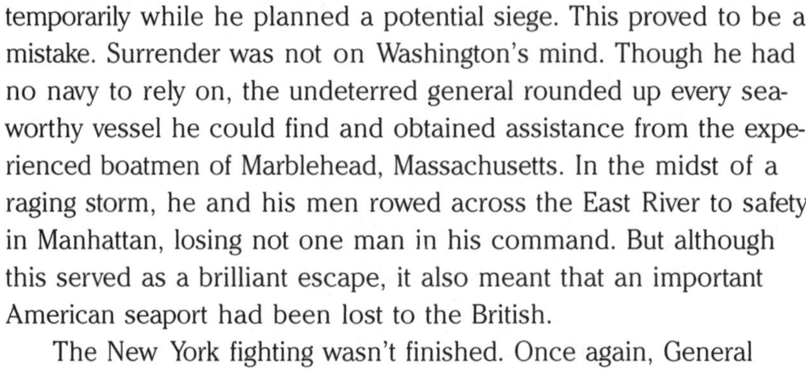

The New York fighting wasn't finished. Once again, General Howe took his time, hoping to negotiate a peace agreement. When those attempts failed, Howe landed his force at Kip's Bay, Manhattan, on September 15, accompanied by British warships cruising the East River. Washington, riding among his men, had trouble keeping the troops together. Rather than take advantage of the disarray, Howe displayed his leisurely posture, feeling perhaps a little smug that he controlled most of Manhattan.

Washington had already shown enough brilliance that it more than made up for his early strategic errors. Most important, as a good military strategist, he had the knack for learning from his blunders. He knew he wouldn't do battle with the British any time soon if he couldn't preserve his own army first. Washington withdrew his troops for a while, retreating to Harlem Heights, then to White Plains. The British prevailed at a White Plains skirmish. While they allowed Washington's forces to retreat in good order, the British turned their attention south, capturing Fort Washington and Fort Lee on the New Jersey shore just days later.

Things were looking a little bleak for General Washington and his men. In three months, they had lost New York and Long Island, and his army of 19,000 was reduced to fewer than 3,500. Desertion among the troops was rampant, and Washington was facing criticism for his performance. British General Howe declared victory—it was that bad. Even the Congress fled Philadelphia for Baltimore. Such times inspired Thomas Paine to write in *The American Crisis*, "These are the times that try men's souls."

Washington led his contingent across the Delaware River into the relative safety of Pennsylvania. As a precaution, he ordered all boats along the New Jersey side of the river to go with them. Morale was running low as winter set in, and many troops were without proper shoes and clothing. Never deterred, Washington found his answer that frigid December.

Christmas Crossing

When reinforcements arrived, Washington's strategic mind went to work. He knew the British had pulled back most of their troops into New York City, leaving only scattered garrisons of the Hessian soldiers the British paid to help them. Those Hessians nearest to Washington were camped at Trenton.

Remember those Marblehead fishermen who helped with their boats before? Well, Washington called on their tactical aid once again as he launched a surprise attack on the sleeping soldiers, on the morning of December 26. He was fairly certain that these foreign troops, celebrating the holidays away from home, would imbibe heavily, and that this was the optimal moment to attack. Washington gained serious ground by killing, wounding, or capturing every one of the Hessian soldiers while suffering only six casualties among his men. James Monroe was one of the four wounded.

This surprise attack reconfirmed in many an American mind that victory could be within their grasp. To the British, Washington's victory proved the Continental Army was worthy of their respect. British General Cornwallis rushed south from New York City toward Princeton with reinforcements. In early January, he reached Trenton, where he decided to rest.

You would have thought the enemy had learned by now, but Washington slipped past Trenton in the night and attacked the British the next morning. Surprise! The Americans not only were victorious on the battlefield, but were able to acquire much-needed supplies.

In fact, the British felt so alarmed and threatened that they evacuated most New Jersey garrisons.

With victories in the Battle of Trenton and the Battle of Princeton, and with Philadelphia no longer in peril, Washington moved north to winter quarters in Morristown, New Jersey. There, Washington turned his attention to recruitment.

The War Up North

The British didn't use their time wisely, for they spent the first six months of 1777 on skirmishes in northern New Jersey. British General John Burgoyne felt that by striking down the Hudson River, he would cut off New England and New York from the rest of the colonies and end the colonial rebellion. After recapturing Fort Ticonderoga, Burgoyne headed toward Fort Edward. When the Patriots saw them approaching, they scattered into the woods for cover, but continued to attack from behind their shield of trees. The end result was British losses of close to 1,000 men. This slowed the British down, and by the time they reached Saratoga, New York, the Americans were ready. American General Horatio Gates positioned his troops to overlook the road to Albany so that when Burgoyne came along, he pretty much had to fight. After losing even more soldiers, Burgoyne did what he swore he'd never do—he surrendered on October 17, 1777.

Valley Forge

Though Saratoga had turned the war in America's favor, Washington still had his struggles. Trying to protect the capital of Philadelphia, he lost the Battles of Brandywine and Germantown, and he withdrew his besieged forces to nearby Valley Forge, the site of his winter encampment.

On the positive side, the 11,000 soldiers who spent the winter of 1777–78 here were positioned high enough to have a grand view of anyone approaching (including British General Howe). However, the conditions at Valley Forge were dismal. An estimated 2,500 troops died from exposure or disease, further reducing Washington's

Visit Valley Forge and Yorktown Today

Valley Forge National Historical Park, administered by the National Park Service, commemorates the historic winter and the army's epic struggle to survive against terrible odds. Start at the visitor's center where a fifteen-minute film gives you an introduction to the encampment. Follow the exhibits—an extensive collection of firearms, swords, and accessories—and browse in the bookstore. Your tour options include the self-guided tour that takes you past the Artillery Park, Washington's headquarters and officers' quarters, and the Grand Parade where General Von Steuben rebuilt the army. Bus tours are given from May through September.

Picnic areas and bike rentals make this a park to spend some time in along the six-mile bicycle or foot trail. For more information, call (888) VISITVF or visit the Web site at *www.valleyforge.org*.

Another famous commemoration of the Revolutionary War is at Yorktown, where you can learn about General Lord Charles Cornwallis's surrender to George Washington. The Yorktown Victory Center, a site erected by the Commonwealth of Virginia, starts with the Road to Revolution open-air exhibit that traces the shift in sentiment toward rebellion. The film *A Time of Revolution* dramatizes recollections of soldiers and their officers. Of course, there is a small arsenal of antiques, including a pistol that belonged to the Marquis de Lafayette and some Hessian boots. Don't miss the Continental Army encampment and the 1780s farm that's been reconstructed. Kids play eighteenth-century dress-up in the Discovery Room.

The National Park Service operates the Yorktown Visitors Center where you can watch a sixteen-minute film shown every thirty minutes, browse exhibits, and choose between two tours—a guided thirty-minute walking tour of the battlefield or the self-guided auto version complete with cassette player.

To reach the Yorktown Victory Center, call (804) 253-4838. For accommodations, call (800) 446-9244, or the Jamestown–Yorktown Foundation at (888) 593-4682 or try the Web site at *www.historyisfun.org*.

fighting force. The men needed everything from food and soap to blankets and warm clothing. Many deserted the Continental Army. Making matters worse, discontented officers tried to oust Washington and replace him with General Horatio Gates. When this attempt failed it ended up doing more to solidify Washington's influence than break it.

The commander refused to take more comfortable quarters until his men were provided for. With the few tools they had, the troops erected shelters of logs and clay. Thanks to Washington's leadership and the efforts of drillmaster Baron Augustus von Steuben, a Prussian officer who volunteered for the American cause, they restored discipline, morale, and training at Valley Forge that winter. Spring's approach brought brighter spirits, as did the heartening news that France had allied itself with the Americans. Within six months, the Continental Army was ready once more. The last major battle in the northeast occurred at Monmouth in June 1778, when British General Sir Henry Clinton, who had preceded Howe, pulled troops out of Philadelphia and moved them north toward New York. Washington's army caught up with them at Monmouth, New Jersey, where General Washington ordered his second in command, Charles Lee, to attack the rear of the British forces. Lee, disliking Washington's plan, fought half-heartedly and ordered retreat. This infuriated General Washington. He rallied the troops to follow his command, and Clinton's army fell back some before withdrawing to New York. Washington had once again restored sagging morale, and Lee, while trying to clear his name of wrongdoing, was court-martialed and suspended from command. When he refused to accept this, Lee was removed from the Continental Army altogether.

Attack on Philadelphia

While the English Major General John Burgoyne was fighting in the north, Howe loaded his troops aboard approximately 250 ships and sailed up the Chesapeake Bay for Philadelphia, leaving Burgoyne to face potential disaster. Washington didn't exactly expect to keep

Howe out of the city. Nonetheless, he couldn't just hand it to him. Thus, he fought with an outnumbered army. The Battle of Brandywine occurred in September 1777 and was followed by the Battle of Germantown, where the British outflanked the entrenched Continental Army.

On October 4, 1777, Howe took Philadelphia, the American capital (though government leaders had previously fled). This might have impressed the British, but it didn't do much for the French, who were beginning to take notice of the American victories in other battles.

French Aid

At the outset of the Revolution, the Americans realized their limitations. All the resources seemed to lie across the ocean. Benjamin Franklin was dispatched to France to foster financial support as well as troops. Remember that King George III had already bought support with Hessian mercenaries from Germany.

Benjamin Franklin

Franklin's diplomatic prowess certainly succeeded, but the victories, especially at Saratoga, spoke volumes. After seeing proof that the Continental Army was a capable fighting force, and upon hearing rumors that Britain might offer America territorial concessions to reach peace, the French government ministers had enough confidence in General Washington to recommend to King Louis XVI that he sign a treaty of alliance with the Americans. In February 1778, this alliance was made formal, with France diplomatically recognizing "the United States of America." Soon after the signing, Spain, which had offered to remain neutral if Britain returned Gibraltar, threw in support since its demands were not met. Spain and France were already allies as well.

French aid was certainly welcome, but French egos were not. Many of the officers who arrived in the summer of 1777 demanded exalted rank and commensurate pay for their limited military experience. An exception was the young Marquis de Lafayette, who arrived in Philadelphia volunteering to serve on America's behalf at his own expense. This quickly won Washington's praise and the admiration of American troops. Lafayette had been rushed into battle at Brandywine, and by December he had his own command and commission as a major general. In 1779, Lafayette returned to his native country to continue lobbying for further aid, thus proving to be a valuable liaison between the Continental Army and the French government.

Valuable Rebel States

Gradually, the real action in the war had shifted south to Virginia, the Carolinas, and Georgia, states that were home to the crucial export crops of tobacco, rice, and indigo, making the southern states perhaps the most valuable of the rebel states.

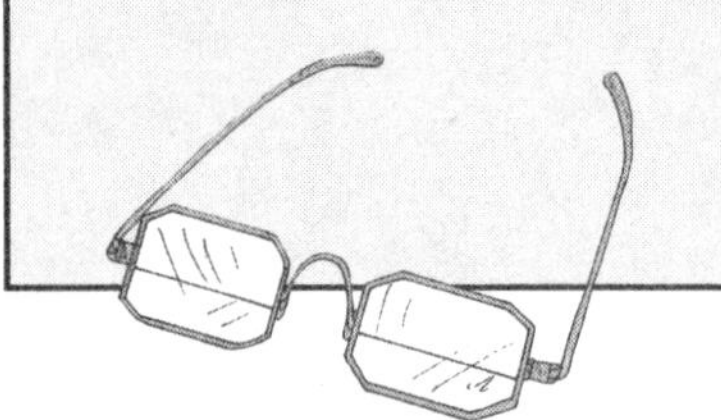

The War in the West and South

American frontiersmen continued to settle and their numbers in the region grew. This was significant because Britain had forbidden the American colonists to move beyond the Appalachians. In fact, Great Britain had recruited Native Americans as allies to attack any colonial settlements out west. But George Rogers Clark, a Virginian, seized British forts along the frontier in 1778 and braved the Ohio River. By spring 1779 he arrived in the Illinois territory.

Also in 1779, British General Cornwallis had 5,000 troops stationed in the South with the goal of forcing the "King's obedience" into the Carolinas. Loyalist sentiment was stronger here. The British secretly hoped that southern Loyalists would provide support as well as much-needed supplies.

In the autumn of 1778, a large British force sailed from New York to launch a sea assault against Savannah, Georgia. The city fell to the British in December. Augusta, Georgia, fell one month later. When the French joined forces to counter the assault, they were shot to tatters. By the end of 1779, most of Georgia was firmly under British and Loyalist control.

While Charleston, South Carolina, had fended off attack for nearly three years, the city's defenses slowly deteriorated. The British besieged Charleston, cutting off supplies, and in May, the Americans were forced to surrender. The Patriots lost many military supplies in the process.

The War at Sea

Great Britain, the world's leading maritime power, hardly feared the infant colonial navy. The British ships plied coastal waters, supplying the Redcoats with whatever was needed, including more of His Majesty's troops. Still, the small Patriot navy won a few surprising victories, especially when a small American squadron captured the port of Nassau in the Bahamas.

Farther out at sea, American naval power did far better, capturing some British ships and cargo. Continental Navy captains—the likes of John Paul Jones from Scotland, Joshua Barney, and Irishman John Barry—proved to be heroic at sea. John Paul Jones is by far the most famous Revolutionary naval hero. In 1778, Jones raided the port of Whitehaven in England, and then captured the British sloop called the *Drake*. On September 23, 1779, when the British attacked his converted merchant ship the *Bonhomme Richard* and demanded his surrender, Jones answered with the famous words, "I have not yet begun to fight!"

By 1781 there were more than 450 privately owned vessels that had received commissions to attack British shipping. And although these did not impede the British troops and their supply provisions, they added tremendous cost to the war Britain waged.

Thanks to the French navy, Britain's supremacy was sufficiently threatened, and the war at sea saw fewer American defeats with added victories. French naval forces fought off the Virginia coast, successfully trapping British General Cornwallis and his army.

The Battle of Yorktown

The Revolutionary War had raged for six years when in the summer of 1781 the second French fleet arrived. Washington had sent General Lafayette to confront Cornwallis near the Chesapeake Bay. There, the British were awaiting supplies from New York. But upon hearing of the French fleet, Washington changed plans, leaving New York himself and heading south.

Washington coordinated the land and sea operation that brought the final climax of the war. It was as if the commander had been

Benedict Arnold

Pharmacist, enlisted member of the militia during the French and Indian War, prosperous shipping mate, spendthrift—all aptly describe Benedict Arnold, but he's best known as a traitor.

Arnold joined Ethan Allen to take Fort Ticonderoga in New York at the start of the Revolution in 1775. The need for money led him to sixteen months of treason writing to the British commander Sir Henry Clinton. Arnold had agreed to surrender key American defenses at West Point and even signed the plans he handed over to Major John André, the British spy who was intercepted before he could deliver the message.

André was hanged, but Arnold fled to British safety and later sailed with his family to England where he lived out his days.

waiting for this very moment to unleash his most brilliant military strategies and fighting energy.

First, the French fleet blockaded Yorktown early that September, followed by a combined Franco-American army that Washington commanded. It took up siege positions on land and by early October had trapped the British against the York River. In a gross misjudgment, Cornwallis had his back to the sea. Daily he endured gunfire and continual pounding from the cannons until he was forced to ask the Americans for terms of surrender on October 17, 1781. Two days later the once mighty (and haughty) British army paraded its units between the victorious French and American soldiers, laying down their arms, while a British band played the popular tune "The World Turned Upside Down."

Unable to concede the war, Cornwallis sent a representative, General O'Hara, to surrender his sword. General O'Hara approached a French commander, who indicated that the sword should go to General Washington. However, Washington felt that an officer of equal rank should receive it. Thus, his second in command, Major General Benjamin Lincoln, received the British sword in surrender.

Back in England, King George III was prepared to fight on, but the British Parliament put an end to that notion. It had taken more than six years of war, and skirmishes before that, to drive its greatest overseas possession toward independence. In February 1782, Lord North's ministry in Britain fell. Parliament would no longer support a war in America.

Peace Negotiations Proceed

You might think Washington's official duties had ended, but although hostilities had ceased, peace was precarious while formal negotiations took place. Four American diplomats—John Adams, Benjamin Franklin, John Jay, and Henry Laurens—were dispatched to Paris to begin the peace process.

Washington stayed on as commander of the American forces. He knew King George had acceded to the wishes of Parliament, and we can presume that Washington didn't put anything past the frustrated and defeated king. To be on the safe side, he maintained a state of military preparedness.

General Washington could have easily usurped power and taken the role of a military dictator, or perhaps become a king himself. Instead, he chose the route of obedience to the Continental Congress and worked tirelessly to establish a strong central government by and for the people. Not only did Washington stress the need for a Constitutional Convention, he presided over it and helped gain ratification of the Constitution of the United States. Peace was officially proclaimed on April 15, 1783, but it wasn't until November that the last British boats left. The formal signing of the Peace of Paris occurred in September 1783, nearly two years after Cornwallis's surrender at Yorktown. Though Britain had hoped to give the Americans less than complete independence, it finally did just that, recognizing the thirteen United States of America.

Purple Heart

The first Purple Heart, a military decoration awarded to those wounded or killed in action, was designed by General Washington and established in 1782.

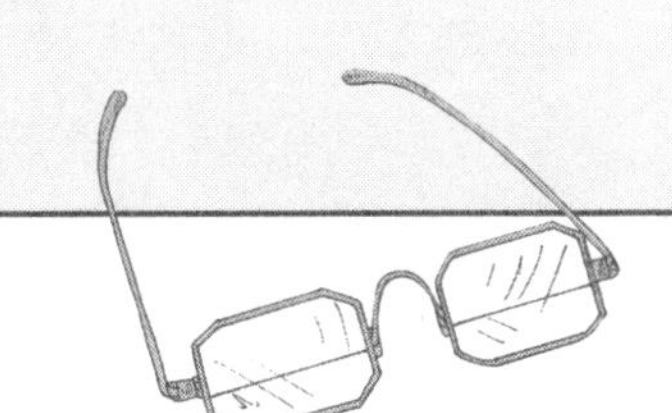

Farewell to Arms

On December 4, 1783, Washington took leave of his principal officers at New York City's Fraunces Tavern. He'd enjoyed the sweet taste of victory several times, but had also swallowed a few bitter defeats. The general had also pacified his former officers, many of whom had not been paid what they'd been promised. He implored these impatient patriots to back down from their threats of military takeover. As he relinquished command, he pledged further service to his new country to "the utmost of my abilities."

Seeking a quiet life, he returned home to his estate at Mount Vernon in Virginia. En route, he stopped at Annapolis, Maryland, where Congress was meeting, to surrender his commission as commander in chief. But in the months and years that followed, others would hold him to his pledge of service.

5

SHAPING A NEW NATION AND GOVERNMENT

Articles of Confederation

Voted on by the Second Continental Congress, these agreements gave the larger balance of power to individual states. Among the powers not vested in the national government was taxation. The Articles of Confederation began the ratification process in November 1777, and concluded in March 1781. Years later, discussions to modify them led to the creation of the U.S. Constitution, transforming the rather loose confederation of colonies into the solidified United States of America.

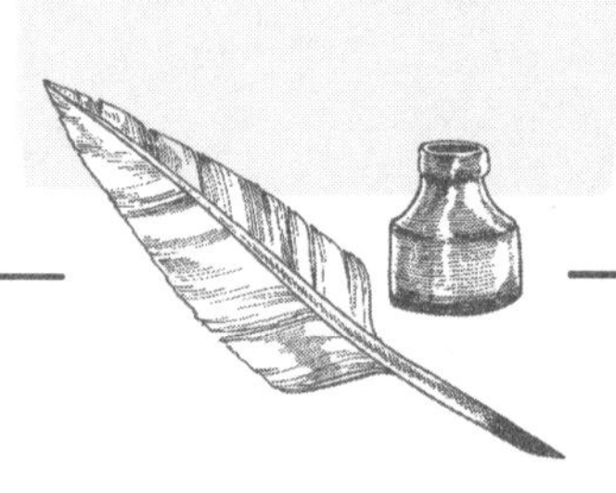

Imagine four scorching months in the summer of 1787, in Philadelphia, trying with all of your mind and heart to hammer out a new system of government. If you were a delegate sent to work on this project, you not only knew you were making history, but you had a fledgling nation threatening to break apart once more—and this, after a long, bloody war. In essence, you got what you asked for, and now you needed to make the best of it.

Shaping a System of Government

The Articles of Confederation, which governed the United States, were simple. They were good for the war effort, but too limiting to guide the new nation down its fought-for path of independence.

There was no governor, no chief executive, and no court to try cases. Each state had one vote, regardless of its population. The Congress had military and diplomatic power but could not levy taxes to pay for any of it. It couldn't regulate commerce. Any shift in power, or any change for that matter, required unanimous consent of the states. Mind you, this wasn't always a congenial bunch!

Under the Articles of Confederation, Congress could do little without the consent of the affected states. George Washington saw this as a sign of weakness and disorganization. In 1785 he wrote, "The Confederation appears to me to be little more than a shadow without the substance." For instance, when Rhode Island and Connecticut failed to pay tax on imported goods, the central government was helpless to take action. When a group of debt-ridden farmers led an insurrection against Massachusetts (called the Shays's Rebellion), Washington grew alarmed and feared that the eight years of bloodshed and expense invested in the United States would be wasted unless some better structure was brought forth. Well, remember how a retiring General Washington pledged his support and service?

The Constitutional Convention

Delegates from all states, with the exception of Rhode Island, which as we'd say today "had an attitude," converged on Philadelphia in May 1787 to revise the Articles of Confederation. The legislature unanimously chose Washington as president of the convention, and most agreed on a few prevailing principles once Alexander Hamilton convinced the crowd that the Articles had best be scrapped and another document created.

George Washington

Original Thirteen States

State	Date Admitted
Delaware	December 7, 1787
Pennsylvania	December 12, 1787
New Jersey	December 18, 1787
Georgia	January 2, 1788
Connecticut	January 9, 1788
Massachusetts	February 6, 1788
Maryland	April 28, 1788
South Carolina	May 23, 1788
New Hampshire	June 21, 1788
Virginia	June 25, 1788
New York	July 26, 1788
North Carolina	November 21, 1789
Rhode Island	May 29, 1790

Work Begins

An array of men were among the fifty-five delegates who gathered in Philadelphia. There were merchants and planters, landlords and other men of wealth and prestige. There were some who owned slaves and some who did not. There were famous war generals and outspoken patriots. All assembled to carve out the Constitution, and little did they know that the entire process from debate and drafting to signing and ratification would take more than a year's time.

George Washington led this group, which included Benjamin Franklin, Alexander Hamilton, and James Madison. Off in Europe on diplomatic matters, Thomas Jefferson and John Adams missed the work and the rancor. Patrick Henry, who supported the limited central government of the Confederation, staunchly refused to attend.

If the purpose was to speak their minds, the delegates were successful from the start. New Jersey's William Paterson proposed reforming the Articles of Confederation, thus allowing the Confederation to levy taxes and regulate commerce and trade. His New Jersey Plan would recognize Congressional acts as supreme beyond the laws of the respective states. However, the convention rejected Paterson's plan.

A few delegates protested that states with large populations were due considerably more votes than the single vote the Confederation allowed. Other delegates felt that too much power rested with the individual states.

The Virginia Plan

James Madison, representing Virginia, presented his alternative for a national republic with a powerful central government, which limited the sovereignty of individual states. Madison's Virginia Plan drew its authority not from the thirteen states but from the population as a whole. The Convention voted to accept the Virginia Plan, with its idea of a lower house based on population, and left a committee to work out the composition of the upper house. On July 16, 1787, the committee proposed the "Great Compromise" that each state have two members in this upper house of legislative government. As part of this concept, there was a three-part national government with lower and upper houses, an executive branch, and a judiciary component chosen by the entire legislature.

Early Compromises

This was a vociferous bunch. While the delegates agreed to the basic principles that Madison and his Virginia Plan outlined early in June, they began to address contentious topics including this issue of population in regard to representation, as well as regional issues such as slavery.

Many southern states had large numbers of black slaves, and northern delegates argued that since slaves could not vote, they should not be counted for purposes of representation. Doing so would yield more power to the southern agenda. Of course, the southerners didn't see it this way, arguing that slaves should be counted as part of the population. Compromise came when it was agreed that three-fifths of a state's enslaved populace would be counted for representation and taxation.

The issue of slavery didn't end there. Moral arguments over the practice entered into the convention's debate. The delegates once again compromised, with the Constitution permitting slaves to be imported until 1808, when Congress could ban their importation and trade. Northerners reluctantly agreed to the Fugitive Slave Clause that allowed owners to reclaim runaway slaves who fled to other states.

POWERS VESTED

The Constitution required more work when it came to defining judicial power. The delegates created a Supreme Court and left the rest of the planning to the first Congress, which then had to tackle how this court system would be established.

Having accepted the "Great Compromise," they agreed that the Senate would be the governmental body filled with two delegates from each state, and that the House of Representatives would be based on population in those states. In addition, rather than have the people vote for the president and vice president, they would select members of a small Electoral College to do so. In the event that one candidate did not receive a majority of votes cast by this Electoral College, the House of Representatives was charged with making the selection. Until the year 2000 (when the Electoral College made front-page news), many of us failed to realize that this system had prevailed for more than 200 years in presidential elections.

Books about the Constitution

- *The Constitution of the United States of America (Little Books of Wisdom)* (Applewood Books, 1995)
- *The Declaration of Independence and the Constitution of the United States* (Bantam Books, 1998)
- *American Constitution: Its Origin and Development* by Alfred Hinsey Kelly, Herman Belz, and Winfred A. Harbison (Norton, 1991)
- *The Bill of Rights: Creation and Reconstruction* by Akhil Reed Amar (Yale University Press, 1998)
- *Our Defense: The Bill of Rights in Action* by Ellen Alderman and Caroline Kennedy (Morrow, 1991)

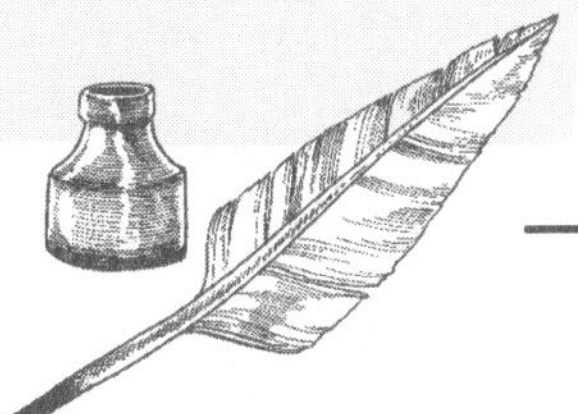

Books about the Constitution for Children

- *Shh! We're Writing the Constitution* by Jean Fritz, illustrated by Tomie dePaola (Putnam, 1987)
- *If You Were There When They Signed the Constitution* by Elizabeth Levy, illustrated by Joan Holub and Richard Rosenblum (Scholastic, 1992)
- *The Constitution* by Marilyn Prolman (Children's Press, 1995)
- *My Fellow Americans* by Alice Provensen (Harcourt Brace, 1995)

The executive office would be responsible for carrying out all laws, and the executive officer, the president, would serve as commander in chief of the armed forces. In addition, the president would oversee foreign relations and appoint federal judges and other federal officials.

Regarding issues of finance, the delegates gave the powers of taxation and currency issue to the new national government. This took away from the individual states the right to issue money.

Checks, Balances, and Everyone's Blessing

Delegates to the Constitutional Convention were astute in setting up a system of checks and balances. For instance, even though the president also served as the commander in chief, only Congress could declare war. The delegates gave the president veto power over Congress, although with a two-thirds majority, the Congress could override such an action. The judicial checks were less thought out at this juncture, but years later, when the chief justice of the United States declared a law unconstitutional, the judicial review process became more firmly established.

Dealing with issues of power and setting limitations on that power proved to be dicey. On September 17, 1787, after much debate, the convention completed the Constitution of the United States. Now, the conventioneers had to gather the delegates' formal signatures, and the states had to ratify the new document outlining the new form of government. Actually, nine states had to ratify the Constitution before it would take effect. Five states—Delaware, Pennsylvania, New Jersey, Georgia, and Connecticut—were the first to approve, and New Hampshire provided the decisive ratification vote in 1788. Some states, including New York and Pennsylvania, insisted more work be done to safeguard fundamental individual rights. Congress submitted twelve amendments, ten of which were adopted as Articles I through X of the U.S. Constitution—collectively known as the Bill of Rights. When Congress introduced the Bill of Rights in 1789, North Carolina and Rhode Island gave their formal approval to the Constitution, which was by now already operating as the law of the land.

The Preamble of the U.S. Constitution reads: "We the People of the United States, in Order to form a more perfect Union, establish Justice, insure domestic Tranquility, provide for the common defence, promote the general Welfare, and secure the Blessings of Liberty to ourselves and our Posterity, do ordain and establish this Constitution for the United States of America."

The Bill of Rights

The first ten amendments to the U.S. Constitution were ratified on December 15, 1791, and form what is known as the Bill of Rights. It's interesting to note that while the Constitution itself has been amended over the years, the Bill of Rights has been untouched—a testament to our nation's early leaders.

Amendment I

Congress shall make no law respecting an establishment of religion, or prohibiting the free exercise thereof; or abridging the freedom of speech, or of the press, or the right of the people peaceably to assemble, and to petition the Government for a redress of grievances.

Amendment II

A well-regulated Militia, being necessary to the security of a free State, the right of the people to keep and bear Arms, shall not be infringed.

Amendment III

No Soldier shall, in time of peace be quartered in any house, without the consent of the Owner, nor in time of war, but in a manner to be prescribed by law.

Amendment IV

The right of the people to be secure in their persons, houses, papers, and effects, against unreasonable searches and seizures, shall not be violated, and no Warrants shall issue, but upon probable cause, supported by Oath or affirmation, and particularly describing the place to be searched, and the persons or things to be seized.

Amendment V

No person shall be held to answer for a capital, or otherwise infamous crime, unless on a presentment or indictment of a Grand Jury, except in cases arising in the land or naval forces, or in the Militia, when in actual service in time of War or public danger; nor shall any person be subject for the same offence to be twice put in jeopardy of life or limb; nor shall be compelled in any criminal case to be a witness against himself, nor be deprived of life, liberty, or property, without due process of law; nor shall private property be taken for public use, without just compensation.

Amendment VI

In all criminal prosecutions, the accused shall enjoy the right to a speedy and public trial, by an impartial jury of the State and district wherein the crime shall have been committed, which district shall have been previously ascertained by law, and to be informed of the nature and cause of the accusation; to be confronted with the witnesses against him; to have compulsory process for obtaining witnesses in his favor, and to have the Assistance of Counsel for his defence.

Amendment VII

In Suits at common law, where the value in controversy shall exceed twenty dollars, the right of trial by jury shall be preserved, and no fact tried by a jury, shall be otherwise re-examined in any Court of the United States, than according to the rules of the common law.

Amendment VIII

Excessive bail shall not be required, nor excessive fines imposed, nor cruel and unusual punishments inflicted.

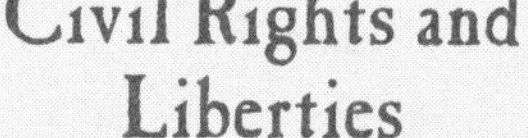

Civil rights and civil liberties refer to the guarantees of freedom, justice, and equality for all citizens. More precisely, civil rights imply equal protection and opportunity under the law, as we know it today. Civil liberties refer to freedom of speech, press, religion, and due process of the law.

Amendment IX

The enumeration in the Constitution, of certain rights, shall not be construed to deny or disparage others retained by the people.

Amendment X

The powers not delegated to the United States by the Constitution, nor prohibited by it to the States, are reserved to the States respectively, or to the people.

Two Factions Forge Ahead

Once the delegates signed the U.S. Constitution, they returned to their respective states and set forth to see it ratified. But two factions had different notions. Federalists believed in a strong central government; merchants and professionals made up this faction. Their opposing party, the Antifederalists, were mainly farmers, many of whom owed large debts. Antifederalists were alarmed by the Constitution's first phrase of "We the people of the United States . . . " thinking that the Constitution might nullify the independence of the states. But the Federalists accomplished a lot. They organized the administrative detail of the national government, began the liberal interpretations of the Constitution, and kept the new nation at peace with a stance of neutrality.

Antifederalists argued that too many differing agendas in large states would make it impossible for one way to prevail. They feared a strong central government, thinking that at some juncture state rights would become null and void.

The Federalist Papers, written by Alexander Hamilton, James Madison, and John Jay, defended the new Constitution. This trio of authors wrote under the pen name of Publius.

New York newspapers ran the individual papers beginning in October 1787, and the collective work was published in 1788 in book form. James Madison effectively put to rest the Antifederalist argument. He stated that its size would indeed make a central

government work best (not impede its functioning) because no one special interest could gain much ground with such diversity throughout the land.

The Federalist Papers did influence New York's ratification, but did little else around the new nation. Only when they were analyzed later was their brilliance realized. The authors' outline of the U.S. Constitution helped others to further understand the intricacies of our nation's government.

George Washington after the War

Though worn out by battle, George Washington reluctantly accepted the call to become the first president, relinquishing his genteel retirement at Mount Vernon. Mindful that his leadership was sorely needed to unify the infant nation, he pressed for ratification of the U.S. Constitution, which he firmly believed was the best that could be written at the time. Washington was so popular that if he gave this new document and governmental creation his blessing, then others would also. But, wise as ever, Washington also knew that he had no example to learn from. "I walk on untrodden ground," he said. "There is scarcely any part of my conduct which may not hereafter be drawn in precedent."

The First Presidency

On April 30, 1789, Washington took the oath of office in the portico of Federal Hall on Wall Street, New York City. Also present were Vice President John Adams, both houses of the newly organized Congress, and an exuberant crowd of onlookers. His first inaugural address was brief and modest, containing only one suggestion to the new Congress—that its members "would carefully avoid every alteration which might endanger the benefits of an united and effective government, or which ought to await the future lessons of experience."

Washington knew there was widespread support for the original amendments that made up the Bill of Rights. He supported these, but also had the foresight to know that further attempts to amend the document too quickly would hinder the fledgling nation.

Washington Eases into Power

Washington was careful not to set precedents that would start dangerous trends toward a monarchy or dictatorship. He respected the divisions of power created in the Constitution, and he spent his first days in office listening to divergent viewpoints as he organized the executive branch. Land owners tended to have more conservative views, and as George Washington was a propertied gentleman himself, he tried to recognize the more liberal outlook of farmers and artisans who made up the majority of the population.

Congress delivered a tariff or tax bill to Washington in June for his signature. The measure would provide the new government a source of much-needed revenue. The issue of where to establish the permanent seat of government was postponed to the next congressional session, but by the close of the first one, bills had been passed establishing three executive departments representing the president's cabinet–State, Treasury, and War. In addition, Congress established a federal judiciary comprising the Supreme Court of one chief justice, five associate justices, and thirteen district courts. An attorney general would be the nation's highest law officer. In keeping with his careful decisions, Washington chose a balance of liberals and conservatives for his cabinet. Alexander Hamilton became secretary of the treasury and Henry Knox the first secretary of war; Edmund Randolph of Virginia was offered the post of attorney general. Washington awaited the return of Thomas Jefferson, who was the U.S. diplomatic representative to France, in order to offer him the position of secretary of state. Our first president nominated John Jay of New York as chief justice of the United States.

Viewing the Constitution

The entire Constitution is displayed at the National Archives in Washington, D.C., only once a year—September 17, the anniversary of the date on which it was signed. On other days, the first and fourth pages are displayed in a bulletproof case. At night they are lowered into a vault strong enough to withstand a nuclear explosion.

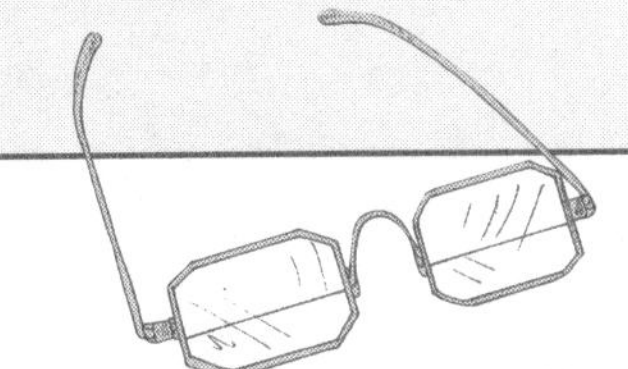

The Federal Government Expands

During the first administration, the seat of government proposal was passed in July 1790 establishing Philadelphia as the capital until

1800, when a federal district on the Potomac would be established. The Bill of Rights was approved in 1791, and President Washington also signed a bill creating the first bank of the United States. The banking issue proved to be the first test of the Constitution's flexibility. Jefferson asserted that a bank bill was unconstitutional, but Hamilton insisted that a national bank was essential.

Overseas, trouble was brewing. Although the French Revolution had begun in 1789 and there was support for the French allies, Washington knew the country was still too weak to risk involvement in another war so soon.

Two Parties Arise

As the president celebrated his sixtieth birthday, he wasn't exactly overjoyed that his two principal advisors—Jefferson and Hamilton—had fundamental differences. Each represented divergent philosophies of government, at a time when Washington felt all public servants should work amicably for the good of the country.

Soon, however, he could not ignore the factions set forth. Hamilton's backers evolved into the Federalist Party backing a strong central government, while those supporting Jefferson for the Republican Party, which later became known as the Democratic-Republican Party, held firm to the opinion that states should have the right to decide matters relating to them.

As the 1792 election drew near, Washington's close advisors unanimously agreed that times were too perilous to risk a transfer of the executive branch to anyone other than the current president. The northern states were disagreeing with their southern neighbors over the reapportionment of seats in the House of Representatives. Washington vetoed a plan that would have favored the North, viewing it as unconstitutional, and he grew anxious over the tendency for northern and southern states to part ways on political issues. Though he wanted to bid farewell to public life, Washington agreed to a second term and was the unanimous choice, along with Vice President Adams, in the 1792 election.

Learn about George Washington at Mount Vernon

Situated along the Potomac River in Fairfax County, Virginia (just fifteen minutes south of Washington, D.C.), is Mount Vernon, the beautiful mansion and plantation home of George and his wife Martha Custis Washington. George's brother Lawrence built the home in 1743, naming it in honor of Admiral Edward Vernon, under whom he had served in the British navy. George Washington inherited Mount Vernon in 1752. In fact, he lived there for forty-five years, from age twenty-two until his death from a throat infection in 1799.

Washington tripled the size of the mansion and expanded the plantation to 8,000 acres, proving that this father of our country could do much more than lead us to freedom. Indeed, Washington read voraciously about progressive agriculture, including crop rotation. He soon found that planting only tobacco (the chief cash crop in Virginia) was not wise because it was too dependent on the weather, the British market, and other factors. Washington taught his slaves cloth-weaving, and he increased wheat production. Visit the round, sixteen-sided threshing barn on your tour.

Costumed guides show you the mansion, pointing out the eighteenth-century artifacts and presenting anecdotes about the Washington family life. Sit a spell out on the long, white-columned porch where you can take in the Potomac view that the Washingtons enjoyed. When you realize that the General refused pay for his wartime leadership, and that the estate faced its share of financial problems and years of neglect, one has an even greater admiration for Washington.

Both George and Martha Washington are buried in the ivy-covered mausoleum not far from the house. Today, the Mount Vernon Ladies' Association maintains the mansion that it acquired in 1860. Kids will be delighted trying on colonial clothing, learning to harness a mule, or making a wooden bucket. Even the mansion tour comes alive with the puzzle treasure map kids complete. Enjoy the wreath-laying ceremony on Washington's Birthday and the holiday candlelight tours during December. On George Washington's actual birthday (February 22), anyone who also shares this birthday and those named George are admitted to Mount Vernon free of charge. Dine at the Mount Vernon Inn for regional and colonial cuisine. You can start your visit at *www.mountvernon.org*.

Washington's Second Term

Just two weeks after the inauguration in March 1793, news reached Philadelphia that King Louis XVI of France had been executed, followed by news that Revolutionary France had declared war on Britain, Spain, and the Netherlands. Washington posed questions vital to America's national security to Hamilton and Jefferson, his top advisors. Should the treaties of 1778, concluded with Louis XVI, be renounced or suspended? How could America remain strictly neutral in this international conflict? Should he issue a proclamation of neutrality? Should he receive "Citizen" Edmónd Charles Genet, the newly appointed diplomat from the French Republic?

Well, if the two divergent advisors and their parties were any indication, Washington knew fairly well there wouldn't be an easy consensus. But compromise came in the Proclamation of Neutrality, issued in 1793. Citizen Genet would be received, and the earlier treaties stood, although they would be interpreted quite cautiously.

As the year drew to a close, Thomas Jefferson desired a retreat from public life. Thus, he resigned as secretary of state and was succeeded by Edmund Randolph, the attorney general (a post taken over by William Bradford from Pennsylvania).

Troubles Brewing

The danger of war with Britain increased by spring 1794 as British warships seized neutral vessels trading with the French West Indies. This caused Washington to approve a thirty-day embargo on all sailing from American ports to avoid any future clashes, and it served as the impetus Congress needed to authorize the construction of six frigates, the first naval requisitions since the Revolutionary War. By signing the Jay Treaty with Great Britain, Washington allowed American ships to be inspected at sea, but the treaty also removed British troops from the Northwest Territory.

Washington Leaves Office

Having guided the new country through a war for independence and through eight years of its early government, a weary President

Washington was determined to leave office and retire to Mount Vernon. It had been an eventful tenure—averting war, opening the economic gateways of the West, and proving that the Constitution did work.

In his famous Farewell Address, Washington outlined the reasons for his decision not to seek a third term. He delivered the address to his cabinet, and it was published the following day in newspapers.

Early Separation of Church and State

Before 1776, most Americans (except for Pennsylvania's Quakers and Rhode Island's Baptists) lived in colonies with established churches. Independence significantly changed religious practices. Patriots who were once proud members of the Church of England repudiated their allegiance to the now-defeated king. Instead, they formed the Protestant Episcopal Church of America. In fact, in order to win support for the war in Virginia, a Declaration of Rights was passed guaranteeing religious toleration.

But even as the southern and mid-Atlantic states moved toward separation of church and state, some maintained that the traditional European system of established churches promoted morality and better respect for authority. This sentiment was stronger in New England where states and the Congregational churches were more closely linked.

The Country's Economy

During the Revolutionary War, British warships had temporarily destroyed the New England fishing industry and seized many American merchant ships. Southern states, where tobacco and rice were key exports, and even the grain regions of the North, suffered a disruption of trade following the long fight for independence.

When British troops had occupied port cities such as Boston, New York, Philadelphia, Charleston, and Newport, trade virtually ceased. Peace didn't bring back prewar prosperity. British merchants,

The Whiskey Rebellion

The first real test of federal law enforcement came in the series of disturbances in 1794 known as the Whiskey Rebellion. A federal law of 1791 imposed an excise tax on whiskey, but the burden fell largely on Pennsylvania, one of the chief whiskey-producing regions. Organized resistors burned the house of the district inspector, and citizens were taking up arms over the issue. Pennsylvania Governor Thomas Mifflin could not muster enough militia to suppress the rebellious lot, so President Washington ordered the mob to disperse and requested state militias from nearby Maryland, New Jersey, and Virginia to come to the aid of Pennsylvania. Washington's decisive action came in August. By the end of November, the rebellion was quelled.

angry over the war as well as unpaid debts, refused tobacco from the Chesapeake, and in South Carolina the indigo industry collapsed. American ships no longer traded with the sugar islands in the British West Indies, thanks to the British Navigation Acts. The result was a commercial recession spanning nearly two decades. By 1790, the value of American exports was a fraction of what it had been twenty years earlier, and with the standard of living in decline, America was ripe for economic conflict.

Adams and Jefferson as President

Though he wasn't a popular war hero like his predecessor, John Adams had participated in framing the Declaration of Independence (although Jefferson was the author), and had served as a diplomat in Europe. When John Adams became our second president in 1797, Great Britain and France were at war, and to his credit, Adams kept the United States out of the conflict. In an attitude of preparedness, however, Adams did establish a naval department and ordered warships to be built. During this time, the USS *Constitution* sailed for the first time (see "Visit Boston Today" sidebar in Chapter 3).

The White House

John and Abigail Adams were the first president and first lady to enjoy the newly created presidential mansion as Washington, D.C., became the nation's capital in 1800. Adams is reported to have written during his second night in the President's House (what would come to be known as the White House), "I pray Heaven to bestow the best Blessings on this House and all that shall hereafter inhabit it. May none but honest and wise Men ever rule under this roof."

Thomas Jefferson succeeded Adams as President. He felt that "the

Visit Philadelphia Today

Also known as the "city of brotherly love," Philadelphia is home to Independence National Historical Park, which includes the area from 2nd to 6th Street and buildings in Independence Square and elsewhere dating back to the colonial era. City Hall, now a National Historic Landmark, is the tallest building without steel girder support. It's topped with a thirty-seven-foot statue of William Penn, the founder of Pennsylvania. Liberty Bell Pavilion houses that famous bell. Too fragile to ring on July 4th, the Liberty Bell had more to do with celebrating the fiftieth anniversary of Penn's Charter of Privileges when it was cast in 1752 than Jefferson's Declaration of Independence. Its Biblical inscription from Leviticus, however, inspired abolitionists fighting against slavery years later. It reads: "Proclaim liberty throughout all the land unto all the inhabitants thereof." The bell was moved from Independence Hall in 1976 for the bicentennial celebrations.

Speaking of celebrations, the National Constitution Center broke ground in 2000 for the 215th anniversary of the signing of this important document in 2002.

Penn's Landing marks the site where William Penn landed in 1682 and is home to several historic ships. At the Independence Seaport Museum, explore the maritime heritage of the Delaware River through interactive exhibits. At Franklin Institute Science Museum, explore hands-on demonstrations about science—and of course, you'll notice the personal effects of Ben Franklin, who used the first lightning rod in Philadelphia and founded the Philadelphia Library, the first library in America. At the Please Touch Museum, children younger than eight will really experience history and other subjects with their senses of sight, smell, touch, and hearing.

The U.S. Mint is located near the historic district and offers visitors a glimpse of how the country transforms metal into money and military medals. You can take a historical tour at Washington Crossing State Park, where General Washington and his troops crossed prior to the Battle of Trenton. Before leaving Philly, be sure to stop at the Philadelphia Museum of Art and Longwood Gardens, housing twenty indoor and twenty outdoor horticultural displays. For more information, contact the Greater Philadelphia Tourism Marketing Corporation or *www.gophila.com*. You can also follow the construction progress at *www.constitutioncenter.org*.

government that governs best governs least." Indeed, he was a proponent of limited power, and a protector of individual and state rights. Jefferson is one of the most learned men in American history, with early Patriot ties, diplomatic tenure abroad, and a keen interest in architecture. He spoke six languages, designed his own home at Monticello in Charlottesville, Virginia, and founded the University of Virginia.

The Louisiana Purchase

In 1803, Jefferson seized the opportunity to purchase a vast expanse of land from France for $15 million (no doubt one of the greatest real estate bargains in U.S. history), even though the Constitution did not authorize him to do so. France was willing to sell the land from Louisiana in the south to present-day Montana in the north because of the fear that it was about to fall into British hands anyway. Jefferson then sent Meriwether Lewis and William Clark to explore the newly acquired territory. The Louisiana Purchase made westward expansion possible and effectively doubled the size of the country.

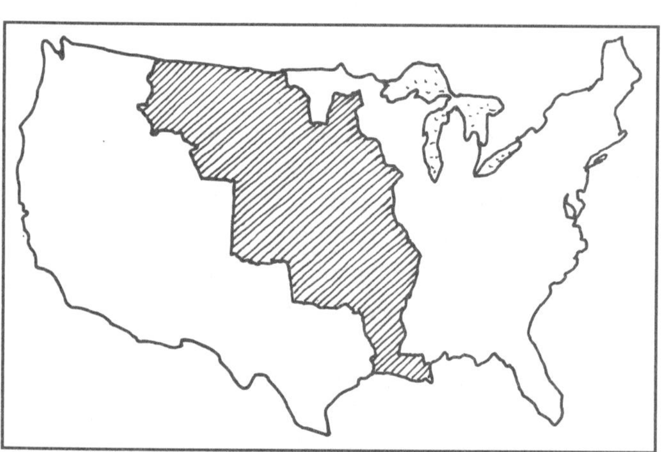

The Louisiana Purchase

In 1808, Jefferson prohibited the import of slaves from Africa. Having been re-elected to a second term, Jefferson stepped down with the belief that no president should govern longer than eight years. He retired to Monticello where he died on July 4, 1826, just hours before John Adams passed away. Buried at the estate, Jefferson left behind his own epitaph which read: "Here was buried Thomas Jefferson, Author of the Declaration of Independence, of the Statute of Virginia for Religious Freedom, and the Father of the University of Virginia." He chose to leave out the detail of being our nation's third president.

6

Early American Struggles

When James Madison took office in 1809, he was already well known for his contributions to the Bill of Rights. Much of Madison's presidency was filled with continued tension with foreign governments.

The Embargo Act of 1807, prohibiting U.S. vessels from trading with European nations and passed by Congress over Federalist opposition, seriously harmed the U.S. economy and was replaced two years later with the Non-Intercourse Act, which forbade trade with France and Great Britain. By 1810, Madison realized the American trade boycott was having little effect, for both countries continued seizing American ships. The Non-Intercourse Act was repealed in May 1810, but Madison was ready to prohibit trade again, if necessary.

Prelude to War

U.S.–British relations worsened as a result of these maritime troubles and also because of America's expansion into British-held lands in the West, in Canada, and in Florida (Spanish-held at the time). Anti-British factions in Congress accused Britain of provoking Native American attacks on American frontier communities. In November 1811, Indiana Governor William Henry Harrison fought the Shawnee nation with American troops at the Battle of Tippecanoe. Though the president had not authorized the use of troops, the incident roused support for military preparedness as war with Britain looked probable.

By the spring of 1812, Madison urged Britain to revoke trade restrictions. Great Britain ignored the requests, and Madison asked Congress to place an embargo, implying that even stronger measures might be warranted against the country.

The British, at war with France's Napoleon, had a pressing need to increase the ranks of the Royal Navy. They boarded U.S. vessels and impressed American sailors into His Majesty's service. Adding to the turmoil, a Congressional faction dubbed the "War

Hawks" viewed war with Britain as potential relief from the Indian hostilities Great Britain had backed and also as a means of further expansion in Spanish Florida, since Spain was allied with Britain in the battles against Napoleon.

Telling Congress that "our commerce has been plundered in every sea," Madison made it clear he felt Britain was intent on destroying American commerce, while sidelining any action against French hostilities.

On June 19, Madison signed a declaration of war, passed by both houses of Congress. What wasn't known, however, was that Britain had actually revoked the practice of intercepting American ships a few days prior, and apparently the French had repealed their own restrictions on American trade.

The War of 1812

Unfortunately, Madison's call for preparedness had not been heeded, and the country was ill prepared for war. This brought only ridicule to the administration that had already heard the northern and southern differences of opinion. Northerners showed no interest in annexing Florida, a southern conquest, and southerners saw any move into Canada as strength added to the northern states. New England Federalists called the War of 1812 "Mr. Madison's War."

Although the U.S. Navy won several victories in the war's first year, 1813 saw the British navy seize many ports and capture several American ships. One American vessel—the USS *Constitution*—had earned a reputation for getting the best of British ships. In August 1812, it had sighted the British warship *Guerrière*, sailing close enough that the *Constitution* could open fire, essentially shredding *Guerrière*'s sails and rendering her dead at sea. After demolishing the ship, the *Constitution* sailed to Brazilian waters, turning the H.M.S. *Java* into a flaming ruin. With all the heavy fire she weathered, the *Constitution* was quickly dubbed "Old Ironsides." (Turn to Chapter 3 for more on the USS *Constitution*.)

The Star-Spangled Banner

The sight of the American flag still flying over Fort McHenry at daybreak inspired Francis Scott Key, an American lawyer, to write his famous poem titled "The Star-Spangled Banner" in 1814. Key had boarded a British frigate under a flag of truce to arrange a prisoner's release, and scrawled the poem on a handbill. Later printed in the newspaper the *Baltimore Patriot*, it was set to tune of an infamous English drinking song "To Anacreon in Heaven." Congress passed an act on March 13, 1931, that recognized the song as the national anthem.

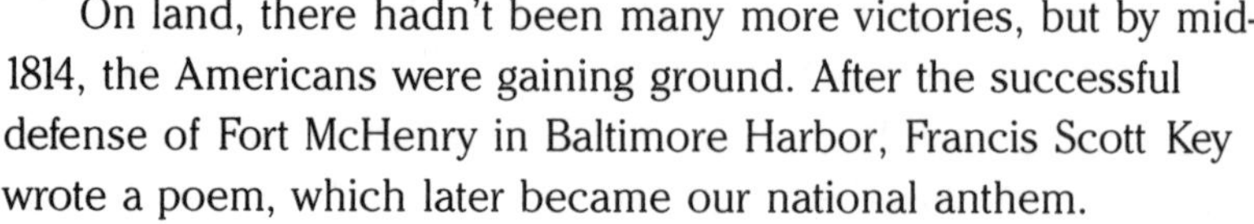

On land, there hadn't been many more victories, but by mid-1814, the Americans were gaining ground. After the successful defense of Fort McHenry in Baltimore Harbor, Francis Scott Key wrote a poem, which later became our national anthem.

> **D.C. Resources**
>
> The Washington, D.C., Convention and Visitors Association can offer you assistance, especially with a free booklet of tourist attractions and a map. Contact them at (202) 789-7000 or at *www.washington.org*. For accommodations call (800) 823-9652. Be sure to read *The Everything® Guide to Washington, D.C.* by Lori Perkins.

Battles

Battles were fought along the Great Lakes and into the Canadian Frontier. The Battle of Lake Erie, under Oliver Perry's command, was the turning point in the northwest for the Americans and tipped the balance of power. Around the time that Key wrote his poem, both American and British negotiators were meeting in Belgium to agree on settlement terms. But while peace was being procured, the British decided to invade the Gulf Coast.

Andrew Jackson won a decisive victory over the British in the Battle of New Orleans on January 8, 1815. This was perhaps the greatest battle of the War of 1812. News of peace and the Treaty of Ghent finally reached Jackson in March, months after the final resolution had been agreed upon on December 24, 1814. The treaty essentially restored matters to prewar conditions. Neither side left the war with more territory than it had commenced fighting with, though the United States claimed victory.

The war had altered the American landscape, however. Western expansion came with little to no opposition, and the issue of slavery took center stage. Defense spending increased as leaders saw the real need for military preparedness. European countries viewed the United States as a hardy opponent and ceased their efforts to regulate American trade and commerce.

Burning

An unfortunate outcome of the war resulted in the British taking the city of Washington, D.C. and burning the White House. The British saw this torching as justifiable retaliation for the American burning of York (now Toronto), the capital of Upper Canada, the previous year.

When Dolley Madison was warned that the British were en route and was told to flee the White House, she calmly collected the president's papers, the national seal, and the Gilbert Stuart portrait of George Washington, and sent them off for safekeeping. Her actions earned her a reputation as the plucky first lady who kept her head in crisis.

On August 24, 1814, President Madison joined his armies retreating from the nation's capital. Three days later, he returned to the burnt rubble the British had left behind.

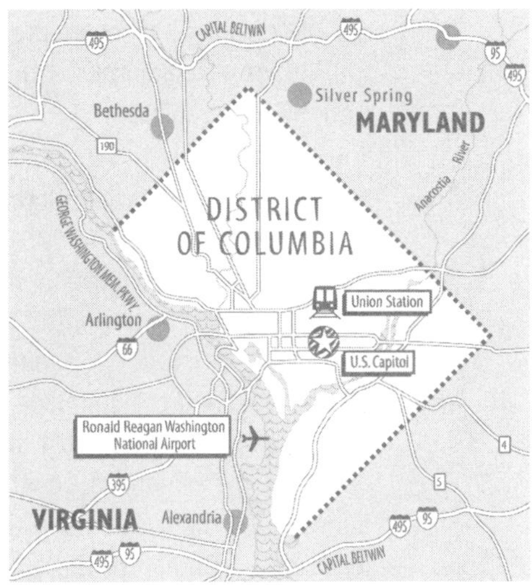

The Creation of Washington, D.C.

The 1783 Congress decided that the nation's capital would move from Philadelphia in 1800. After much debate, members passed the Residence Act, which outlined a ten-miles-square site on the Potomac River along the Virginia–Maryland border, an area that President George Washington had selected.

President John Adams was the first leader to govern from Federal City, later named Washington, D.C., in honor of our nation's first president. Today, the city of Washington exists as the District of Columbia (D.C.), the federal district of the United States, named after Christopher Columbus.

While the area was being surveyed, Washington and Thomas Jefferson selected French architect Pierre L'Enfant to design the city, which at the time it was surveyed, included Georgetown (Maryland) and Alexandria (Virginia). L'Enfant's plan featured broad avenues radiating out from Capitol Hill, interrupted by a series of rectangular and circular parks, all overlaid with a perpendicular grid of streets. The grid was then slashed with diagonal avenues named for the thirteen original states.

The French architect began supervising construction, but lacked a cost-containment attitude. After his many quarrels with public officials, he was dismissed

Visit Washington, D.C., Today

In future chapters, read more about the Smithsonian, the White House, and Ford's Theatre, as these are only a few favorites in our nation's capital. There are a variety of tour options including DC Ducks (amphibious vehicles), Old Town Trolley Tours, Tourmobile buses, Potomac River cruises, and walking and bike tours.

One great perk is the more than 100 free attractions, recreational activities, and special events, including the Smithsonian, the White House, the Washington Monument, and the Jefferson and Lincoln Memorials. Visit the largest library in the country—the Library of Congress, housing almost 110 million items in three buildings. At the Bureau of Engraving and Printing, you'll see where currency is printed at the rate of 8,000 sheets per hour. The thirty-five-minute tour here is self-guided, but at the gift shop, don't count on free samples! The National Archives and Records Administration houses the original Declaration of Independence, Constitution, Bill of Rights, and of course, billions of additional records. Don't miss the National Cathedral, part of Pierre L'Enfant's grand plan for the city. The architect didn't favor any particular religion, but rather envisioned it open to all faiths. It's the sixth largest cathedral in the world.

The National Zoo has been widely acclaimed for the 3,000 exotic animals, birds, and reptiles, including the new pandas.

At the Corcoran Gallery of Art, you can see many works of fine art such as Gilbert Stuart's famous portrait of George Washington (seen on the dollar bill). The atmosphere is somber at the U.S. Holocaust Memorial Museum, where artifacts, films, and oral histories tell the story of the mass killing of Jews during World War II. And the V-shaped Vietnam Veterans Memorial pays tribute to veterans, its black granite walls inscribed with the names of more than 58,000 Americans missing or killed in that conflict.

Georgetown is the toniest neighborhood, but don't miss Chinatown, too. Cultural offerings abound at the John F. Kennedy Center for the Performing Arts and the National Theatre.

In nearby Arlington, enjoy free admission to the Newseum (see Chapter 16) and Arlington National Cemetery. Follow the evolution of news and see classic footage when news stories first broke. Visit the graves of John F. Kennedy and Jacqueline Kennedy Onassis, along with those of Robert F. Kennedy and Supreme Court Justice Thurgood Marshall, as well as the Tomb of the Unknown Soldier.

in 1792. L'Enfant died in poverty in 1825, but appreciation of his architectural vision grew in later generations. Over the years, most of his ideas were realized.

When the government transfer took effect in 1800, the town boasted fewer than 5,000 people. Of course, the British burning of important buildings (including the White House) in 1814 did much to halt early growth.

In 1847, that part of the District lying on the Potomac's western banks was returned to Virginia, and thus today Washington, D.C., covers only about two-thirds its original size. The residential population grew to approximately 52,000 by 1850, and then increased dramatically, reaching 132,000 by 1870.

Erie Canal

The 363-mile-long Erie Canal, which opened the West to commerce, proved to be an engineering marvel as well as a grand commercial success. Completed in 1825, this artificial inland waterway extended from Lake Erie, at Buffalo, New York, to the Hudson River, near Albany. With increased commerce, New York City grew to become the nation's leading financial and commercial center.

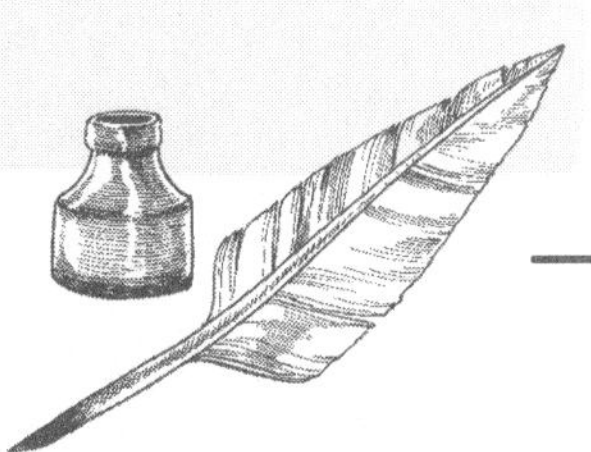

Native American Tensions

The British indeed used the fighting power of Native Americans in the War of 1812. William Henry Harrison fought the Shawnee nation at the Battle of Tippecanoe while Andrew Jackson commanded the Tennessee militia winning the Battle of Horseshoe Bend. The Treaty of Fort Jackson in 1814 signaled the end of Native American supremacy in Mississippi.

The Indian Removal Act

Following the war, Native Americans were moved to lands west of Mississippi, commonly referred to as Indian Territory. Although removal had gone on since the early 1800s, the Indian Removal Act of 1830, implemented during Andrew Jackson's presidency, resulted in the uprooting of entire tribes from their homelands.

As some Native Americans refused to resettle, several smaller wars or skirmishes ensued. The Black Hawk War in Illinois and Wisconsin was one of these, ending in 1832. The Cherokee were removed from Georgia, the remaining Creek were uprooted from Mississippi and Alabama, and the Seminole Indians fought to resist the U.S. Army's attempts to force their retreat from Florida. By the end of the 1850s, only scattered groups of Native Americans remained in the eastern half of the country.

The Monroe Doctrine

In 1823 in his seventh annual message to Congress, President Monroe set forth his opinion that no European nation should attempt to further colonize in the Western Hemisphere, and that they shouldn't interfere with the newly independent Spanish-American republics. He added that the United States would not interfere with existing European colonies or in the European continent itself. Monroe also implied that the United States should complete any further settlement in North America.

While the president's views were not labeled as he spoke them, the remarks became known as the Monroe Doctrine after the mid-1840s. At the time, the United States did not possess the naval power to enforce these sentiments, but the Monroe Doctrine would be used in future generations to justify American occupation of Haiti, the Dominican Republic, and Nicaragua in order to protect them from foreign influence.

Opening Other Frontiers

After the Louisiana Purchase spurred the go-West attitude in the early 1800s, the country experienced the continued growth of its boundaries. Many had the idea that the vast grasslands west of the Mississippi were unsuitable for farming, a theory that was promoted by explorers such as Lieutenant Zebulon Pike, an army officer who led a group from St. Louis into Minnesota. Pike won command of a Southwest expedition that took him far into Spanish-held lands in 1806–07. In what we now know as Colorado, the lieutenant discovered a mountain 14,110 feet (4301 meters) high, now bearing the name Pikes Peak. Pike described much of the territory he discovered as a wasteland, and subsequent explorers concurred with the notion that the Great Plains region was bleak. Early settlers understandably avoided the plains.

In 1818 and 1842, treaties settled Canadian border disputes with Britain from northern Maine to the Continental Divide.

Other Early Presidents

John Quincy Adams, son of our nation's second president, followed James Monroe into the highest office. A scholarly man, he found citizens not quite as willing to allot their tax dollars to specific advancements he deemed important, including new roads and canals, along with scientific exploration. Adams served only four years in office, though he went on to a distinguished career as a member of the House of Representatives, where he was a vigorous opponent of slavery. In 1848, at the age of eighty, John Quincy Adams suffered a stroke while fulfilling his House duties, and died days later.

Andrew Jackson, known for his heroic battlefield experiences in the Battle of New Orleans, took office as the seventh president in 1829. He served two terms, resulting from his popularity with voters. Jackson saw himself as a champion of the average citizen, continually battling Congress and vetoing legislation he thought favored the wealthy elite. Thus, his policies became known as "Jacksonian democracy."

Martin Van Buren, Jackson's vice president, succeeded him in 1837. Unfortunately, the nation was mired in an economic recession, and Van Buren never did find the cure voters sought. Thus, they voted him out of office, and William Henry Harrison was inaugurated in 1841. Harrison's father had signed the Declaration of Independence, and the president himself earned military recognition at the Battle of Tippecanoe, defeating Shawnee warriors in the Indiana Territory. But alas, Harrison never got to prove himself in office, for one month after his inauguration, he died of pneumonia. He now is known as the president serving the shortest term.

John Tyler became the first vice president to succeed to the presidency. Though a Whig, he departed from party projects such as a national bank and federally funded roads and canals. Worse, however, he supported slavery, making him an outcast in his own political party. It was no surprise that he served only one term. James Polk won election in 1845.

A Step Back for Some

In the Mexican–American War's aftermath, Mexican-Americans lived as second-class citizens on territory they once owned. Many lost their land and livelihoods. In addition, the war reopened the sticky issue of slavery.

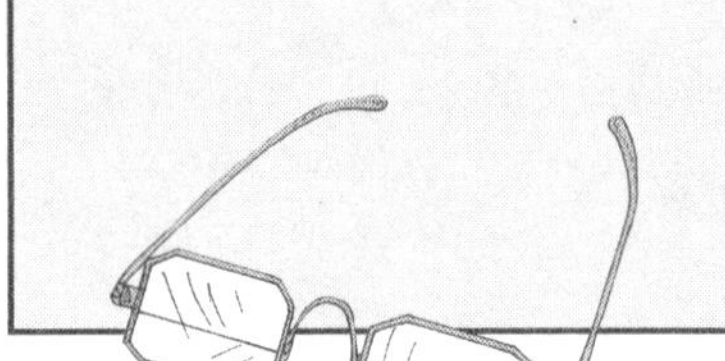

Mexico and Manifest Destiny

The idea of Manifest Destiny—that the United States had the God-given right to expand across the North American continent—was a popular and fervently held belief in the mid-1800s. The idea justified taking Indian territory, and it incited claims to even more land.

Tensions with Mexico coincided with America's quest for expansion. Mexico, which had just won its independence from Spain, had originally encouraged U.S. settlers in Texas, but its dictator, General Antonio López de Santa Anna, later banned further U.S. immigration. And when Texas declared its own independence from Mexico in 1836, Santa Anna marched to San Antonio with a force of 3,000 men to put down the insurrection. He surrounded 200 Texans at the Alamo, an old abandoned mission. Refusing to surrender, the Texans held firm for ten days, but the Mexicans captured the Alamo and killed its defenders.

Texas Gains Independence

"Remember the Alamo" became a rallying cry for the Texans who were steadfast in their quest for independence. Weeks later, while Santa Anna's troops took their afternoon siesta, Texans attacked. They were under the command of Sam Houston, who had fought against the Native Americans with Andrew Jackson in the War of 1812. By the end of this Battle of San Jacinto, the Texans captured Santa Anna, who promised, in exchange for his life, that he'd retreat from Texas. Thus, the Republic of Texas (nicknamed the Lone Star Republic because its flag bore a single star) received its independence.

Sam Houston immediately asked for Texas to be annexed to the United States, but as the balance of states stood at the time, there were thirteen states opposed to slavery and thirteen states in favor of it. Northerners felt that admitting Texas, where slavery was legal, would tip the balance of power in favor of the South. Thus, annexation was tabled until President John Tyler succeeded in pushing a joint resolution through Congress allowing Texas to join the Union in 1845.

The Mexican–American War

When annexation occurred, Mexico severed all diplomatic ties to the United States. Mexicans were even more outraged when U.S. officials insisted that the Rio Grande be used as the southern border of Texas. Thus, border skirmishes ensued even as the new president, James Polk, offered to purchase California and New Mexico and to assume Mexico's debts in exchange for the Rio Grande border. When rumors of Mexican invasion caught the capital's attention, the president sent General Zachary Taylor and 3,500 troops to the Rio Grande to defend Texas. After Mexicans killed several of Taylor's men, Polk asked Congress to declare war, which it promptly did.

The U.S. soldiers who marched across the dry ground became covered with a white dust, similar in color and texture to Mexican adobes. Soon, Mexicans dubbed their opponents "dobies" or doughboys, and the name stuck for generations of soldiers.

It didn't take long to capture California, and Americans also forced a Mexican surrender at Monterrey. Yet the war effort met with criticism, for some saw this as an aggressive, unprovoked war on disputed territory. Undeterred, President Polk ordered troops south to capture Mexico City. Shortly thereafter, both sides reached peace.

After two years of fighting, the Treaty of Guadalupe Hidalgo resulted in Mexico's ceding California and large stretches of the Southwest to the United States, as well as its acceptance of the Rio Grande border. In return, the United States paid the Mexican government $15 million and assumed unpaid claims by U.S. citizens against Mexico. Zachary Taylor emerged as a hero and was elected president in 1848.

Go West, Young Man

Britain's and America's disputed control of the Oregon Country was settled in 1846, with the United States gaining sovereignty of the

Morse Code

Samuel F. B. Morse invented the telegraph in 1844, allowing for the transmission of a message from one city to another by using electrical current. Morse abandoned an artistic career to concentrate on a coded system of dots and dashes that was used for telegraphic transmissions, revolutionizing communication.

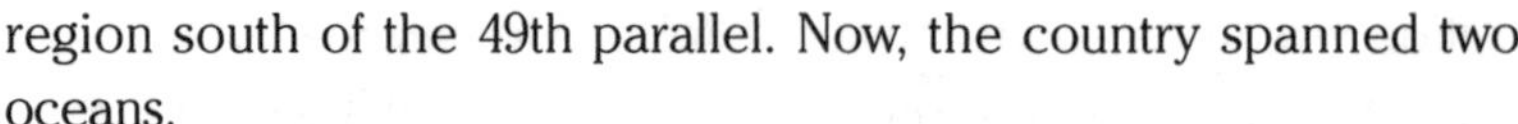

region south of the 49th parallel. Now, the country spanned two oceans.

Around this time, members of a religious sect founded by Joseph Smith in 1830 sought isolation in the West, as they had been hounded in Ohio, Missouri, then Illinois and Iowa. Mormons, or members of the Church of Latter-Day Saints, practiced polygamy and roused growing suspicion. In 1847, a group of Mormons ventured over the prairie through the Rocky Mountains until they reached the dreary flats beside the Great Salt Lake in Utah. Over the next several years, thousands followed the Mormon trail their leader had blazed. They called this homeland Zion, and like the Israelites of old, they made their desert bloom. By 1860, approximately 12,000 Mormons lived in the Salt Lake City environs.

Making Money

In 1862, the U.S. government bought the private mint at the corner of Market and 16th Street in Denver, Colorado, owned by Clark, Gruber and Company. It became a government mint where coins are still made today (as well as at the mint in Philadelphia created in 1792). The U.S. Bureau of the Mint has gold warehouses in Fort Knox, Kentucky, and West Point, New York, as well as a mint and museum in San Francisco, California. Paper currency is printed at the Bureau of Engraving and Printing in Washington, D.C. Gold and silver coins are made at West Point.

Gold Is Discovered

On January 24, 1848, just days before Mexico signed the treaty giving California to the United States, men working at a sawmill in the Sacramento Valley struck gold along the American River. Mill owner John Sutter implored his workers to keep the discovery quiet, but of course, news spread, particularly from the lips of those who stood to profit. Samuel Brannan was one such shrewd merchant, who stocked his store near Sutter's fort with mining supplies before alerting others to the potential for riches.

By spring, chaos erupted as men quit their jobs, leaving ghost towns in their wake. Hundreds of soldiers abandoned their posts, and in San Francisco harbor, sailors literally left their ships to rot as everyone flocked to the frenzy of finding gold. Those in hot pursuit of the precious metal became known as Forty-Niners.

The Gold Rush

It took about six months for news of the gold discovery to make it back East, but when it did, President Polk included word in his message to Congress. Thousands rushed west over the Great Plains, or by using the Oregon or Mormon trail. Some took the Santa Fe, Sonora, or other southern trails, and still others went by boat to Panama and across to the city of Panama in order to catch another boat headed for San Francisco. Although it was a much longer voyage, some made their passage by sailing around Cape Horn, the southernmost point of South America—the demand was that great.

Of those who trekked west, few struck it rich, but many stayed on to establish themselves in farming or business, increasing California's population nearly tenfold between 1848 and 1853. In 1850, California was admitted as a state. Gold rushes took place in the present-day states of Colorado, Nevada, Montana, Arizona, New Mexico, Idaho, Oregon, and Alaska. Wherever a gold strike was made, miners gathered to build a camp or community that usually had a saloon and a gambling house, and very few women or children. Miners lived in shanties, hastily built structures of wood frame, abandoning these "shantytowns" when the gold ran out and everyone pulled up stakes to head for the next strike. Frontier justice reigned with each camp meeting to set forth the size of the gold claim that an individual could possess, and the way it should be registered. Sheriffs administered the codes, and justice was harsh and swift when necessary. Although most of the miners were Caucasian men who drew no social distinctions, they did try to keep gold out of Mexican, Chinese, and Native American hands. By 1851 industrial mining became the trend where organized businesses with more advanced technology replaced individual efforts, and by the late 1850s, the California Gold Rush was over. Four decades later, others, never minding the biting wind and frigid cold, trekked to Alaska when rich strikes were made near Nome and Fairbanks.

Forty-Niners Lead the Way

Forty-Niners did more than blaze new trails for settlement. They boosted the American economy by adding billions of dollars to the treasury. These billions, in turn, financed industrial growth during the nineteenth century.

The Wave of Immigrants

It's interesting that most immigrants to the United States did not sail to America for political or religious reasons, as the early settlers may have done. Most immigrants in the 1800s came because of economic deprivation in their home countries, and African-Americans came involuntarily from Africa as forced laborers to southern plantation owners.

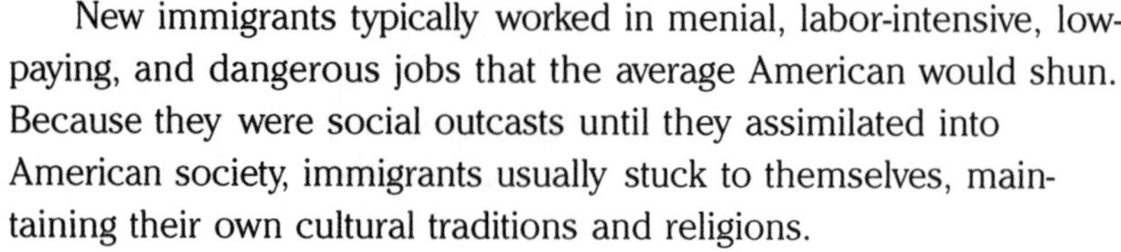

New immigrants typically worked in menial, labor-intensive, low-paying, and dangerous jobs that the average American would shun. Because they were social outcasts until they assimilated into American society, immigrants usually stuck to themselves, maintaining their own cultural traditions and religions.

The Melting Pot is Forged

The influx of so many immigrants, especially once they began intermarrying, brought about the phrase "melting pot," meaning that many immigrant traditions and bloodlines were blended together, creating a new society. Alarmed, Americans began to limit the numbers of immigrants as early as 1790, when Congress passed an act requiring a two-year residency period before one could qualify for U.S. citizenship. In 1795, that residency period rose to five years, and in 1798 during John Adams's administration, Congress passed the Alien and Sedition Acts. One of these new laws (the Naturalization Act) increased the waiting period to fourteen years, while the Alien Act allowed foreigners to be expelled if they were thought to threaten American interests. These acts were either repealed or expired in the early 1800s, but their passage was historic.

No doubt the greatest wave of immigrants to U.S. soil occurred between 1840 and the 1920s. During this period approximately 37 million immigrants arrived, mostly of German, Irish, Italian, English, Scottish, Austro-Hungarian, Scandinavian, Russian, Baltic, and Jewish descent.

Driving Forces

The Industrial Revolution, which began in England in the late eighteenth century and spread across Europe, changed the economic and social realities for many families, as did the potato famine that ravaged Ireland in the 1840s. Immigrants facing poverty at home believed American streets were paved with gold. Coming across in ships' steerage, many were swiftly disillusioned.

About 70 percent of all European immigrants initially landed in New York City. If they came after 1892, most went through their

Statue of Liberty Inscription

Not like the brazen giant of Greek fame,
With conquering limbs astride from land to land:
Here at our sea-washed, sunset gates shall stand
A mighty woman with a torch, whose flame
Is the imprisoned lightning, and her name
Mother of Exiles. From her beacon-hand
Glows world-wide welcome; her mild eyes command
The air-bridged harbor that twin cities frame.
"Keep, ancient lands, your storied pomp!" cries she
With silent lips. "Give me your tired, your poor,
Your huddled masses yearning to breathe free,
The wretched refuse of your teeming shore.
Send these, the homeless, tempest-tost, to me,
I lift my lamp beside the golden door!"

—Emma Lazarus, 1883

processing and questioning at Ellis Island, which was opened after Castle Garden on Manhattan Island was inundated by immigrants. Some groups preferred to stay in New York City, while others made homes in Boston, Philadelphia, Baltimore, and New Orleans. Chinese immigrants during the 1850s entered through San Francisco and understandably stayed in this region. But with railroads contributing to a transient society, many immigrants settled wherever they could find a particular line of work. Those seeking heavy industry often moved inland to Buffalo, Pittsburgh, Cleveland, Detroit, Chicago, and Minneapolis. German immigrants settled extensively in Texas, the Midwest, New York, and Pennsylvania, where plenty of work was available in skilled labor or agriculture. While Italian Americans worked in light manufacturing, retail business, or the construction industry, Jewish Americans preferred to settle in major cities such as New York, Chicago, or Boston. Members of Slavic groups (Polish or Slovak Americans) found work in heavy manufacturing towns. Chinese Americans worked mostly on building the railroads, in light manufacturing, or in domestic, retail, or mining trades. In 1882, Congress passed the Chinese Exclusion Act, which prevented Chinese immigration for ten years. This stemmed from economic hardship during the Arthur administration where Chinese and Irish immigrants vied for the few available jobs, and the tensions led to street fighting in San Francisco.

Women immigrants worked in laundries, retail shops, or light manufacturing; some, such as Irish American women, were employed as domestic servants. It often took two or three generations for immigrants to move up the socioeconomic ladder and earn wages that could provide the comfortable standard of living that other Americans enjoyed.

VISIT ELLIS ISLAND

If you ever visit New York City, there's no better place to learn about immigration than Ellis Island. Ferries leave from Battery Park in Manhattan and from Liberty State Park in New Jersey.

Ellis Island was the gateway to the United States for at least 16 million immigrants between 1892 and 1954. It became part of the Statue of Liberty National Monument in 1965 and is run by the National Park Service. In the late 1980s, the main building for processing immigrants was restored as the Ellis Island Immigration Museum, featuring three floors of exhibits, a research library, and an ongoing oral history project that records and preserves the stories of many immigrants. Visiting gives you an appreciation for what it must have been like to arrive with one suitcase in hand, not knowing the language, and with much uncertainty in a strange land. Exhibits chronicle the medical and intelligence tests given to the arriving immigrants, who were also grilled about their personal finances and job prospects. You'll see three sets of stairs, known as the "stairs of separation," because those likely to become public charges were turned back. However, as many as 5,000 per day were admitted. For information about the Statue of Liberty Ferry, call (212) 269-5755.

7

A Country Unraveling

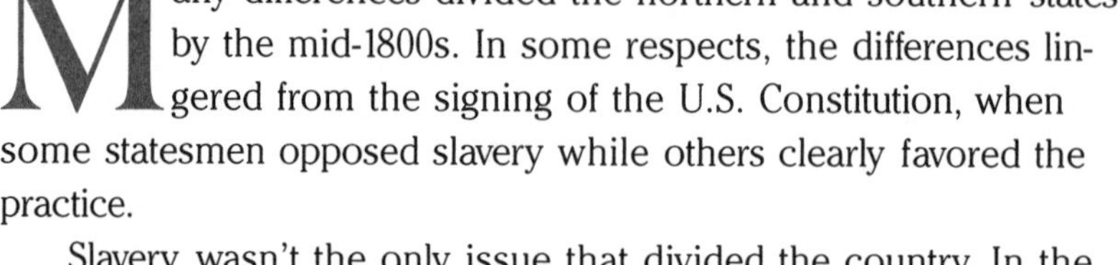

Many differences divided the northern and southern states by the mid-1800s. In some respects, the differences lingered from the signing of the U.S. Constitution, when some statesmen opposed slavery while others clearly favored the practice.

Slavery wasn't the only issue that divided the country. In the North, agricultural, commercial, and industrial development led to fast-growing cities, whereas in the South, the economy was dependent on foreign sales of cotton, its cash crop. In addition, the South opposed tariffs on imported goods, but the northern manufacturing economy demanded tariffs to stave off foreign competition. The federal government's chief revenue source was tariffs to pay for roads and canals, but the South felt it could do without these improvements. Southerners simply felt no need to strengthen the government with this type of spending.

Slavery was a major factor in the country's collapse, albeit not the only one. The northern industrial society needed labor for its economic prosperity, but the commencing wave of immigration provided a labor pool without resorting to slavery.

The Cotton Gin

The cotton gin might even be blamed for the North–South turmoil. Invented by twenty-seven-year-old Eli Whitney in 1793, it made cleaning cotton seeds fifty times faster than by hand. Thus, cotton became king, and slavery the king's literal servant.

The Issue of Slavery

When slaveholding Missouri applied for statehood in 1818, there was a balance of slave states and free states, with eleven of each. Each faction viewed any attempt by the other faction to tip the scales as dangerous. Such paranoia delayed the annexation of Texas. Thus, Congress found a middle ground with what became known at the Missouri Compromise, enacted in 1820 and regulating the extension of slavery in the country for three decades until its repeal by the Kansas–Nebraska Act of 1854.

This new act authorized the creation of Kansas and Nebraska, territories west of Missouri, and stipulated that the inhabitants of these territories would decide the legality of slavery. The bill's sponsor, Democratic Senator Stephen A. Douglas of Illinois, wanted to assure southern support for white settlement into otherwise Native American territory. He hoped such settlement would facilitate construction of the transcontinental railroad. Southern votes were absolutely necessary. Removing the restriction on slavery's expansion ensured passage, and indeed President Franklin Pierce signed the bill into law May 30, 1854.

With passage, however, political parties went into turmoil, and tensions between the North and South grew more passionate. The vicious fighting that resulted became known as "bleeding Kansas," and one of the names made famous over this dispute was John Brown, a self-ordained preacher with a fervor against slavery.

The issue and the political fallout split the Democratic Party and destroyed the badly divided Whig Party, particularly in the South. The northern Whigs joined antislavery sentiment, forming the Republican Party in 1854.

A Dred-ful Decision

In 1857, the U.S. Supreme Court decided the case of Dred Scott, a fugitive slave, who argued for his freedom after his master died when the two traveled to another state. When the Missouri state court ruled against Scott, he took his case to the high court where Chief Justice Roger B. Taney had the final word, denying him the right to sue for his freedom, reasoning that a slave wasn't a citizen. This outraged abolitionists.

Farming the Land

When colonists first began farming, their intent was to produce cash crops—sugar, cotton, and tobacco—for the colonies to prosper, and to supply enough food for survival and for trade with other colonists. The production of animal products such as wool and hides also kept farmers busy.

The slave trade provided much-needed laborers to fill the work force of the typical southern plantation. Indentured servants from Europe also provided both skilled and unskilled labor to many colonies. Invention also led the way. By the mid-nineteenth century, proper drainage brought more land into cultivation, and farming implements had also advanced.

As far back as 1797, Charles Newbold, a New Jersey blacksmith, introduced the cast-iron moldboard plow. John Deere, another blacksmith, improved this plow in the 1830s, manufacturing it in steel. In 1831, twenty-two-year-old Cyrus McCormick invented the reaper, a machine that in only a few hours could cut an amount of grain that had taken two or three men a day to scythe by hand. Numerous other horse-drawn threshers, grain and grass cutters, cultivators, and other equipment made farming easier.

The Pony Express

The Pony Express, begun by Russell, Majors and Waddell, a freighting firm, was a novel means of carrying letters. Western freighting prior to 1860 occurred with wagons, but it was a slow means of transport. On April 3, 1860, a lone rider carried letters only—no passengers and no wagons used—through some of the country's toughest terrain, by horseback. One rider carried the materials to another station, exchanging the letters with another rider and even switching horses along the way. Buffalo Bill Cody joined, becoming a legend for filling in when his relief rider was killed. Unfortunately, the venture was not profitable. In its brief tenure of nineteen months, the Pony Express lost only one article of mail.

By the late 1800s, steam power frequently replaced animal power in drawing plows and operating farm machinery.

Advancements in transportation with the construction of roads, canals, and railways meant that farmers could receive needed supplies and market their products to areas at a distance. Food stayed fresher for longer periods with the development of refrigeration in the late 1800s.

Some say the growing tensions in America were the result of conflict between wheat and cotton. The southern farmers put all their faith in the cotton crop, which helped them earn money. This success encouraged them to secede. However, as history would later show, their growing reliance on this sole crop created food shortages. In the North, farmers prepared for a more diverse harvest and were putting new inventions to work in the fields. With crop failures in Britain and France, these countries desperately needed the grain exports the North could provide. Unwilling to risk famine, they refused to recognize the southern states' cause.

The Cry for States' Rights

Since the birth of the republic, states were fearful of tyranny and slow to release any powers to the federal government. In fact, the principle of nullification was supported by many of the early founders, among them James Madison and Thomas Jefferson. And the stubborn nature of some states had already been shown. The New England states nullified an unpopular embargo from 1809 to 1810, and years later, Georgia nullified federal laws relating to Native Americans.

In 1830, U.S. Senator Daniel Webster made some rather prescient remarks before his Senate colleagues as he successfully combated the nullification theory, advocating the pre-eminence of federal authority. With foresight, he warned that nullification would cause the Union to fall apart in a fratricidal war. But in 1832, South Carolina declared a tariff null and void, forcing President Andrew Jackson to consider sending troops to enforce the tariff in the port of Charleston. John C. Calhoun was a staunch supporter of states' rights who was causing the stir among the South Carolina radicals. Both sides of the dispute claimed victory, however, as they reached a compromise days before nullification was to occur, essentially tabling the question until future years.

The Underground Railroad

The antislavery faction, comprised mostly of northerners, helped fugitive slaves reach safety in a loose, secret network dubbed the Underground Railroad, sometimes called the Liberty Line. This enabled runaway slaves to achieve safety in the free states or in Canada. Begun in the 1780s by Quakers, the Underground Railroad grew legendary after the 1830s. It's thought that approximately 60,000 slaves gained freedom through this lifeline.

Many hiding out in the Underground Railroad traveled less conspicuously at night, using the North Star for guidance. Isolated farms or towns sympathetic to a slave's plight would effectively conceal them. Harriet Tubman, an escaped slave, became known as the Moses of the blacks for her work in rescuing slaves to freedom.

Harriet Tubman

Even under these circumstances, escaping slavery was an arduous task. Vigilant officers in search of rewards often spotted runaway slaves, seizing them as they made their passage north. But even if the slaves didn't always reach safety, their efforts did give validity to the antislavery cause, forcing many to publicly acknowledge the wrongs of slavery. Even the federal Fugitive Slave Laws of 1793 and 1850 became difficult to enforce as northern judges restricted the rights of many a slave's master. This further enraged the southern states, galvanizing sentiment toward Civil War.

The Rise of Abraham Lincoln

From backwoods origins, Abraham Lincoln held many jobs in his lifetime—rail splitter, ferryboat captain, store clerk, surveyor, and postmaster among them. But the job that solidified his place as a

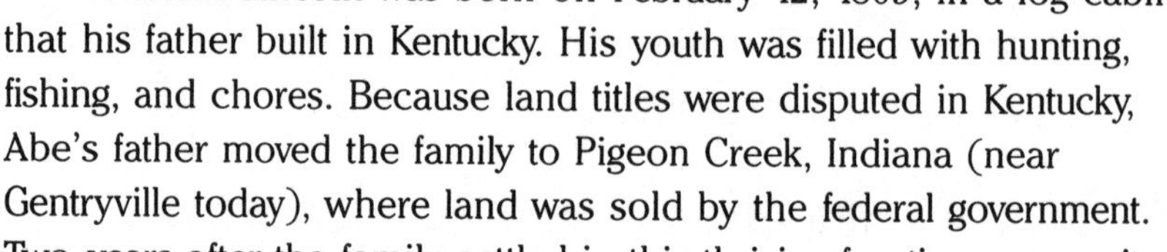

great figure in history was his role as the sixteenth president of the United States during a time of great strife.

Abraham Lincoln was born on February 12, 1809, in a log cabin that his father built in Kentucky. His youth was filled with hunting, fishing, and chores. Because land titles were disputed in Kentucky, Abe's father moved the family to Pigeon Creek, Indiana (near Gentryville today), where land was sold by the federal government. Two years after the family settled in this thriving frontier community, Abe's mother died in an epidemic (caused by ingesting poisonous cow's milk). The next year, Abe's father married a widow with three children, and Abe seemed to bond well with his stepmother.

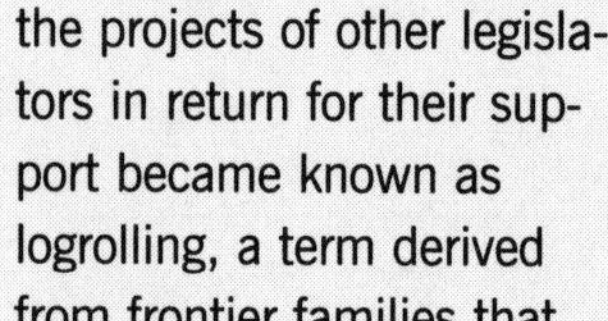

Logrolling

The practice of supporting the projects of other legislators in return for their support became known as logrolling, a term derived from frontier families that helped each other to build log cabins.

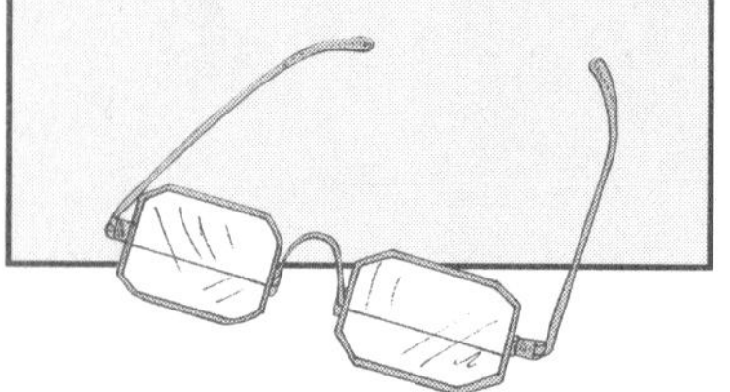

Abe learned at a young age to wield an axe to clear the frontier forest, and he attended a log cabin school when he wasn't tending to chores. In later years, his campaign hearkened back to these "rail splitter" days to prove that Abe came from humble roots. Though the lad had less than one year of formal education, his stepmother encouraged his thirst for knowledge. Lincoln learned to read, write, and do simple arithmetic at an early age, and it's said that a book about George Washington made a deep impression on him. With his family's move to Illinois, Abe helped his father build a log cabin. That year, he attended a political rally and spoke on behalf of one of the candidates. You might say the political bug bit Lincoln, and he never quite recovered!

At a lanky 6'4", Lincoln's appearance was somewhat awkward, especially given his long arms and big hands. He held various jobs, but because he could read and write, he was called on to draw up legal papers for the less literate around him. And when Lincoln expressed his views, he did so with grace and discernment that caught people's attention.

Lincoln Enters Politics

In the spring of 1832, Lincoln decided to run for a seat in the Illinois House of Representatives. Before the election, he volunteered in the suppression of a rebellion by Native Americans led by Chief Black Hawk, though he saw no actual fighting. Despite a platform of better schools, roads, and canals, Lincoln was defeated and he began a venture with a general store, followed by his job as a postmaster, a position that gave him ample time to read ravenously, especially the newspapers.

Now better known, Lincoln ran for the Illinois legislature in 1834. He was elected every two years, and he studied law between legislative sessions. This experience as a state legislator sharpened his political savvy. Lincoln's first public stand on slavery, which he'd encountered years earlier when he viewed a slave auction, came in 1837 when the Illinois legislature voted to condemn abolition societies that wanted to end the practice by any means. Although Lincoln was opposed to slavery, he also felt strongly that extreme measures were not necessary and that lawful conduct could end the practice.

Though Lincoln became a licensed lawyer in 1836, and continued as a state legislator, economic achievement didn't automatically follow. He also spent this time without love. Some said he was plunged into sadness by the death of Ann Rutledge, the woman he loved, and that a period of melancholy marked his adult years. Others believe this romance was a myth. He proposed marriage to another woman who turned him down. It wasn't until he met Mary Todd in 1840 that courtship blossomed, and the two were married two years later.

Lincoln Family Life

Abraham and Mary Todd Lincoln had four children, but only their eldest son, Robert Todd Lincoln, would survive to adulthood. It's said that Mary Todd Lincoln made her husband's life miserable, for she was unable to handle the loss of their children in later years. Though she was perhaps unstable, Lincoln remained devoted to her, and she in turn supported his political rise.

The ambitious legislator and lawyer soon looked beyond Illinois to the U.S. Congress, and he was elected in 1846 to the House of Representatives. Despite the difficulties of being a freshman congressman, Lincoln never lost confidence in his abilities. He opposed the Mexican–American War begun by President Polk, though his Illinois constituents denounced him as a traitor (for they supported the war). Once war was declared, however, Lincoln supported all appropriations, despite his private opinions.

Abraham Lincoln

John Brown

Abolitionist John Brown grew so obsessed with winning freedom for slaves that he took his crusade to Harper's Ferry, Virginia (today's West Virginia). On October 16, 1859, Brown and approximately twenty others incited an uprising. Federal troops commanded by Robert E. Lee retaliated, killing about half the group, wounding Brown and taking him prisoner.

Lincoln resumed his law practice after serving one term in Congress. Travel between county seats allowed him to reflect, read, and mingle with other lawyers. Though he sometimes lacked time to prepare for cases, he made up for it with oratory skill far greater than many of his peers.

Lincoln's Antislavery Sentiments Grow

Lincoln was outraged by passage of the Kansas–Nebraska Act in 1854, a measure that allowed the territories to decide the issue of slavery for themselves. Democratic Senator Stephen Douglas was the author of the act, and Abe Lincoln's passion for the plight of slaves rose to the surface. When Douglas defended the Kansas–Nebraska Act in October of that year, Lincoln spoke the next day, attacking the act with well-researched arguments that forced citizens to contemplate not only the political ramifications of slavery but also the moral ones. Lincoln was quoted as saying, "If the Negro is a man, why then my ancient faith teaches me that 'all men are created equal,' and that there can be no moral right in connection with one man's making a slave of another." As impassioned as his conviction was that slavery was wrong and a national problem to contend with, Lincoln remained fairly nonjudgmental regarding the South. "I will not undertake to judge our brethren of the South," Lincoln said in what became known as his Peoria, Illinois, speech.

By 1856, the Whig Party that Lincoln belonged to had died out, and the young politician officially identified himself as a Republican. Soon, the slavery issue was gaining national momentum with the Dred Scott case and memories of bleeding Kansas. As Senator Stephen Douglas ran for re-election, the Republicans nominated Abraham Lincoln to oppose him. Accepting the nomination, Lincoln used his harshest words, declaring, "A house divided against itself cannot stand. I believe this government cannot endure permanently half slave and half free. I do not expect the Union to be dissolved; I do not expect the house to fall; but I do expect it will cease to be divided. It will become all one thing, or all the other."

The Lincoln–Douglas Debates

In a series of face-to-face debates that captivated Illinois citizens, the two Senate candidates debated the morality of slavery. Douglas used Lincoln's "house divided" speech against him, accusing Lincoln of trying to divide the nation. Lincoln, in turn, cited the Declaration of Independence and asserted that all men are created equal. By now Lincoln was well known as an extraordinary political stump speaker.

Though Lincoln was confident he could defeat Douglas, the Democratic majority won, re-electing Douglas. Lincoln handled his loss with grace, glad he could speak out on a truly crucial issue. He wrote to a friend, "I believe I have made some remarks which will tell for the cause of civil liberty long after I am gone."

Real Estate Bargains

The Homestead Act of 1862 gave settlers 160 acres of federal land for a nominal filing fee if they would farm it for five years. This federally owned land included property in all states except the original thirteen and Maine, Vermont, West Virginia, Kentucky, Tennessee, and Texas. An incentive to go west if there ever was one!

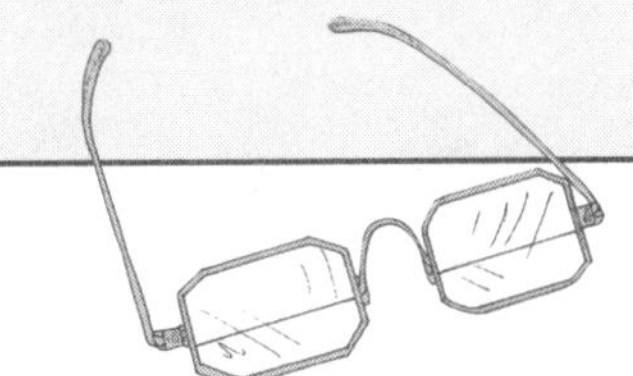

Lincoln is Put on the National Stage

The debates had more impact than the defeated candidate would imagine. They launched Lincoln onto the national stage, giving him opportunities to speak in other states. His moderate views won him praise as he insisted the Republican party was not one solely of northern origin but that it encompassed the South as well. Lincoln spoke out against the extreme abolitionist John Brown, who incited violence. After speaking in New York, Lincoln became the leading contender for the Republican presidential nomination in 1860.

When the party convened, they did in fact select Lincoln as their presidential nominee. With the Democratic Party split, Lincoln felt confident of victory. Though he won only 40 percent of the popular vote, he received the majority of electoral votes (though none in the South) and won the race to become the sixteenth president of the United States.

The country would look to Lincoln for his measured words and thoughtful leadership, for it was unraveling fast. He faced challenges no former president could have imagined, yet Lincoln stood firm with the heartfelt conviction that the country needed to remain whole.

Southern militants had already threatened to secede from the Union if Lincoln was elected president. Sure enough, when election results became known, South Carolina became the first southern state to leave the Union in December 1860. By February, several other states followed as they developed their own government.

Lincoln Takes Office

President James Buchanan did nothing to stop the secessionists. At that time, Lincoln was still a president-elect. As he bid farewell to Illinois, Lincoln remained hopeful that peace could be restored. "Today I leave you," he told friends. "I go to assume a task more difficult than that which devolved upon George Washington." And with additional words reflecting his belief in God, he asked his followers to pray for the country and his efforts.

Because rumors were rampant that Lincoln could be assassinated, he quietly sneaked into Washington at night for his inauguration on March 4, 1861. Ironically, Lincoln was sworn in as president by Chief Justice Roger B. Taney, who also issued the Dred Scott decision—a deed that spurred the crisis that would consume Lincoln's presidency.

Creation of the Confederacy

With the momentum increasing to follow South Carolina's secession, Mississippi, Florida, Alabama, Georgia, Louisiana, and Texas adopted similar ordinances. The seceding states sent representatives to a convention in Montgomery, Alabama, where they adopted a provisional constitution, gave themselves a name, and chose a president of their own. Thus, the Confederate States of America (known as the Confederacy) was born against the government in Washington, D.C. Jefferson Davis of Mississippi was named president of the Confederacy, and the delegates ratified their separate constitution.

Jefferson Davis

After selecting cabinet members that represented other southern states, Davis turned his attention to the necessary preparations for the impending conflict with the North (Union). Confederates had already seized eleven federal forts and arsenals in the South, and they'd caused trouble at Fort Sumter in

Visit Lincoln Sites

If you want to learn about the Lincoln family and combine that with a visit to New England, find your way to Manchester, Vermont. When you're finished with the outlet shopping and enjoying the landscape, tour Hildene, the estate of Robert Todd Lincoln, the only child of Abraham and Mary Todd Lincoln to reach adulthood.

The story has it that Mrs. Lincoln and the children loved visiting this area. Had he lived, the president was to stay at the Equinox Hotel where a specially designed suite would have accommodated him. The love of Vermont stayed with the younger Lincoln, who built his home there at the turn of the century. Descendants of President Lincoln lived on at the property until 1975 in what is today a twenty-four-room Georgian Revival mansion preserved with original furnishings and personal family effects. Robert Todd Lincoln used Hildene as a summer home, but tourists will enjoy learning a little about the family by seeing what was important to them. For instance, the Aeolian organ with its 1,000 pipes is played for each tour. It was installed in 1908.

You can purchase tour tickets at the visitor's center, where you can begin with a brief film about the Lincolns and purchase souvenirs. Regular tours are offered mid-May through October, and special candle-light tours make the Christmas season come alive at the mansion. If you're an avid gardener, spend time in the restored cutting and kitchen gardens. For more information, contact Hildene at (802) 362-1788 or at *www.hildene.org*.

Travelers will also enjoy the Equinox Hotel, not far from the property. This hotel enjoys a rich history for hosting many past presidents including Taft, Grant, Harrison, and Teddy Roosevelt. Though Lincoln never stayed in the presidential accommodations built especially for his needs, with enough money you can reserve the suite. It has its own outside entrance and nearby rooms (originally designed for the president's security). Call the Equinox at (800) 362-4747.

Harriet Beecher Stowe

Charleston, South Carolina. Shortly after he took office, President Lincoln sent reinforcements to Fort Sumter. Within weeks, eleven southern states had broken away, leaving a handful of border states south of the Mason–Dixon line—Delaware, Maryland, Kentucky, and Missouri—that stayed with the Union (although some citizens joined the Confederate cause).

On May 24, 1861, the Confederates moved their capital from Montgomery, Alabama, to Richmond, Virginia. When created, the Confederacy had a population of almost 9 million, including nearly 4 million slaves. But that paled by comparison to the Union population of approximately 22 million. Land values were higher in the North, as was economic strength, making the South extremely dependent on Europe for many material items. A basic lack of resources forced the Confederacy to levy taxes and deal with rising inflation. Southern railroads proved to be inadequate, and the South also lacked manufacturing equipment to make large field guns and even basic military equipment.

JEFFERSON DAVIS

Jefferson Davis was born on June 3, 1808, in Kentucky. He was educated at Transylvania University in Lexington, Kentucky, and at the U.S. Military Academy. He served on the frontier following graduation until his health forced him to leave the army in 1835. From then on, Davis was a planter in Mississippi until he was elected to the U.S. Congress in 1845. When the Mexican War broke out a year later, he resigned his seat to serve, fighting at Monterrey and Buena Vista.

Following the war, Davis served as a U.S. senator from Mississippi, as secretary of war for President Franklin Pierce, and again as U.S. senator from 1857 to 1861. As you might guess, his legislative voice was heard arguing in support of states' rights, and he used his influence during the Pierce administration to pass the Kansas-Nebraska Act, favoring a pro-slavery sentiment. Ironically, Davis didn't favor secession. As a senator, he tried to keep the southern states in the Union, although when his own state of Mississippi seceded, he gave up his Senate seat.

After his election as president of the Confederate States of America, Davis failed to raise the much-needed war chest to pay for Confederate fighting. He was equally unable to interest foreign governments in helping their cause.

The Confederate government was in a state of constant turmoil, it seemed, with judges from the various state courts interfering in military matters. However, Davis did appoint General Robert E. Lee as commander of the Army of Northern Virginia, and Davis remained true to his task until the bitter end. He staunchly believed the South could achieve independence, until he realized that defeat was imminent. He fled the Confederate capital of Richmond, and on May 10, 1865, federal troops captured him in Georgia. For two years, he was imprisoned at Fortress Monroe in Virginia. He was indicted for treason, but released one year later on bond. The federal government dropped its case against Davis in 1868. He lived many years engaged in a string of unsuccessful business ventures, though he did write *The Rise and Fall of the Confederate Government*, published in 1881. Davis died in 1889 and is buried in Richmond.

States That Left the Union

State	Secession Date	Readmission Date
South Carolina	December 20, 1860	June 25, 1868
Mississippi	January 9, 1861	February 23, 1870
Florida	January 10, 1861	June 25, 1868
Alabama	January 11, 1861	June 25, 1868
Georgia	January 19, 1861	June 25, 1868*
Louisiana	January 26, 1861	June 25, 1868
Texas	February 1, 1861	March 30, 1870
Virginia	April 17, 1861	January 26, 1870
Arkansas	May 6, 1861	June 22, 1868
North Carolina	May 20, 1861	June 25, 1868
Tennessee	June 8, 1861	July 24, 1866

* Georgia was readmitted a second time on July 15, 1870.

Harriet Beecher Stowe

Born in 1811, Harriet Beecher Stowe was an American writer and abolitionist who was horrified by the passing of the Fugitive Slave Act of 1850. In the early 1850s, she wrote a powerful novel—*Uncle Tom's Cabin*—which became a source of enlightenment regarding the wrongs of slavery. It precipitated the Civil War as it strengthened the antislavery movement.

Stowe was born and raised in New England, and she wrote her famous work while living in Maine. The abolitionist paper, the *National Era,* serialized *Uncle Tom's Cabin,* but it failed to attract much attention. Later, when issued in book form in 1852, its success was unprecedented as it sold 500,000 copies in the U.S. alone within five years.

8

The Civil War

Three words adequately introduce the Civil War: It was inevitable. With each new state admitted to the Union, it seemed the squabbles never ceased, with the issue of slavery a paramount concern. With tensions mounting over North–South differences, citizens could no longer deny the outbreak of war as their new president, Abraham Lincoln, took office. As the southern states seceded, the Confederates seized most of the federal forts within their borders. Only four remained under Union control: Fort Sumter (Charleston, South Carolina), Fort Jefferson, Fort Pickens, and Fort Taylor (all in Florida).

Fire on Fort Sumter

As moderate as Lincoln tried to be in his policies, there was no fence-sitting when Confederate rebels fired on Fort Sumter in South Carolina in April 1861. He had to act swiftly.

Fort Sumter, which lay at the entrance to the Charleston harbor, remained under the command of Major Robert Anderson and a small detachment of federal troops. It was by far the most important of the four forts remaining under Union control.

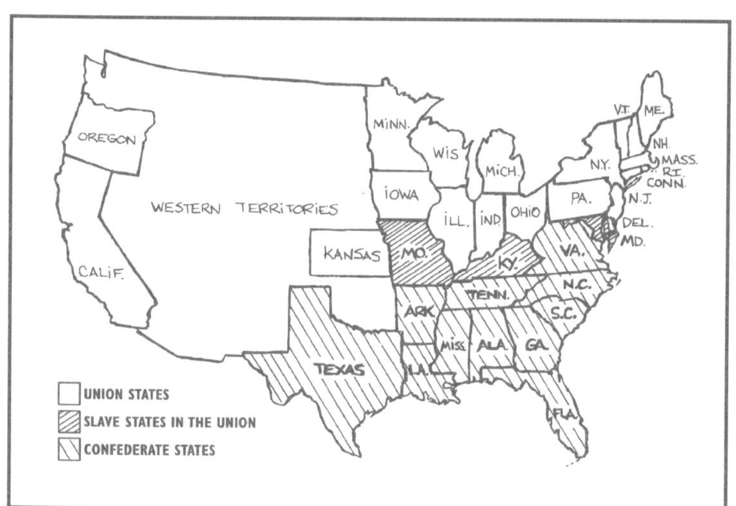

Map of United States During the Civil War

Reluctantly, because he feared igniting war, President Lincoln sent supplies to reinforce Fort Sumter, but the Confederates blocked the harbor. With orders from Confederate President Jefferson Davis, Confederate General Beauregard demanded that the Union surrender the fort. When Major Anderson ignored the ultimatum, Confederate fire erupted on April 12, 1861, and Anderson had little choice but to surrender.

Abraham Lincoln called on local militia in the Union states to suppress any uprisings against federal territory or laws. In essence, the Civil War had begun, and the Union rallied around its new president. A lesser man or leader might have yielded to the insurrection, but Lincoln upheld what he believed were his duties under the oath of office to protect and defend the Constitution and the country, with the powers vested in him to mobilize militia and blockade Confederate ports.

Four Years at War

Neither side knew at the initial firing that the Civil War would last four years and rank among the bloodiest wars ever fought. Although the issue of slavery loomed large, it didn't by any means diminish the goal of reconciling the country. Lincoln, to his credit, refused to recognize the legitimacy of the Confederate government, insisting instead that it was a rebellion that could be quelled.

Lincoln's resolve was to the North's advantage, for he became the towering symbol in body and in deed of the nation's strength. While the North enjoyed other advantages in terms of population, troops, and resources, the South found it far easier to defend its territory than to invade. The North had to push forth, carrying battles south in order to cripple the South's capacity to wage war. Of course, this proved to be more costly and time consuming. Strategically, the South felt it could learn from the example set in the Revolutionary War: to win meant exhausting the other side, dragging out the conflict until the North would no longer want to commit resources to the effort.

Early in the Civil War, Lincoln removed Brigadier General Irvin McDowell from his command of the federal army and placed Major General George B. McClellan in the role. While McClellan restored morale and raised the caliber of the fighting forces, he lacked decisiveness and was very slow.

Union soldiers dressed in blue government-issued uniforms, whereas the South's official color was gray. However, as some clothing worn by Confederate soldiers came from Union casualties or their own clothing reserves, the dress code varied a bit.

Flying the Confederate Flag

Even in the year 2000, South Carolina's allegiance to its Confederate past was strong. Angry protests have surrounded the flying of the Confederate battle flag, which flew over South Carolina's statehouse dome between 1962 and 2000. On July 1, 2000, the flag was moved from the dome to another location on the statehouse lawn.

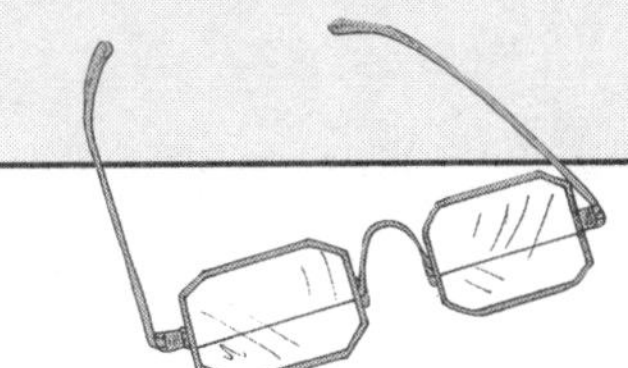

Famous Battles in the South

Although at the outbreak of the war the Union may have had skewed expectations, the first Union offensive put an end to any hopes of quick and easy victory.

In July 1861, at the Battle of Bull Run, or what the South called First Manassas, the Confederates used some of the brightest and best in military talent to defeat the rather haphazard Union soldiers marching into Virginia. Not only were McDowell's troops inexperienced, not to mention threatened with Confederate forces so near Washington, D.C., but they also suffered from overconfidence.

The Confederate army of General Beauregard maintained a line along Bull Run Creek, and the Virginia brigade led by Thomas J. Jackson was at the line's center. His stubborn defense earned him the moniker "Stonewall Jackson," for his troops remained standing like a stone wall!

In February 1862, Union gunboats led by Commodore Andrew Foote steamed up the Tennessee River to reach Fort Henry, where the plan called for an amphibious attack en route to Fort Donelson on the Cumberland River. Ulysses S. Grant led forces on land, but the muddy roads they traversed slowed them. Foote grew impatient and fired, wrecking havoc with the forts walls and Rebel guns. With flood waters flowing in, the southern forces raised the white flag.

Most of the escaping Confederates sought shelter at Fort Donelson. Grant's army pursued by land, reinforced by the gunboats making their way up the river. But with this fort situated high on a bluff, the fire by water did little but cause a retaliatory hail of bullets. While the Confederates damaged Yankee vessels, the fleet retreated down river. This left Grant's army without reinforcement, though it seemed to hold its own in the fighting. Union soldiers broke Confederate lines and caused acting General Buckner to surrender. Buckner, who had known Grant before the Civil War, expected generous surrender terms. That was wishful thinking, for Grant demanded unconditional and immediate surrender, earning him the nickname "Unconditional Surrender" Grant.

Soon after these forts were taken, Union troops took Tennessee's capital at Nashville, giving them a commanding presence in southern territory, especially along the rivers. The march farther south commenced.

Habeas Corpus

The writ of habeas corpus is a constitutional guarantee that a person cannot be imprisoned indefinitely without being charged with a specific crime. During the Civil War, however, Lincoln suspended habeus corpus in order to hold many southern agitators. Following the war, the Supreme Court ruled that a president could not suspend habeas corpus without Congressional consent.

In early April 1862, Grant was in a holding pattern in Tennessee while he waited for another Union commander to join him in a campaign toward Corinth, Mississippi. However, Confederate commander Albert Johnston's troops struck Grant's army by surprise. Grant lost approximately 13,000 men and the Confederates almost as many in a bloody battle known as Shiloh (ironically, the Hebrew word for "place of peace"). Shiloh's savagery shocked many on both sides of the war.

The Peninsular Campaign

Also that spring, with General McClellan in charge, the Union army began its Peninsular Campaign, advancing by way of the peninsula between the James and York rivers in Virginia in order to reach Richmond, the Confederate capital. But McClellan was not a decisive leader, and he was dreadfully slow, delaying the assault on Richmond. The resulting Seven Days battles, fought in late June 1862, led to an alarming number of casualties. Lincoln's administration held McClellan responsible for not taking Richmond, while McClellan blamed the president for not sending reinforcements.

Capturing New Orleans

Though most of the nation's attention was focused on the peninsula, the Union needed to gain control of New Orleans if it ever wanted to navigate the Mississippi River and effectively blockade the South. In April 1862, Flag Officer David Farragut, with a squadron of ships carrying federal troops, started up the Mississippi and arrived on April 25, demanding surrender. As the Confederates numbered only 3,000, they gave up easily, inflicting a painful loss on the South.

The Second Battle of Bull Run

Upon the failure of the Peninsular Campaign, Lincoln named Henry Halleck as the top general of the Union armies. Halleck ordered McClellan to bring his men back to Washington, for Lincoln was not about to leave Washington, D.C.,

unguarded. Organized in June 1862, the Army of Virginia had 45,000 troops and a fresh commander, Major General John Pope. Pope soon marched south with hopes of taking Richmond.

Robert E. Lee was determined to keep the Union out of his native Virginia. He sent Stonewall Jackson and 12,000 Confederate troops to block Pope's advance. The Yankees struck first, sending Jackson's men back until they regrouped and drove the Union from the field. The still-green Pope felt he'd better retreat, so he withdrew to the north side of the Rappahannock River while waiting for McClellan's troops.

However, Lee sensed an opportunity. With others in his company, Lee rushed to join Jackson, and on August 25, 1862, Confederate forces moved in on the Union at Manassas (site of the First Battle of Bull Run), capturing their supply station and treating themselves to a feast of food. The weary Rebels were now better nourished, and probably happier as they marched away with sacks full of provisions and supplies, including new shoes. On August 29, Pope's men attacked Jackson's soldiers. The Confederate defensive was weak, and Pope fully believed he'd defeated Jackson. He even wired Washington of his victory. Then on the following day, the Confederates reinforced Jackson, defeating the Union's forces.

A humiliated Pope retreated toward Washington with enormous losses after what became known as the Second Battle of Bull Run. Victorious, Lee determined that it was time to move his campaign across the Potomac, into the North.

FREDERICKSBURG

When McClellan continued to be a hesitant leader, Lincoln replaced him with Major General Ambrose Burnside. But in December 1862, Lee defeated Burnside at Fredericksburg, Virginia, south of the Rappahannock River, in a long day of needless slaughter. Refusing to heed the warnings of fellow generals, Burnside sent his troops into Lee's fire. Again, the cry came forth for better military leadership.

Thus, Lincoln relieved Burnside of his command and put Major General Joseph Hooker in place. "Fighting Joe," as he was called, was certainly more aggressive, and he restored the troops' spirits. In late April 1863, he set off to outfox Lee.

The Union general jumped most of his troops upstream of Lee's forces on the Rappahannock, but Hooker must have gotten spooked, for he quickly ordered his men onto the defensive. Now Lee had the advantage and used it, striking hard. The fighting was so intense that fire erupted in the dry leaves and brush, choking the battle lines with smoke and burning some soldiers alive. Hooker pulled back his army across the Rappahannock, having lost 17,000 of his fighting force.

Victory was short-lived for the Confederates, however, as Stonewall Jackson succumbed to pneumonia after being wounded. He died that May, and the Confederates would soon miss his military skill. President Lincoln, fairly fed up with Hooker's lack of military prowess, replaced him with Major General George Meade in June.

Video Classics

The Civil War made it to Hollywood with *Glory, Gettysburg, The Red Badge of Courage,* and *North and South.* And of course, who could forget the 1939 film *Gone With the Wind?* Although based on fiction, it captured the hearts of Americans everywhere as Atlanta burned and the Confederates fled.

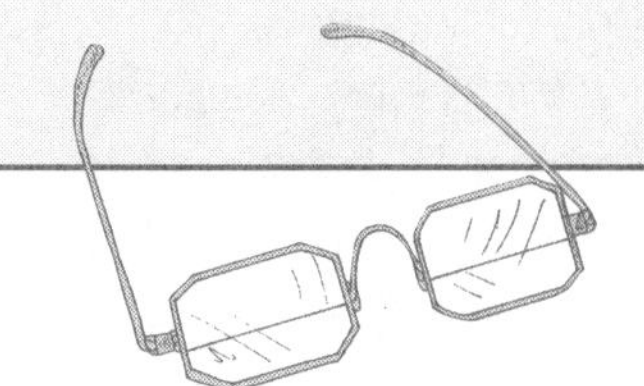

Northern Fighting

Lee's ulterior motive for winning a battle in the North was to finally convince foreign governments to back the South, and he believed that sympathizers in the border states would also join the Confederate cause. As his army headed into Maryland, they were a pathetic sight—dirty, hungry, and often barefoot. Just the least bit unnerved by Confederate troops in his backyard, Lincoln relieved Pope of his command, giving McClellan, or "Little Mac," another chance to fend off Lee's troops.

Unfortunately for Lee, a Confederate soldier left behind a precious piece of military intelligence—General Lee's troop orders. The Union corporal who stumbled on it turned it over to McClellan, but in another surprise, a southern sympathizer tipped off General Lee that the North knew of his plans. As a result, Lee pulled back his forces, and instead of attacking quickly, the cautious-as-ever McClellan hesitated, believing that Lee outnumbered him. But truth

An Incredible Charge

On July 3, 1863, at 1 P.M., Confederates opened an artillery bombardment—with 175 cannons firing on the Union line—during the Battle of Gettysburg. General Pickett, with a fresh division, led a charge on Cemetery Ridge. General Lee gave Pickett the orders to proceed, even though others cautioned against this type of attack. Lee might have done better by heeding the warning. The Union Army fired on the Confederate troops, inflicting heavy casualties. The bloody charge failed to crack General Meade's line. The Confederates fell back, having lost nearly three-fourths of their ranks. Pickett's charge ensured that the Battle of Gettysburg was just about over. Indeed, on the evening of July 4, General Lee began retreating to Virginia.

be told, McClellan had amassed about 70,000 troops in front of Lee at Sharpsburg, Maryland, along Antietam Creek. In the fighting that September 1862, McClellan drove Lee back into Virginia in the bloodiest one-day battle ever fought. The Battle of Antietam, or Sharpsburg as the South called it, cost both sides dearly, but the outcome was Union victory.

A Chance Meeting at Gettysburg

By summer 1863, General Lee's army was at its fighting peak, anxious to threaten northern territory. Lee commanded his army through Gettysburg, Pennsylvania, in order to march further north.

Early on July 1, a group of Rebels in search of badly needed shoes stumbled on northern cavalry units, which were ordered off their horses to keep the Confederates in check until Union reinforcements arrived. By midday, Lee sent in his own reinforcements, who drove the Union away. Soon, blue-clad soldiers were spotted traipsing through the town of Gettysburg.

Lee tried to get General Richard Ewell to seize Cemetery Hill, just south of the town, but Ewell was too cautious, and the Union set up a line along the ridges during the night. Meade formed a fishhook line to the southeast whereby the curve of the hook was Cemetery Hill with the shaft running down Cemetery Ridge. Lee ordered charges to the right and left flanks, hoping to crush the Union line.

Confederates did capture Devil's Den, a boulder-strewn area in front of the hill known as Little Round Top. Had they put cannons atop Little Round Top, they could have blasted the Union line. Once the Rebels were spotted, however, fighting recommenced, and Little Round Top was saved. The Rebels had charged Cemetery Ridge and Cemetery Hill, but they hadn't forced the Union troops from there. Meade chose to stay on the defensive, repeatedly repulsing Lee's assaults.

Confederate General Longstreet had warned Lee not to attack the Union's center of the line. On the third day, in what became

Visit Gettysburg Today

Three days in July 1863 put this town forever on the historical travel map. If you visit Gettysburg today, you'll find the Gettysburg National Military Park to be one of the best in the country, with a well-equipped Visitor's Center filled with two floors of exhibits and a bookstore perfectly suited to adults and kids. The displays include Civil War uniforms, rifles, sabers, cannons, and medical kits, with explanations of their use on the battlefield. The electronic map vividly demonstrates troop movements, and in another building, the Cyclorama Center features a light and sound show surrounded by Paul Philippoteaux's 1884 painting of Pickett's Charge.

Tour the miles of battlefields by bus, individual car (with audio tapes or licensed guides), or on a bicycle in good weather. Numbered stops with markers describe battle action, and you can take as much or as little time as you want if you explore on your own. Elsewhere in this little town, you'll discover the National Civil War Wax Museum and perhaps take part in the Ghosts of Gettysburg Candlelight Tours.

Finally, you don't have to be de Gaulle, Churchill, or Khrushchev to visit Ike and Mamie Eisenhower's only home at the Eisenhower National Historic Site, a 230-acre farm. You'll quickly discover that their station in life didn't influence this famous couple. Notice the brick barbecue where Ike grilled steaks for his guests, or the barn where he raised his show cattle. Tours depart from the Visitor's Center during the warmer months. For more information, contact the Gettysburg Convention and Visitors Bureau at (717) 334-6274.

known as Pickett's Charge, Confederates opened a huge artillery bombardment concentrating on the line's center. But in the scorching heat during the first three days of July, the carnage of the Battle of Gettysburg was as incredible as the failed decisions many generals made. This lapse in judgment forced Lee to retreat back across the Potomac.

Lincoln's Gettysburg Address

Lincoln was called upon to deliver just a few appropriate remarks on November 19, 1863, to dedicate a military cemetery at Gettysburg. He delivered his remarks following those of Edward Everett, a distinguished speaker in his own right. Though Lincoln's speech was much more concise than the two-hour oration Everett rendered, the president's remarks were profound and masterful, imparting another persuasive vision for America:

Four score and seven years ago our fathers brought forth on this continent, a new nation, conceived in Liberty, and dedicated to the proposition that all men are created equal.

Now we are engaged in a great civil war, testing whether the nation, or any nation so conceived and so dedicated, can long endure. We are met on a great battlefield of that war. We have come to dedicate a portion of that field, as a final resting place for those who here gave their lives that that nation might live. It is altogether fitting and proper that we should do this.

But, in a larger sense, we cannot dedicate—we cannot consecrate—we cannot hallow—this ground. The brave men, living and dead, who struggled here, have consecrated it, far above our poor power to add or detract. The world will little note nor long remember what we say here, but it can never forget what they did here. It is for us the living, rather, to be dedicated here to the unfinished work which they who fought here have thus far so nobly advanced. It is rather for us to be here dedicated to the great task remaining before us—that from these honored dead we take increased devotion to that cause for which they gave the last full measure of devotion—that we here highly resolve that these dead shall not have died in vain—that this nation, under God, shall have a new birth of freedom—and that government of the people, by the people, for the people, shall not perish from the earth.

War on the Western Front

During August and September 1862, the Confederate army invaded Kentucky, a slave state that had chosen not to secede from the Union. With the people divided concerning the war effort, it wasn't uncommon to have people from the same community enlist in both the Confederate and Union armies. Unfortunately, both sides clashed at the Battle of Perryville on October 8, 1862. Though neither side could claim clear victory, the Confederates did retreat.

The Political Climate

Lincoln, under much pressure from abolitionists, saw his main objective as saving the Union, regardless of how the slavery issue played out. With the political climate simply too volatile, Lincoln trod carefully so as not to offend slaveholding border states, very key to the North. Kentucky was one of these. Because of its strategic location on the Ohio River, it had to remain in the Union. Besides, in his inaugural address, Lincoln had promised not to interfere with slavery. To do so would have meant additional states joining the Confederacy.

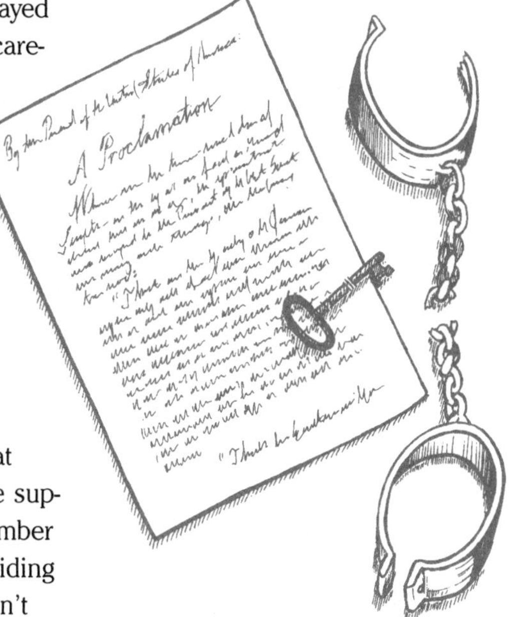

On April 16, 1862, Lincoln signed a bill abolishing slavery in Washington, D.C. Lincoln wanted to free all the slaves in the seceding states, but Secretary of State William Seward advised him to make such a momentous announcement only after a Union victory. When the Battle of Antietam brought that opportunity, and as he became more confident of border state support, Lincoln issued his Emancipation Proclamation. On September 22, 1862, he announced that on January 1, 1863, all slaves residing in the Confederate states would be free. The proclamation didn't apply to border states that were not in rebellion against the Union, though Lincoln did urge voluntary compensated emancipation. In fact, Lincoln did not have the power to free slaves except under the powers granted during war to seize enemy property. As president, he had to abide by the Constitution, which protected slavery in slave states. Due to their rebellion, he could act in states that had seceded. The 100-day warning in the proclamation was intended to give Rebel states ample opportunity to rejoin the Union with slavery intact.

An End to Slavery

The Thirteenth Amendment, which Lincoln pushed for, made up for the limitations of the Emancipation Proclamation: it barred slavery from the United States in perpetuity. Later, it became a condition that southern states had to accept the Amendment to be readmitted to the Union. It became law in January 1865.

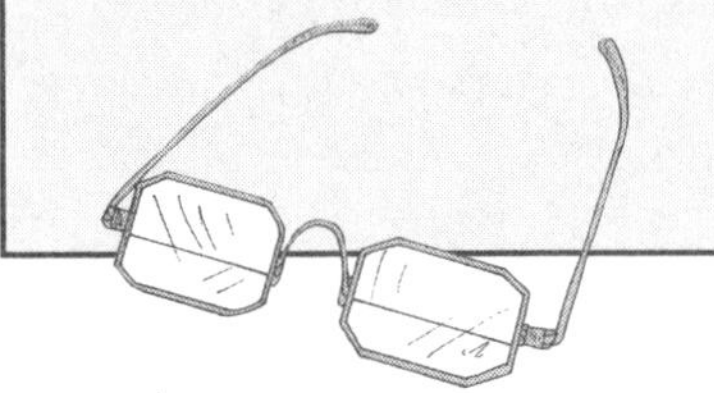

Signs of the Times

The draft (conscription) began in 1862 when the Confederacy called all men between eighteen and forty-five to serve in the army. In March 1863, the Union passed a similar act calling men between twenty and forty-five into military service. However, you could hire a substitute or pay $300 instead. The act was branded a rich man's law, and troops had to quell riots that flared, but Lincoln dared not suspend the draft.

The Union faced additional burdens with financing the war. As a result, new federal taxes were levied on inheritances, legal documents, and personal income. The government also printed paper money, dubbed "greenbacks" because of the color. By 1863, $450 million worth of greenbacks were in use. The value of these greenbacks varied and was usually lower than that of gold. And because there was an increase in the money supply, prices rose.

More Fighting in the South

On the day Lee withdrew his forces from Gettysburg, Lincoln received word that General Ulysses S. Grant had captured Vicksburg, Mississippi, a key Confederate fort along the Mississippi River. Indeed the Battle of Vicksburg had spilled over from October 1862 until July of 1863. Throughout the winter and spring, Grant's army had tried one tactic after another to attack the city, but with stump-clogged canals, tangled forests, massive flooding, and Confederate fighting power, the Yankees had a hard time

The Emancipation Proclamation

When Abraham Lincoln was working on drafts of his Emancipation Proclamation, he had the foresight to say, "If my name ever goes down into history, it will be for this act, and my whole soul is in it." Drafted in 1862, it went into effect by presidential signature on New Year's Day, 1863, with these words:

. . . Now, therefore I, Abraham Lincoln, President of the United States, by virtue of the power in me vested as Commander-in-Chief, of the Army and Navy of the United States in time of actual armed rebellion against authority and government of the United States, and as a fit and necessary war measure for suppressing said rebellion, do, on this first day of January, in the year of our Lord one thousand eight hundred and sixty three, and in accordance with my purpose so to do publicly proclaimed for the full period of one hundred days, from the day first above mentioned, order and designate as the States and parts of States wherein the people thereof respectively, are this day in rebellion against the United States, the following, to wit:

Arkansas, Texas, Louisiana, (except the Parishes of St. Bernard, Plaquemines, Jefferson, St. Johns, St. Charles, St. James[,] Ascension, Assumption, Terrebonne, Lafourche, St. Mary, St. Martin, and Orleans, including the City of New-Orleans) Mississippi, Alabama, Florida, Georgia, South-Carolina, North-Carolina, and Virginia, (except the forty-eight counties designated as West Virginia, and also the counties of Berkley, Accomac, Northampton, Elizabeth-City, York, Princess Ann, and Norfolk, including the cities of Norfolk & Portsmouth [)]; and which excepted parts are, for the present, left precisely as if this proclamation were not issued.

And by virtue of the power, and for the purpose aforesaid, I do order and declare that all persons held as slaves within said designated States, and parts of States, are, and henceforward shall be free; and that the Executive government of the United States, including the military and naval authorities thereof, will recognize and maintain the freedom of said persons . . .

Usually, Lincoln signed bills in abbreviated form using "A. Lincoln." However, he signed his full signature onto the Emancipation Proclamation, and said to those cabinet officers standing near, "Gentlemen, I never, in my life, felt more certain that I was doing right than in signing this paper."

Lincoln's proclamation gave slaves a beacon of hope. As they spotted Union troops approaching their towns, slaves simply refused to work for their masters. Further along in his address, Lincoln invited slaves to join the Union army. By the end of the Civil War, one Union soldier in eight was African-American. This hastened the South's demise, and foreign governments (namely France and Great Britain) took notice as well.

succeeding. Grant's men had to literally dig their way to Rebel lines, but the Union troops managed to keep up a steady bombardment, forcing civilians to go underground for safety. With no relief army in sight, the Confederates asked Grant for surrender terms, and on July 4, 1863, the Rebels stacked their arms before marching out of their fallen city. Grant's victory opened the Mississippi River to the Union and effectively broke the Confederate army in two.

Fighting at Chickamauga Creek that September had devastated both the Union and Confederate forces, rendering the survivors weary of war. The Yankees, anxious for the arrival of General Grant, had staggered back into trenches near Chattanooga, Tennessee, and the Confederates rested on a hill with the intention of starving their enemies into surrender. Though it took Grant nearly a month to arrive, when he did, he ordered a surprise night attack, with relief troops from the Army of the Potomac.

The Confederates looked down on Chattanooga from the slopes of Missionary Ridge, and Grant ordered troops under the leadership of Major General George Thomas to move forward but stop at the base of the ridge. Inspired, enthused, adrenaline pumping, the Yankees kept going straight to the slope where the slightly panicked Confederates clambered up, losing Chattanooga in addition to another 6,700 men that November 1863.

By the end of 1863, the Union had achieved two main objectives—control of the Mississippi River, which split the South in two, and a strangling blockade of southern ports. Severely lacking, however, was a coordinated strategy to finish the war, until in March 1864, Lincoln selected General Ulysses S. Grant to command the northern troops.

Grief Overwhelms the Lincoln Family

Besides the daunting burden of war, Lincoln endured many personal trials during his White House years. Mrs. Lincoln lost four of her brothers who fought for the Confederacy, but the ultimate blow was the death of the couple's son Willie in 1862. The strain left Mrs. Lincoln depressed and morbidly afraid to allow her eldest son Robert to sign up with the army (though at the war's end, Lincoln secured Robert a fairly safe post on Grant's staff). Yet despite the family turmoil, the president worked long hours seeing to his duties, greeting White House visitors, and personally reviewing matters unrelated to the Civil War. When reviewing court-martial sentences, he urged leniency by scrawling on one such case, "Let him fight instead of being shot."

Lincoln mastered the 1864 re-election against Democratic candidate General McClellan, who was still very popular with soldiers from his Army of the Potomac. McClellan's followers felt Lincoln unjustly relieved him of his military command following Antietam. Showing himself to be a staunch fighter, McClellan ignored his party's platform, which called for the war's immediate end. Instead, he urged that the fighting continue. Lincoln chose Andrew Johnson as his vice president and ran on the platform of abolishing slavery and ending the war.

Final Battles

General Grant gave General William Tecumseh Sherman full command of the West, while he himself moved east to lead Meade's Army of the Potomac against General Lee's Confederate forces. His strategy: attack the South's strong armies rather than take key southern cities. While Grant would focus on Lee, Sherman's March Through Georgia went after General Joe Johnston's force of 45,000 men. While en route, he hoped to destroy much of the Confederate infrastructure, especially the vital rail and industrial strength of Atlanta. On September 1, 1864, Sherman succeeded in his mission, sending a telegram to the president that "Atlanta is ours." The capture did much to solidify Lincoln's re-election.

Meanwhile, Lee's Army of Northern Virginia spent much of the fall and winter of 1864–65 hunkered down in trenches. Grant tried to cut off Lee's resources. With fewer supplies making it to the front lines, and with

Ulysses S. Grant

Confederate soldiers deserting the ranks, Lee knew he had to make a move. In March 1865, he decided to attack the Union's Fort Stedman long enough to divert Grant and, he hoped, effect an escape to join Joseph E. Johnston's forces farther south. But the attempt failed, and with Grant commandeering Lee's last rail supply line, Lee advised Jefferson Davis to move his Confederate government out of Richmond. Nonetheless, Lee took his dwindling troops toward Lynchburg, but the Rebel lines collapsed at Sailor's Creek. Finally, desertion, disease, near-starvation, and the Union's relentless attacks brought the Confederacy to its knees.

Lee's Surrender

In a quiet country village near a rail stop, General Robert E. Lee brought his weary regiments into the Appomattox Courthouse. His men didn't even resemble warriors. Their supplies captured, they could no longer fight, especially with a wall of blue-clad soldiers surrounding them.

Calling a truce, Lee asked for a meeting with Grant to discuss surrender terms. On the afternoon of April 9, 1865, the two generals met at the home of Virginian Wilmer McLean. While they chatted about the Mexican War initially, Grant knew that whatever they discussed regarding the Civil War's end would have a profound effect on the country's restoration. Grant, a man of Lincoln's choosing and, so it appeared, beliefs, decided not to humiliate the Confederate side. In his offer to Lee, he stated that Confederate forces could keep their own horses, baggage, and side arms, returning home with the assurance that U.S. authorities would not harm them. Grant even made arrangements to feed Lee's troops before the two parted.

Robert E. Lee

Lee's army stacked its arms and surrendered battle flags on April 12, 1865, though it took until June for all Confederate forces to lay down their arms. When the Union forces gloated over their victory with artillery salutes, Grant demanded they stop. Later he wrote, "We did not want to exult over their downfall. The war is over. The rebels are our countrymen again."

Amendments and Aftermath

As a result of the Civil War, several amendments were added to the Constitution. The Senate and House passed the Thirteenth Amendment eliminating slavery in 1864 and 1865, respectively, while the country was still waging war. Those states that had seceded had to approve of the amendment in order to be readmitted to the Union.

After the war, the Republican majority in Congress pushed through the Fourteenth Amendment, which defined American citizenship to include all former slaves and declared that individual states could not unlawfully deny citizens their rights and privileges. As might be expected, passing this amendment took deft political maneuvering, as almost every southern or border state initially rejected it. Just like the amendment that had preceded it, seceding states had to adopt the Fourteenth Amendment to be readmitted. The required three-fourths of the states ratified the Fourteenth Amendment on July 9, 1868, though the measure had passed Congress two years earlier.

The Fifteenth Amendment, granting African-American men the right to vote, also took a two-year path to ratification. It was presented to the states in 1868, and southern states grudgingly passed the measure. Years later (in the 1890s), former Confederate states required African-Americans to take literacy tests as a requirement for voting. Since few slaves were literate at the time, this all but eliminated voting among this group until a more modern civil rights movement protested these strictures in subsequent years. Interestingly, this amendment said nothing about affording women the right to vote, an issue which wasn't addressed until 1920.

In addition to the legislative fallout from the war, the economic toll was substantial. The war took more than 600,000 lives, destroyed property valued at $5 billion, and created social wounds that never completely healed. It did, however, end slavery, making many believe the moral objectives of the war were indeed accomplished.

The Lincoln Library

Fans of Abraham Lincoln are lucky, as plans are well underway for a 160,000-square-foot Lincoln Presidential Library to be built on two city blocks donated by the city of Springfield, Illinois. The new facility, housing manuscripts written and signed by Lincoln along with posters, photos, books, and other memorabilia, is set for completion by 2002.

ONE FATEFUL NIGHT AT THE THEATER

On Good Friday, April 14, 1865, Lincoln and his wife, along with General and Mrs. Grant, were to attend a performance of *Our American Cousin* at Ford's Theatre in Washington, D.C. Those attending Lincoln's cabinet meeting earlier in the day reported seeing him cheerful and happy, for the surrender at Appomattox had taken place days earlier.

That night, although the Grants could not attend, the Lincolns went to the theater with their other guests. At approximately 10:30 P.M. and at a planned moment when all eyes were focused on the stage, John Wilkes Booth, a southern sympathizer, crept into the poorly protected presidential box and fired his pistol at Lincoln's head just once. The president slumped into his seat, unconscious, while Booth leaped to the stage shouting, "*Sic semper tyrannis*," the Virginia state motto, which meant "Thus ever to tyrants."

Though he had injured his foot, Booth ran away. Lincoln's body was taken to a lodging house across the street, where Mrs. Lincoln, cabinet members, and friends waited through the night for doctors to perform a miracle that never happened. On Saturday, April 15, 1865, Lincoln was pronounced dead, and within hours Vice President Andrew Johnson was sworn in as president. This marked the first presidential assassination in the United States.

On the same day that Booth shot Lincoln, friends of Booth made attempts on Secretary Seward's life, but he lived. In fact, one friend was to have carried out a plan to assassinate Vice President Johnson, but decided against it.

Booth, it was discovered, was a vengeful, half-crazed actor from a fairly famous theatrical family who had planned for some time to kidnap the president and take him to Richmond. There, he hoped to exchange him for captured Confederate prisoners of war. However, when that city fell and with the conflict now resolved, Booth resorted to murder, claiming that he was God's instrument to punish Lincoln for all the trouble he caused the country.

Lincoln's body lay in state in the East Room of the White House. On April 19, he was given a military funeral in Washington, and two days later, his coffin was placed on a special train that carried his body back to Springfield, Illinois, for burial in Oak Ridge Cemetery. The slain president's funeral procession retraced the route he'd initially taken to reach Washington for his inauguration in 1861.

As for the fate of John Wilkes Booth, he did escape with the help of friends and an unsuspecting physician who tended his injuries, but he was discovered twelve days later in a shack near Bowling Green, Virginia. When he refused to surrender to authorities, they set the barn ablaze. Some say that Booth was struck by a sniper's shot, and others assert that he pulled a gun on himself. Regardless, Booth was dragged out of the inferno and died shortly thereafter. His coconspirators went on trial for aiding the assassin.

If John Wilkes Booth felt his pro-southern objectives were accomplished, he was mistaken. Lincoln's tragic death galvanized the country, plunging it into profound grief. Had Lincoln been able to lend his steady, reassuring hand to the Reconstruction process, tensions would have certainly healed sooner between the two factions. Booth took down a great leader at a time when the country still needed him, and every citizen paid a price for that act of vengeance.

Presidential Succession

In the event of a president's death, removal from office, or resignation, the vice president is sworn in as the nation's commander in chief. Should the vice president be unable to serve, the Speaker of the House is next in line to assume the presidency, followed by the president pro tempore of the Senate, the secretary of state, the secretary of the treasury, the secretary of defense, and then the attorney general. Other cabinet members could technically become president as well, but it's hard to imagine the need. Any successor to the presidency must meet the requirements for the office as established by the Constitution.

9 MENDING AMERICA

At the start of the Civil War, Andrew Johnson, a Tennessee Democrat, was the only southern U.S. senator remaining loyal to the Union. You can imagine this didn't win him many friends, even if it did earn him the vice presidential nomination in the 1864 election.

Thrust into the presidency after a mere forty-one days on the job as second in command, Johnson tried to reunite the bitterly divided land that saw neighbor fight against neighbor, brother against brother. Johnson shared Lincoln's view favoring leniency, but a group of Congressmen called the Radical Republicans resented Johnson's Reconstruction policies.

Reconstruction

Reconstruction was the official name given the rebuilding process following the American Civil War. It forced the country to grapple with pressing questions that came up after southern defeat and the abolition of slavery. Should there be punishment for the Confederate rebellion? What rights would be granted to the newly freed slaves? What criteria did Confederate states need to meet before being judged as "reconstructed"? And how would the southern economy survive and prosper without its traditional labor base?

Johnson offered amnesty to all who took the oath of allegiance (and if the Confederates had postwar wealth surpassing $20,000, they had to apply for a pardon). He returned plantations to their former owners, and he sought to restore political rights to the southern states as soon as possible, with each state drafting a new constitution. Of course, these constitutions had to outlaw slavery and disavow secession. Bitter over their defeat, many southerners still restricted the rights of former slaves, and this angered northerners who felt that Johnson was selling out to the South. Pennsylvania representative Thaddeus Stevens, leader of the Congressional Radicals, declared that "the punishment of traitors has been wholly ignored by a treacherous Executive."

Dissension Grows

The faction against President Johnson grew in its belief that the Union victory had to stand for more than simple restoration. The Republican majority in the House of Representatives refused to seat their colleagues sent by southern states or to accept the legitimacy of their governments. Lengthy debate ensued, with Congress passing its version of the Reconstruction Act in March 1867 over Johnson's veto. With Tennessee having ratified the Fourteenth Amendment, it was seen as having been restored. Other southern states were given a military commander to oversee the writing of new state constitutions that would allow all adult males to vote, regardless of race. If states ratified their new constitutions along with the Fourteenth Amendment, they would be readmitted to the Union.

Compromise eventually won out, but the damage had been done. In 1868, Andrew Johnson became the first president to be put on trial by the Senate, even though no constitutional grounds existed for his impeachment. Johnson was spared from removal by a margin of one vote. But his presidency was effectively over, based on the political disagreements stemming from his Reconstruction policies.

Changes in the South

While the U.S. War Department created the Freedmen's Bureau in 1865 to help former slaves find jobs and obtain an education, southern whites did what they could to keep African-Americans poor and powerless. Confederate war veterans formed the Ku Klux Klan, originally a social group, which quickly became a violent vigilante group preventing freedmen from voting. This hate group originated in Pulaski, Tennessee, with its members, often dressed in white robes with pointed hoods, spreading terror as they rode on horseback at night.

Though treated as second-class citizens, blacks eagerly sought to make a better life for themselves, forming their own churches and other institutions. Sympathetic northerners often helped, winning the label of "carpetbaggers" as they entered

The Alaska Purchase

In foreign affairs, Johnson's secretary of state, William H. Seward, acquired property from Russia. Critics thought he was plain mad to pay $7.2 million for unexplored territory to the north—land we would later incorporate into the nation as the state of Alaska. Seward reached the deal in 1867, and it was quickly ridiculed as "Seward's folly." It wasn't until the Alaskan Gold Rush years later that Seward's shrewd purchase would be appreciated.

southern politics to apply their principles. Most blacks continued to vote Republican, but Democrats returned to power in some southern states by the mid-1870s. As this political transition occurred, Republican fears were confirmed, with Democratic victories sometimes leading to a reversal of Reconstruction accomplishments. Black school funding was slashed, and over many decades to come, a rigid segregation policy pervaded the South. As a result, southern blacks began their migration north to escape the lingering oppression. Many settled in America's largest cities, such as New York and Chicago.

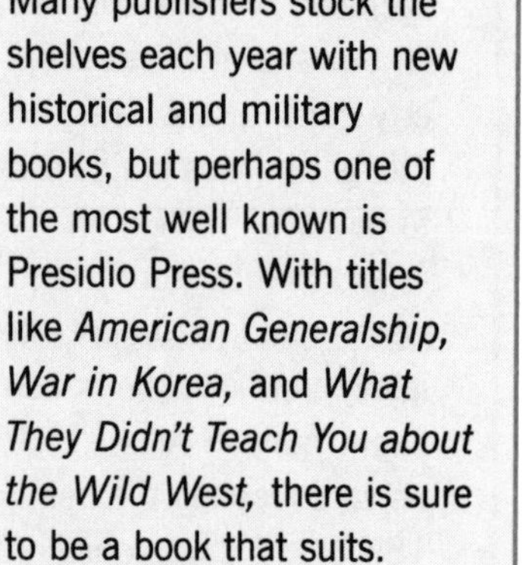

Presidio Press

Many publishers stock the shelves each year with new historical and military books, but perhaps one of the most well known is Presidio Press. With titles like *American Generalship, War in Korea,* and *What They Didn't Teach You about the Wild West,* there is sure to be a book that suits. Check out their Web site at *www.presidiopress.com*.

The Wild West

The Wild West refers to a time and place in American history surrounding the settlement of the western states in the second half of the nineteenth century. Cowboys epitomized a unique type of western character, and they figured prominently after the Civil War through the 1890s when transportation facilities were scanty. Cowboys had to drive cattle to shipping points over long distances, and they often had to keep the livestock safe from thieves and marauding animals. Because these hardy souls were tough at times, the cowboy figure reached mythical status, becoming a legend. Songs and tales were based on cowboy escapades, as were motion pictures and television programs decades later.

Towns such as Abilene, Kansas, prospered in the late 1860s and throughout the next decade as cattle were loaded and shipped by rail to eastern markets. Cheyenne, Wyoming, was made prominent by the Union Pacific Railroad. Dodge City, Kansas, was founded in 1872 with the arrival of the railroad, and developed into a major shipping point for trail herds.

Although the process of pushing Native Americans westward started much earlier, a number of skirmishes, otherwise known as the Indian Wars, occurred in the latter half of the nineteenth century. In 1868, Congress had recognized the Black Hills of South Dakota as sacred to the Sioux and Cheyenne Indians, but the deal was called off when gold was discovered there. It became common practice for the government to move Native Americans onto reservations whenever their current settlements impeded so-called progress. On June 25, 1876, federal cavalry with George A. Custer in the lead attacked the camp of Chief Sitting Bull on the Little Big Horn River in Montana. The Native Americans prevailed, killing Custer and his troops, but their victory was short-lived. Federal troops later forced the Native Americans to surrender.

POST–CIVIL WAR PRESIDENTS

Ulysses S. Grant, who became a national hero leading the Union to victory in the Civil War, was inaugurated as president in 1869. He served two terms despite scandals within his administration involving railroad fraud and whiskey taxes. Rutherford B. Hayes succeeded him, winning a controversial election by one electoral vote over Samuel J. Tilden. As a result, he was sometimes referred to as "His Fraudulency" or "Rutherfraud" B. Hayes. Fairly lenient toward the South, Hayes won over his critics by the end of his single term in office.

James A. Garfield came to the presidency in 1881, making him the third Civil War general in a row to become president. It turned out, however, that Garfield was probably safer on the battlefield, for tragedy struck four months into his presidency: he was shot by Charles Guiteau, a disgruntled man who had failed to obtain a federal job. Garfield lingered with his gunshot injuries for two months, dying on September 19, 1881.

As with many ascending to high office, no one figured that Chester A. Arthur would become president. Upon Garfield's death, Arthur was sworn in. Ironically, this man who had formerly been given political jobs in return for party loyalty became a staunch supporter of earning federal jobs based on merit. In 1883, Arthur signed the Pendleton Act that established the Civil Service Commission, requiring job seekers to pass examinations before being admitted to civil service.

Having failed to win the Republican Party's nomination for a second term, Arthur left office. Grover Cleveland then served two terms as president, though not consecutively. He was ousted from office by Benjamin Harrison in 1889, but returned to the White House four years later. Cleveland won the popular vote 49 to 48 percent, but Harrison triumphed in the Electoral College, becoming president. In his two terms, Cleveland earned the nickname of "Old Veto," for he vetoed more legislation than any prior president. During a severe economic depression, known as the Panic of 1893, Cleveland failed to restore the nation's sagging economy and didn't win a third nomination.

Harrison, the grandson of former president William Henry Harrison, supported the Sherman Antitrust Act of 1890 designed to regulate big business and eliminate monopolies. He also signed the McKinley Tariff Act, which placed tariffs on imported goods, causing a rise in prices.

William McKinley came to office in 1897 and quickly established his reputation in foreign affairs. In 1895, Cubans had risen up against their Spanish rulers, and many Americans sympathized with the revolutionaries. In January 1898, McKinley ordered the U.S. battleship *Maine* to Havana harbor to check on the hostilities. One month later, the *Maine* exploded and sunk, killing 262 sailors, causing headlines to cry "Remember the *Maine*! To hell with Spain!" Having accused Spain of this deliberate attack, the United States declared war on April 25.

Theodore Roosevelt, secretary of the Navy at the time of the attack, quit his post and formed a cavalry unit of volunteer soldiers. Known as the Rough Riders, these men landed in Cuba in June, heading inland toward San Juan Ridge. Armed with pistol on horseback, Roosevelt led his men to victory. The Spanish–American War lasted 113 days, ending with the Treaty of Paris. Under the terms of the treaty, Spain left Cuba, giving Puerto Rico and Guam to the United States along with the Philippines, for which the United States paid $20 million. Also during President McKinley's administration, the nation annexed Hawaii as a territory. The United States was becoming a global force.

Unfortunately, on September 6, 1901, an anarchist from Buffalo, New York, shot President William McKinley. Eight days later the president died from his wounds.

The Pledge of Allegiance

"I pledge allegiance to the flag of the United States of America, and to the Republic for which it stands, one nation under God, indivisible, with liberty and justice for all."

The original Pledge of Allegiance was written by Francis Bellamy in 1892. The phrase "my flag" was in the original. An act of Congress in 1954 inserted the words "under God."

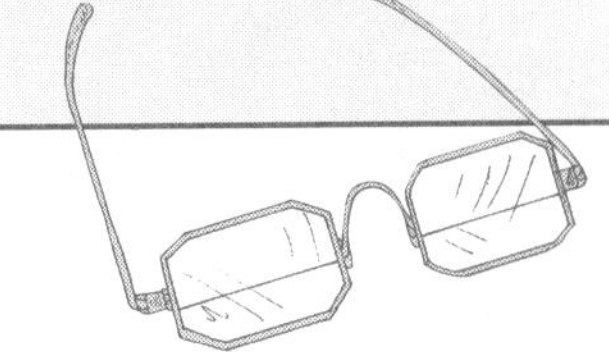

Transportation Evolves

Although train travel was hardly new around Civil War times, it had steadily evolved from the early railroads of the 1820s. Passenger comfort was improving as well. Early on, tiny engines such as the DeWitt Clinton, built in 1831 for the seventeen-mile Mohawk and Hudson Railroad, were used with passengers sitting in open cars resembling stagecoaches just behind the engine. It couldn't have been exciting. Terrifying maybe, but hardly enjoyable as riders were bathed in black smoke and menaced by the smokestack's sparks!

These early trains couldn't go the distance, and with railroad expansion, life got better. The Baltimore and Ohio (B&O) Railroad opened in 1830, and the Pennsylvania Railroad connected Pittsburgh with the Atlantic coast. Later engines distributed the weight via several sets of wheels, were made to round the bends, and incorporated the boiler into the body of the engine. The transcontinental railroad was completed in 1869, and it continued to be the predominant means of transcontinental travel until well after World War II.

New Means of Power Emerge

Electric traction was introduced in 1895 for short stretches of railroad track, especially in urban areas when tunnels were involved. This electrification, which eliminated smoke and steam, was precipitated by a serious accident in New York City when a tunnel filled with smoke. Soon, trains passed under Park Avenue to enter Grand Central Terminal in Manhattan, in compliance with a state law discontinuing the use of combustion engines within New York City.

With diesel-electric, electric, and turbine-powered trains replacing steam engines, only a few of the earlier trains survive today, mostly for display or nostalgia rides. Indeed, it turned out that electric trains could accelerate and meet schedules far better than their predecessors.

The Stagecoach

The stagecoach was also a viable means of transportation in the West. The early railroads could only go so far. Manufactured in the quiet New England town of Concord, New Hampshire, the world-renowned Concord Coach became a symbol of the Wild West in the period following the Civil War. A durable coach, it could withstand harsh jolts on rutted roads, making it ideal for the wilderness.

Wells, Fargo and Co., founded in 1852 to provide mail and banking services for the California gold camps, used these stagecoaches as the fastest means of transportation for that part of the country. In 1861 you could buy a rail and stagecoach ticket, and barring any storms, floods, Indian attacks, holdups, or breakdowns, you might make it coast to coast in twenty-six days!

Transportation, Business, and Politics

Inventions such as the automatic coupler and the airbrake (invented by George Westinghouse) improved safety each decade. In the 1880s, Westinghouse pursued his interest in rail safety, and at the age of thirty-four founded Union Switch & Signal Company in Pittsburgh. Within two years, his company was selling complete systems for switching trains from track to track and indicating the position of every train.

One of the most important strides came when George Pullman built a remarkable new railcar in 1864. These cars, given the name Pullman cars, had sliding seats, upper berths, and comfortable heating. In addition, Fred Harvey, a Kansas restaurateur, introduced meals to the railroad. In 1894, President Grover Cleveland sent federal troops to break up a strike by railroad workers at the Pullman Palace Car Company in Chicago because the strike over pay cuts interfered with mail delivery.

As the railroad phenomenon grew, presidential campaigns adopted whistle-stop tours, in which the candidate would speak from the train's rear platform. During World War II, President Franklin D. Roosevelt used a specially built railcar with armor-plated sides and three-inch-thick bulletproof windows.

A Heritage of Crafts

Americans have long been known for their superior craftsmanship from the time of colonial silversmith Paul Revere. After the American Revolution, Revere devoted much time to making tea services in what's known as the Federal style. A genuine Revere item has the family name enclosed in a rectangle. Revere later worked in brass as well.

American Shaker creations originated with the Shaker sect, whose founder came from England. Since Shaker laws forbade anything too fancy, all creations from buildings to furniture and baskets were functional and unadorned. Light wood stains showed the natural beauty of the wood grain. By the 1880s, you could purchase Shaker replicas by mail order, especially chests, baskets, fabrics, and chairs.

As German Protestant immigrants streamed into William Penn's "promised land" of Pennsylvania, they brought along cherished folk traditions as well as the determination to pass these down through the generations. The Pennsylvania Dutch weren't only folk artists who loved to depict ornamental birds, animals, and flowers. They were also early makers of musical instruments.

Wood and master furniture craftsmen made elegant furniture and cabinets out of popular woods like mahogany. At Colonial Williamsburg, you can see cabinetmakers using the same eighteenth-century woodworking methods as early Americans.

Another famous American artist crafted beautifully stained-glass windows, bowls, and vases. Louis Comfort Tiffany had planned to become a painter, but he soon became known for his exquisite

The Roeblings Build a Bridge

John Augustus Roebling, a German immigrant and civil engineer, left his mark in Pittsburgh and New York with his wire rope used to build suspension bridges. In 1857, Roebling built the Brooklyn Bridge joining Manhattan with Brooklyn over the East River. Thousands celebrated its opening on May 24, 1883, but few realize that Emily Roebling, wife of Washington Roebling and daughter-in-law of John, transformed herself into an engineer to see the project through after John died and Washington collapsed during the bridge's construction.

work in what he called Favrile glass. This he created using a secret process of his own invention by which color, design, and texture are embedded into the glass before it is hand-blown. At the turn of the century, Tiffany Art Nouveau glassware was popular and would later become museum treasures. If you visit the Metropolitan Museum of Art in Manhattan, you'll find many examples of Tiffany's exquisite work on display.

Famous Firsts

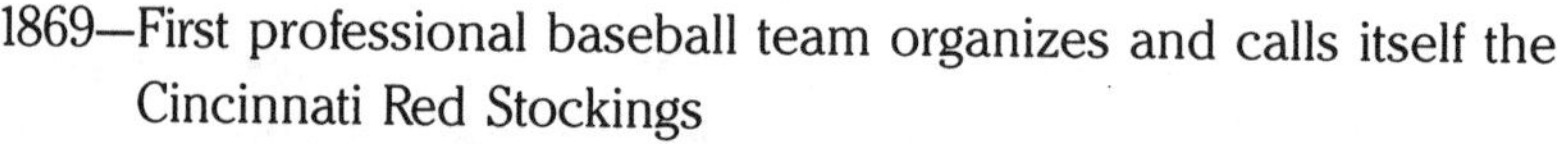

1869—First professional baseball team organizes and calls itself the Cincinnati Red Stockings

1872—Aaron Montgomery Ward founds the first mail-order business (Sears came along in 1886)

1876—Alexander Graham Bell invents the telephone with repair mechanic Thomas Watson

1881—P. T. Barnum teams with James Bailey for Barnum & Bailey's Circus

1886—Atlanta druggist John Pemberton invents Coca-Cola, first as a health tonic and later as a soft drink

1879—Thomas Edison invents the light bulb

1888—George Eastman coins a name that is easy to spell and pronounce for his Number One Kodak camera

1895—Dr. John Harvey Kellogg invents the first flaked breakfast cereal

Famous American Architects

Throughout American history, several esteemed architects have literally shaped the form of our country in the buildings that many work in or continue to visit today. Here are some of the most famous:

- *Thomas Jefferson (1743–1826).* Our nation's third president also distinguished himself by designing the Rotunda at the University of Virginia, a modified version of the Pantheon in Rome. He also designed his home at Monticello.

Architectural Tourism

For architecture aficionados, the concept of architectural tourism is catching on in many U.S. cities. If you want to see works by H. H. Richardson, Frank Lloyd Wright, and Philip Johnson, among others, take part in the "Living Architecture . . . Alive in Pittsburgh" travel package offered by the Greater Pittsburgh Convention and Visitors Bureau. You'll tour the Allegheny County Courthouse and Jail in addition to viewing PPG Place, and receive tickets to the Carnegie Museum Complex (made possible by the philanthropy of industrialist Andrew Carnegie) and the Andy Warhol Museum (devoted to the famous pop artist born and educated in Pittsburgh). Classical and gothic architecture were used when Richardson employed the rounded arch, adapted from Romanesque architecture of the early eleventh century. Once inside, stop to admire the three-story staircase, made of Indiana limestone with original lighting fixtures. It's a celebration of the Richardson Romanesque arch.

You'll also visit two properties in Fayette County designed by Wright—Fallingwater and Kentuck Knob. Wright's design of Fallingwater used glass, steel, and natural stone quarried on the property. The elements cause the eye to focus on the surroundings. Inside the house, Wright created the furniture, and you'll also see Tiffany lamps, Japanese prints, and other artwork. Because of the gradual deflection of the first and second levels, temporary shoring has been installed, and a massive restoration is planned. However, tours are still given. At nearby Kentuck Knob, Wright built a much more modest home of fieldstone boulders and tidewater red cypress from South Carolina. He based the design on a hexagonal modular grid all on one level to allow for openness. The home reflects Usonian design, a precursor to the ranch home that most could afford. For more information about this architectural tourism package, call (800) 359-0758.

- *Charles Bulfinch (1763–1844).* One of the first major exponents of the Federal style, he designed the Massachusetts State House with its great, gold dome soaring high on Boston's Beacon Hill. It was one of the most distinguished public buildings when completed in 1798. Bulfinch also succeeded Benjamin Henry Latrobe as architect of the U.S. Capitol, completing it in 1830.
- *Frederick Law Olmstead (1822–1903).* This major American landscape architect was educated at Yale University and traveled throughout the United States and Europe to study. In 1857, Olmstead, along with Calvert Vaux, originated and supervised the master plan for New York City's Central Park, the first major metropolitan park in a U.S. city. So successful was this that many others commissioned him to design large public parks in their cities. Olmstead planned the grounds of the Capitol in Washington, D.C., and was the first commissioner of Yosemite National Park in California.
- *Richard Morris Hunt (1827–95).* The architect of several summer homes in Newport, Rhode Island, he built the Breakers for Cornelius Vanderbilt II in 1892–95. Modeled after North Italian Renaissance palaces, this house has been preserved as a monument to the bygone era of formal entertaining and ostentatious wealth. Other examples of his works include the Great Hall of New York City's Metropolitan Museum and the Biltmore Hotel in Asheville, North Carolina.
- *Henry Hobson Richardson (1838–86).* Having studied at Harvard and in Europe, he created his own style, called Richardson Romanesque, characterized by deep entrance arches. Richardson used granite in such a way that the stone carver's skill revealed rather than concealed the natural stone. Among his famous works are Trinity Church in Boston and the Allegheny County Courthouse and Jail in Pittsburgh, Pennsylvania, both masterpieces of nineteenth-century architecture.
- *Louis Henry Sullivan (1856–1924).* Applying his influential credo, "Form follows function," Sullivan's brilliant ideas

allowed steel beams to show, becoming elements of the design. He shunned historical styles, believing that one had to consider the building's purpose, and became known as the father of the skyscraper. He built, among others, the Wainwright Building in St. Louis, Missouri (completed in 1891), and the Carson, Pirie, Scott and Company Building in Chicago (completed in 1904).

- *Frank Lloyd Wright (1867–1959).* Perhaps the most famous pupil of Louis Sullivan, Wright distinguished himself as an organic architect with the main objective of harmonizing a building with its natural surroundings, as he did with Fallingwater, built in the 1930s. At Bear Run, south of Pittsburgh, this home has dramatic horizontal planes and stone walls and is built directly over a waterfall. The Solomon R. Guggenheim Museum in New York City explored the possibility of the curve and is certainly one of his most dramatic and controversial designs. It was commissioned in 1943 and opened in 1959, six months after Wright's death.
- *Philip C. Johnson (1906–).* Educated at Harvard, Johnson created unconventional designs that culminated in his own glass box home built in New Canaan, Connecticut, in 1949. Only one room, the bathroom, was enclosed. In addition, Johnson designed glass skyscrapers, including the Seagram Building (1958) in New York City, and PPG Place (1984) in Pittsburgh, Pennsylvania.
- *I. M. Pei (1917–).* This Chinese-American architect fused classical concern for elegance of form with contemporary functional efficiency. Pei studied at the Massachusetts Institute of Technology and at Harvard and designed many famous works nearby, including the John Hancock Tower in 1973 and the John F. Kennedy Library and Museum in 1979. Pei also designed the Jacob K. Javits Convention Center in New York City (begun in 1980 and opened in 1986).

10

The Age of Industry, Invention, and Discovery

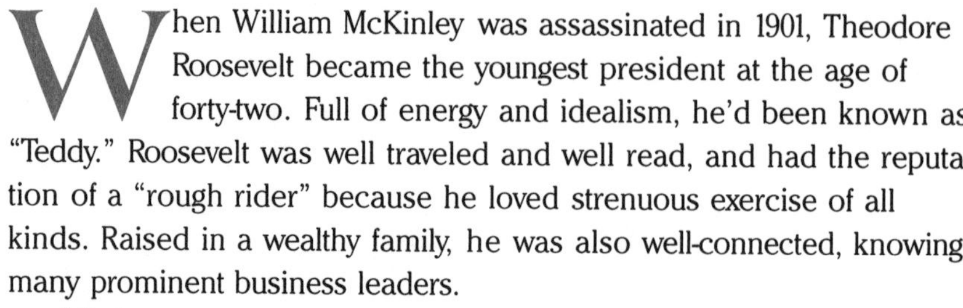

When William McKinley was assassinated in 1901, Theodore Roosevelt became the youngest president at the age of forty-two. Full of energy and idealism, he'd been known as "Teddy." Roosevelt was well traveled and well read, and had the reputation of a "rough rider" because he loved strenuous exercise of all kinds. Raised in a wealthy family, he was also well-connected, knowing many prominent business leaders.

His image as a fairly ordinary citizen enhanced his appeal, and in turn, he championed the causes of the working class by maintaining a balance between wealthy industrialists, business owners, and ordinary workers. When coal miners in Pennsylvania went on strike for higher wages in 1902, President Roosevelt threatened to seize the mines if owners would not agree to arbitration. Similar actions earned him the moniker of "Trust Buster" when he acted to stop unfair practices in the big businesses of tobacco, oil, steel, and the railroads. These industries had established trusts, working together to limit competition. The most famous was the Standard Oil trust run by John D. Rockefeller.

Of course, Roosevelt's reform efforts sparked great political opposition and made for interesting times. In February 1902, Roosevelt brought suit under the Sherman Antitrust Act against the railroad trust of the Northern Securities Company. The people loved him for it, and when the case went before the Supreme Court, the decision came in five to four against the trust. Actually, the president did not want to disband all of these trusts—just the most flagrant ones. He called his moderate approach the "Square Deal."

Trustbusting

The Sherman Antitrust Act of 1890 regulated the operations of corporate trusts and declared that every contract, combination in the form of trust, or other act in restraint of trade was illegal. The act has been amended and supplemented over the years.

The Rise of Organized Labor

Large factories had become the major employers for most people—a result of the Industrial Revolution at the end of the eighteenth century. But the downside to that was that workers lacked protection from almost all contingencies, including inflation, illness, disability, and arbitrary firing. Workers soon banded together, demanding a voice and a change in labor conditions. The 1870s were marked with particular unrest given the sad state of the nation's economy in 1873. A secret fraternal order called the Knights of Labor embraced workers in many occupations, becoming one of the most powerful early unions. In 1881, workers met in Columbus, Ohio, to establish a far more effective group called the American Federation of Labor (AFL). Its first leader was Samuel Gompers, president of the Cigarmakers International Union and of the Federation of Organized Trades and Labor Unions. The AFL gave workers more rights, such as negotiating with employers for better conditions and wages.

Several disastrous strikes, coupled with the depression of this era, stunted union growth. In 1892, large numbers of private detectives as well as National Guard troops quelled striking workers at Carnegie Steel Company's Homestead Mill in Pittsburgh, essentially destroying the union. In 1894, a strike by the American Railway Union against the Pullman Company was defeated by an injunction issued under the Sherman Antitrust Act.

But after the Spanish–American War, the trade union movement grew so that by 1904, more than 2 million workers belonged to trade unions. Almost 1.7 million belonged to the AFL. With great reluctance, employers gradually accepted collective bargaining with the unions as the norm.

Presidents in the last quarter of the nineteenth century typically sided with business owners against workers who went out on strike with their grievances. Sensing new public sentiment, Roosevelt sent in federal troops to a Pennsylvania mine strike, not only to protect the mines themselves, but to protect the strikers as well. Business owners were known to hire thugs to beat up striking workers, and the presence of soldiers prevented violence and led to more peaceful resolution of labor/management disputes.

Income Tax

The 1913 passage of the Sixteenth Amendment ushered in the era of income tax—the original Constitution had prohibited such a tax. Actually, the Bureau of Internal Revenue was established in 1862 to collect temporary taxes during the Civil War. In 1943, automatic payroll withholding began, and in 1953, reorganization resulted in the Internal Revenue Service, precipitating the widely held belief that nothing is certain in life "except death and taxes."

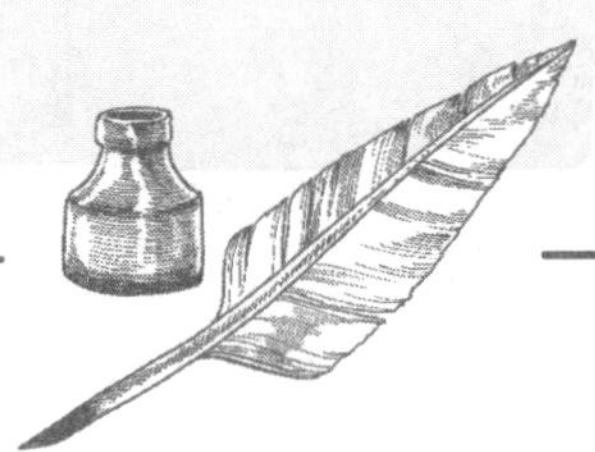

Inventions and Engineering Marvels

American ingenuity continued to advance, with the inception of the railroads and the invention of the telephone in the 1870s. In the early 1900s, two brothers worked closely to develop early aeronautics. Wilbur Wright, along with his younger brother Orville, enjoyed constructing simple mechanical toys, and in 1888 they built a large printing press.

The two soon began publishing a Dayton, Ohio, newspaper and opened a bicycle repair shop and showroom in 1892. Having read about German experiments with gliders, they built their first in 1900.

First in Flight

In September 1900, near Kitty Hawk, North Carolina, the Wright brothers tested their glider invention, carefully noting their findings and correcting the problems they'd discovered. This work continued as they concurred that planes could be balanced best by pilots rather than by built-in engineering devices. Astutely, they patented their idea and went on to construct their first propeller and a machine with a twelve-horsepower motor. At Kitty Hawk, on December 17, 1903, Orville Wright made the first test flight in their first powered glider, the Flyer I, making this the first airplane flight in history (though it lasted a whopping twelve seconds). A subsequent flight on September 9, 1908, at Fort Myer, Virginia, where Orville Wright established several records under government contract for a sixty-two-minute flight, made him an international celebrity.

Despite some public skepticism, the brothers dedicated themselves to further developing better engines and airplanes. The Wright Brothers National Memorial, at the site of their first flight, is now administered by the National Park Service.

The Automobile

Americans found themselves learning about another mode of transportation as Henry Ford introduced the Model T in 1908. "I will build a car for the great multitude," Ford said. His first Model T sold for $850, the price of a car's accessory by today's standards, but a hefty sum back then. Ford kept his promise, developing an assembly-line style of manufacturing that became efficient enough to bring prices down. This assembly-line approach became the industry standard in the manufacture of automobiles. By the time the Model T (commonly known as the Tin Lizzy) was discontinued in 1927, its price of around $300 was widely affordable.

THE PANAMA CANAL

Although not the type of invention the Wrights or Henry Ford created, the Panama Canal (connecting the Atlantic and Pacific Ocean) was certainly an engineering marvel of its day. Without a canal, ships traveling from New York to San Francisco had to take the long route around Cape Horn at the southern tip of South America. Construction of the canal cut this journey by 7,000 miles. The work wasn't easy, for it required damming a river and digging a channel through a mountain range. Although construction began in 1904, epidemics of tropical disease delayed the work. Chief Engineer John F. Stevens came up with a new plan to speed the process, but Col. William C. Gorgas, the sanitary officer, made the greatest contribution when he eliminated yellow fever and malaria. The project became a most difficult undertaking because of its complexity and its cost of $350 million. The fifty-mile-long Panama Canal opened to shipping on August 15, 1914, but not without ongoing dispute. Under a 1903 treaty, the United States controlled both the waterway and some surrounding land known as the Panama Canal Zone. Panamanian resentment over the next century led to new negotiations, and treaties were signed in the 1970s during the Carter presidency. These treaties recognized Panama's ultimate ownership of the canal and surrounding lands. Panama controlled the region from 1979 on, and the United States officially turned over the Panama Canal in 1999.

EARLY MEDICAL MIRACLES

Quality of life throughout American history has been greatly enhanced by medical advancements, improvements that helped people live longer with each successive generation. Here's a list of some early medical pioneers:

- *Benjamin Rush.* Founded the first public dispensary in Philadelphia and became one of the earliest doctors to characterize insanity as a medical condition rather than the influence of evil spirits. Yet Rush practiced bloodletting,

a rather draconian measure of treating patients plagued by illness.

- *Crawford Long.* Georgia physician who experimented with ether, a gas that, when breathed in, numbed a patient's pain but didn't render the person unconscious.
- *William T. G. Morton.* Boston dentist who publicly demonstrated ether as the first truly effective surgical anesthetic.
- *Oliver Wendell Holmes.* In the 1840s he brought attention to unsanitary practices as the cause of many deaths, particularly during childbirth; he also suggested the term "anesthesia."
- *Elizabeth Blackwell.* In 1849, she became America's first female physician, later opening a private dispensary in New York City staffed only by women.
- *American Medical Association.* Known today as the AMA, this group was formed when physicians gathered in 1847 at the Academy of Natural Sciences in Philadelphia. They formed an organization that remains the watchdog over medical practices and lobbies for the sake of its members.
- *Walter Reed.* U.S. Army doctor who in 1900 proved that certain mosquitoes spread yellow fever (this discovery saved thousands of lives during the construction of the Panama Canal).

The Smithsonian

The Smithsonian stems from the generosity of James Smithson, a wealthy English scientist struck by the principles of the United States as well as the amazing discoveries made in our country in the nineteenth century. Upon his death in Italy in 1829, Smithson willed his fortune to his nephew, with the stipulation that if he died without heirs, the entire fortune would be given to the United States to create a fine institution where knowledge would be increased for future generations. President Andrew Polk signed a congressional act establishing the Smithsonian Institution, and construction began in the 1850s.

Thomas Edison, Inventor Extraordinaire

Many famous Americans put their creativity to use discovering new processes and products to save time and money, and most of all, add convenience. But none was as prolific as Thomas Edison, who patented 1,000 of his products. Edison's invention of the light bulb ranks with the advent of the telephone as two of the most important technological advances of the nineteenth century. To name just a few of Edison's noted inventions:

- In 1877, Edison announced the phonograph, which recorded sound mechanically on a tinfoil cylinder.

Visit the Smithsonian

There are museums of national note, but none like the Smithsonian Institution. Made up of sixteen smaller galleries on and off the National Mall, it charges no admission, thanks to government funding and private donations. Perhaps best known is the National Air and Space Museum. Dozens of aircraft hang in suspended animation, showcasing American aviation and space technology. View the Wright Brothers' 1903 *Flyer,* Charles Lindbergh's *Spirit of St. Louis,* Chuck Yeager's *Glamorous Glennis,* the Gemini IV spacecraft, and the Apollo 11 command module.

At the National Museum of American History, step inside American culture and politics, peering in at the first ladies' inaugural ball gowns, Mr. Spock's phaser, even the chair Archie Bunker used on television and the sweater Mr. Rogers wore for children. Scientific and technological advances are chronicled here, from Benjamin Franklin's experiments and Edison's light bulb to inventions such as the Model T, nylon, the atomic bomb, and the radio.

Dazzle yourself with the gem and mineral collection at the National Museum of Natural History. The famed Hope diamond is housed here, as well as impressive collections of dinosaur skeletons, the Orkin Insect Zoo, and collections representing foreign cultures, habitats, and ecosystems.

Art buffs won't want to miss the collection of nineteenth and twentieth century art at the Hirshhorn Museum and Sculpture Garden, which houses permanent collections of Picasso and Warhol paintings and sculptures by Rodin and Matisse, among others. At the National Portrait Gallery, you can see the famous portrait of George Washington by Gilbert Stuart in addition to portraits of all other American presidents. Those interested in the Civil War will be delighted by the special collection devoted to that era. The Smithsonian also offers gift shops and cafes. Because the Smithsonian is government-run, any souvenirs you buy here are tax free. For more information, call (202) 357-2700 or visit *www.si.edu*.

- In 1879, Edison exhibited incandescent electric light bulbs, making electric lighting his most significant discovery.
- In 1882, Edison developed and installed the world's first large central electric-power station in New York City.
- In 1888, Edison invented the kinetoscope, the first machine to produce motion pictures by a rapid succession of individual views.

Although these noteworthy contributions had a profound effect on society, Edison wasn't finished. He invented the alkaline, nickel–iron storage battery, and at the outbreak of World War I, Edison designed, built, and operated plants for the manufacture of benzene, carbolic acid, and aniline derivatives. In 1915, Edison was appointed president of the U.S. Navy Consulting Board, where he made further discoveries and improvements.

The Election of 1904 and Beyond

Although he was popular, President Roosevelt knew he had never been elected to the post in which he now served. Traditionally, Republicans favored big business while Democrats supported progressive candidates advocating reform. At first, it was unclear whether Roosevelt would win his Republican Party's nomination. However, the president was successful, winning not only the nomination, but also a landslide victory that stunned the incumbent president himself.

Although politics kept the president occupied much of the time, his family life filled the remaining gap. Roosevelt was the father of six rambunctious children, some of whom slid down White House staircases on metal trays. His oldest, Alice, was a bit of a handful. She loved to shock people by smoking in public, keeping a pet snake, and behaving in other ways that were unconventional for women of that time, including betting on horses at the racetrack. Teddy Roosevelt reportedly said, "I can be

president of the United States, or I can control Alice. I cannot possibly do both."

The children no doubt obtained much of their charisma from their father, who was also a great supporter of racial equality. He was the first president to invite an African-American to dinner at the White House when he dined with Booker T. Washington, principal of the Tuskegee Institute in Alabama.

Unfortunately, in spite of all of his fine attributes, Roosevelt's strength in keeping his promises proved to be a mistake in at least one case. During the campaign of 1904, he vowed not to seek re-election in 1908. But when the end of his second term rolled around, this young, still ambitious man wanted to stay in the post he excelled in. He felt he could not—he had to keep his promise. Yet because of his great popularity, Roosevelt helped to pick his successor. William Howard Taft won the election of 1908, taking office the following year.

The Taft administration was fairly lackluster, although it continued the previous administration's progressive policies, carrying trustbusting further than Roosevelt had. Taft also took advantage of many new technological innovations. He was the first president to buy White House automobiles. Though good-natured (he was teased about his weight of more than 300 pounds), he had trouble filling the shoes of his predecessor. In the end, Taft served only one term, but went on to become the tenth chief justice of the United States (and the only person ever to hold the highest offices in both the executive and judicial branches).

"Teddy" Bear Origins

On a bear hunt in 1902, President Theodore Roosevelt found only a bear cub, which he couldn't bring himself to shoot. Upon hearing the story, the *Washington Post* ran a cartoon, inspiring a Brooklyn toy maker to place a copy of the cartoon in his window next to a stuffed brown bear. The term "teddy bear" stuck.

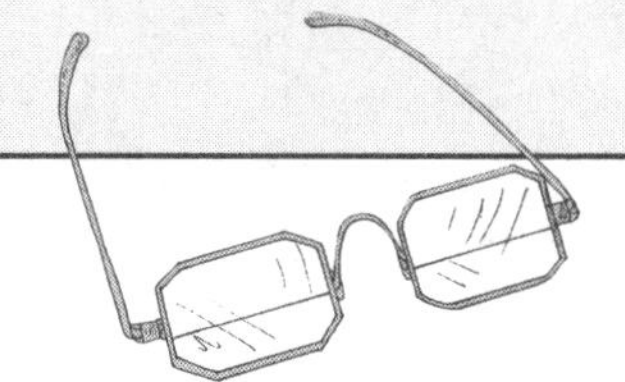

The Nation's Economy

Inventions fueled the economy, creating jobs in railroads, oil, steel, communications, factories, and retailing. The automobile industry remained in its infancy during World War I, but quickly grew after 1918, leading to America's first real consumer buying spree.

At stores such as John Wanamaker in Philadelphia, R. H. Macy in New York City, and Marshall Field in Chicago, Americans enjoyed boosting the economy. These large stores and catalog companies

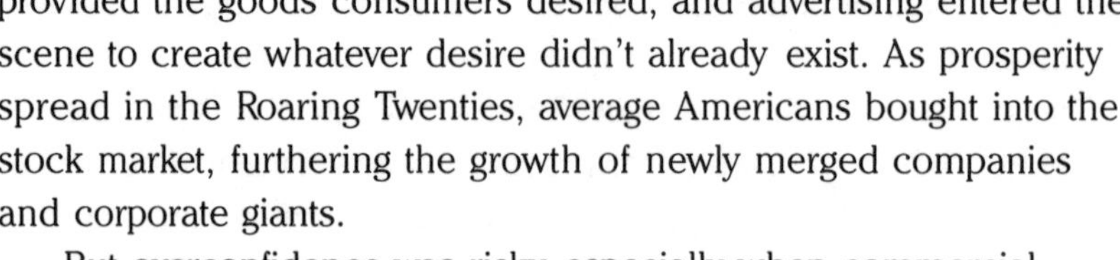

provided the goods consumers desired, and advertising entered the scene to create whatever desire didn't already exist. As prosperity spread in the Roaring Twenties, average Americans bought into the stock market, furthering the growth of newly merged companies and corporate giants.

But overconfidence was risky, especially when commercial banks cast prudent business practices aside, financing the stock market and dabbling in real estate speculation. When farm prices collapsed, smaller banks fell into insolvency. Increasing numbers of consumers racked up debt each year to obtain the goods they wanted or thought they needed.

The NAACP

The National Association for the Advancement of Colored People (NAACP) was founded in 1909 to champion the rights of African-Americans, becoming the most influential black organization in America.

Men of Vision and Wealth

Several industrial and financial power brokers arose in the early 1900s. Their drive, determination, and uncanny ability to see the future led to vast empires. They included the likes of:

- *John Pierpont Morgan.* Son of a prominent international banker, Morgan began his career in banking and after the Civil War reorganized the railroads. By the end of the century, he controlled a transportation empire. In 1895, he founded J. P. Morgan & Co., which lent the U.S. government millions of dollars in gold. In 1901, Morgan organized U.S. Steel, the first billion-dollar corporation.
- *Andrew Carnegie.* Born in Scotland, Carnegie had no wealth to back his rise to power. When he came to America in 1848, he worked as a bobbin boy in a Pittsburgh cotton factory. But he moved forward as a messenger, telegrapher, and in various positions within the Pennsylvania Railroad. During his railroad rise, Carnegie invested in oil, iron, and bridge building. In the 1870s, he concentrated on steel, and soon the Carnegie Steel Company became America's industrial giant. Carnegie, a savvy businessman and ferocious competitor, also became

known for his philanthropy, giving away huge sums for future generations to enjoy.

- *John D. Rockefeller.* Rockefeller made his fortune with the Standard Oil Company, formed in 1870. During the 1880s, Rockefeller's Standard Oil Trust controlled virtually all of the nation's refineries. Not surprisingly, antitrust sentiments prevailed, and as the trust dissolved, Rockefeller formed Standard Oil of New Jersey as a holding company until the Supreme Court broke it up in 1911. Rockefeller retired early, his personal wealth a staggering $1 billion.
- *John D. Rockefeller Jr.* Upon his father's retirement in 1911, the younger Rockefeller assumed the reins in business. He also led the board of directors of the Rockefeller Foundation (among other board posts), and in 1930, he began supervising a massive undertaking in New York City. It was an extensive complex of buildings, completed in 1939, known as Rockefeller Center or Radio City, where the ice rink and Christmas celebrations remain prominent today. Rockefeller's philanthropy extended also to New York City land given to the United Nations (upon which the international headquarters was established) and to the restoration of Colonial Williamsburg in Virginia.
- *Edward H. Harriman.* Harriman was born to wealth, but he built his fortune even farther. Success on Wall Street led Harriman to rebuild bankrupt railroads in 1881. The centerpiece of this effort was the Union Pacific Railroad, but he also acquired controlling shares in other lines.
- *James J. Hill.* Born a Canadian, Hill matched financial wits with some of the finest in business. In the United States in the late 1870s, Hill became a partner in the St. Paul and Pacific Railroad, which he acquired along with other lines. In time he consolidated his holdings into the Great Northern Railway. Later, Hill and Morgan paired against Harriman and financier Jacob Schiff in a battle for the Northern Pacific Railroad, causing tremors in the stock market in 1901.

The Old Ballgame

The first modern game of baseball was played in 1846, and although much credit for the present-day game belongs to Alexander Joy Cartwright, particular players and their talent had a hand in America's pastime. Names such as Babe Ruth, Jackie Robinson, Roy Campanella, Honus Wagner, Ty Cobb, Hank Aaron, Joe DiMaggio, and Roberto Clemente have become synonymous with the game.

In 1903, the National and American Leagues recognized each other as the only major leagues in the sport. The first World Series occurred that autumn between pennant-winning teams. The American League's Boston Red Sox defeated the National League champs, the Pittsburgh Pirates.

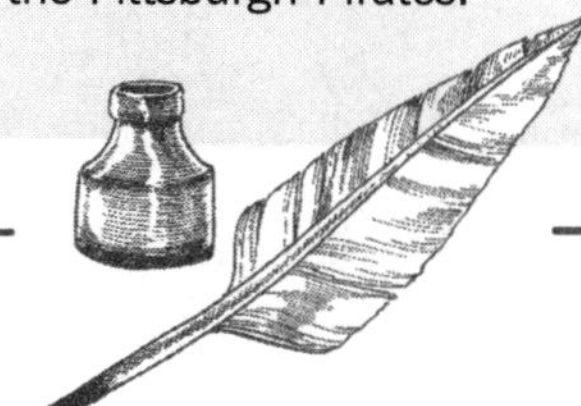

The Power of Publishing

The tradition of newspapers vying for readers based on their divergent perspectives dates back to Thomas Jefferson and Alexander Hamilton, who each found newspaper forums to use as their sounding boards.

Until the 1830s, newspapers were published essentially for the elite, but as printing techniques improved, the number of papers grew. In 1833, Benjamin Day founded the *Sun* in New York; the *New York Morning Herald* followed in 1835, founded by James Gordon Bennett. These two competing dailies led to the creation of a news gathering force known later as the Associated Press (AP).

In the early 1900s, Edward Wyllis Scripps formed the United Press Association, which in 1958, after a merger with International News Services, became United Press International (UPI).

The Printed Page Expands its Coverage

By 1850, monthly magazines such as *Harper's Monthly*, the *Atlantic*, and the *Ladies' Home Journal* informed and entertained Americans. You could buy *The Saturday Evening Post* for a nickel by the end of the century. Around this time, a young California upstart made himself a success with the *San Francisco Examiner*, which he took over from his father. With this newspaper, William Randolph Hearst intended to take on another successful publisher, Joseph Pulitzer, whose newspaper empire (starting with the *New York World*) reached beyond New York City. Pulitzer had pioneered the newspaper business with the advent of sports pages, women's fashion section, and more. Hearst and Pulitzer tried to outdo each other from the comics to coverage of scandals, bringing forth the term "yellow journalism" to describe the sensational techniques often used to attract readers. Joseph

Visit New York City

Peter Minuit snagged the last great real estate deal in New York when he bought the island of Manhattan for $23.70 in trinkets. America's largest city doesn't come as cheap today, but it's memorable.

Stock prices have risen since a group of brokers met under a buttonwood tree on Wall Street in 1792. Visit the New York Stock Exchange (20 Broad Street) to see the informative video and exhibits before watching the frenzy of the trading floor from the observatory. At the Federal Reserve Bank (33 Liberty Street) you can learn about money making, literally, at this branch, one of twelve in the country.

Manhattan boasts some of the finest museums in what's dubbed Museum Mile. Among them, the Metropolitan Museum of Art (1000 Fifth Avenue), founded in 1870, houses perhaps the most comprehensive collection of works in the Western world. In 1930, sculptor Gertrude Vanderbilt Whitney founded the Whitney Museum of American Art (945 Madison Avenue). Architect Frank Lloyd Wright designed the giant white shell exterior of the Solomon R. Guggenheim Museum (1071 Fifth Avenue at 89th) in the 1950s. Reflecting the structure, this museum houses modern and contemporary art. Don't miss the gorgeous Beaux Arts Reading Room at the New York Public Library. The library has amassed vast collections of artwork, prints, and photographs since its founding in 1895.

Don't miss the expanse of Central Park with its lush meadows between 59th and 110th Street. On weekends, the park is closed to most vehicles for the bikers and skaters to enjoy. Theater lovers find their way to 42nd Street and Broadway. Kids will delight in Disney's productions, such as *Beauty and the Beast* and *The Lion King*. Times Square (great when lit at night) was renamed in 1904 when the famous newspaper moved to the New York Times Tower and celebrated with fireworks on New Year's Eve. The extravaganza has been celebrated every December 31st ever since!

The bronze statue of George Washington on the steps of Federal Hall (26 Wall Street, New York City) marks the site where he took office in 1789. Peer up at the vast Rotunda, the nearby Bill of Rights room, and the interactive exhibit on the Constitution.

If you can't travel to New York, rent the PBS Home Videos *The Statue of Liberty* and *Ellis Island.* The first tape takes the statue from concept to construction; the series explores the immigrant experience and how immigration changed America. For more information, go to *www.shoppbs.com.*

Pulitzer donated $1 million to Columbia University for a school of journalism, founded in 1912, and funded Pulitzer Prizes.

San Francisco Shakes

On May 5, 1906, a powerful earthquake measuring 7.9 on the Richter scale rocked San Francisco, causing three days of raging fires that destroyed many downtown and residential areas. Fortunately, San Francisco was quickly rebuilt and hosted the Panama–Pacific International Exposition in 1915.

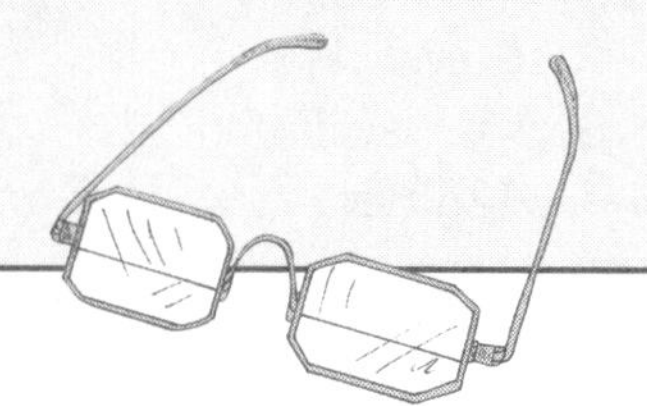

Periodicals Establish Niches

Adolph Ochs kept steering his newspaper, *The New York Times*, founded in 1851, to serious news coverage with the slogan "All the news that's fit to print." Tabloids began around 1919 as more easy-to-read newspapers profusely filled with illustrations and graphics. The *New York Daily News* was one of the first, followed by Hearst's *Daily Mirror*.

By 1922, *Reader's Digest* truly capitalized on the reading and news phenomenon. Published by DeWitt and Lila Acheson Wallace, this small magazine featured informative but condensed articles that had previously appeared elsewhere. It remains successful with that tradition into the twenty-first century. The *Digest*, as some call it, inspired other magazine upstarts such as *Time* and *Newsweek*, and in 1925, *The New Yorker*, with its fine fiction, articles, and cartoons. *Life* hit newsstands in 1936 and proved that pictures could tell a story as well as words.

11

The World War I Era

Woodrow Wilson took the oath of office in 1913 determined to live up to his new commitment, as this son of a Presbyterian minister had high moral principles. Indeed he was tested, for it took much skill to keep the United States at peace in a world moving toward war.

The First World War Begins

In June 1914, Austro-Hungarian Archduke Francis Ferdinand and his wife were assassinated by Serbian nationalists as they rode through the streets of Sarajevo in Bosnia. This event in itself was troublesome, but didn't lead immediately to conflict. It did, however, provoke hostilities in Europe and foster the combat readiness of many armies put on alert. These deeply rooted hostilities were remnants of political and economic struggles that had raged throughout Europe in the previous century. The assassination was not the sole trigger of international tensions, merely a catalyst. In August, the Austro-Hungarian Empire declared war on Serbia.

What were the causes of the Great War? Russia, as the protector of Greek-Orthodox Christians, feared that Austria intended to annex Serbia and wanted to settle the issue in the Hague Tribunal (a court of arbitration). Austria refused. Germany backed Austria, for the two countries were allies. On July 28, 1914, Austria declared war on Serbia, and this caused Russia, an ally of Serbia, to mobilize. Germany sent an ultimatum to Russia to halt its mobilization or face German action. Russia refused, and Germany then declared war on Russia on August 1. As if this wasn't enough wrangling between world powers, France, a Russian ally, refused to urge the Russians to stop. France wanted to regain the Alsace–Lorraine region, which it had lost to Germany in the Franco-Prussian war of 1870–71. Germany declared war on France on August 3, and also invaded Luxembourg and Belgium.

The French joined the fighting, and the Austro-Hungarian Empire declared war on Russia in August 1914. Wilson was committed to neutrality while the other countries began to fight the Great War, named World War I years later. Eventually thirty-two nations became embroiled in the conflict. The French–British–Russian alliance became know as the Allied Forces. Germany and Austria-Hungary formed the Central Powers.

Britain's sea power had effectively halted German shipping, but this created problems for the United States, which had supplied food and arms to both sides. The British tightened their blockade, and as Germany's supply routes were closed off, the Germans faced starvation unless they worked around it. The German Navy used submarines, called U-boats, to torpedo vessels supplying England. Unfortunately, this included U.S. ships.

Submarines Let Loose

In April 1915, the British Cunard liner *Lusitania* prepared to leave New York harbor. While the German embassy had issued a warning to travelers to cross the Atlantic at their own risk, many gave little credence to that admonition. Only one passenger cancelled his ticket. On May 7, the *Lusitania* was passing Ireland on its way to England when a German submarine attacked, sinking the ship with 1,198 passengers on board, including 126 Americans. Germany insisted that the *Lusitania* carried munitions; the United States denied the allegations (though it would be learned later that there was a small amount on board). Even though the ship's sinking enraged Americans, who felt it was defenseless, the Wilson administration was determined to keep the country out of war. The United States forced Germany to modify its method of submarine warfare, but in no time at all, the Germans sunk a French steamer, causing the loss of additional American lives.

Wilson won re-election in 1916 while the war in Europe raged on. The numbers of casualties mounted: in the Battle of the Somme, 1.25 million men on both sides were killed, wounded, or captured, and the Battle of Verdun resulted in 1 million French and German casualties. A year later, Germany declared all-out submarine warfare, and it was unlikely that the United States could remain neutral.

U.S. Entry into World War I

Wilson warned the German command of the United States' strong opposition to unrestricted submarine warfare. Therefore, when Germany announced that effective February 1, 1917, unrestricted

It's All Relative

Few realize that World War I was fought between countries whose rulers were relatives. King George V of England was the first cousin of the German Kaiser and Russian Czar Nicholas. Queen Victoria, grandmother to these royal children, was their determined matchmaker, believing that if she arranged international marriages it would help bring about world peace.

submarine warfare would be launched on all shipping to Great Britain, the president had little choice but to break off diplomatic relations. At Wilson's request, a number of Latin American countries broke off relations also. In a speech before Congress, Wilson suggested that if American ships were attacked, he would be forced to act. Not heeding the U.S. signals, the Germans sent secret telegrams to Mexico promising an alliance in return for help in defeating the United States should it enter the war. The Germans implied that Mexico might win back lost territory in Texas, Arizona, and New Mexico. However, the telegraphed message was intercepted and made public. Of course, it infuriated President Wilson as well as the rest of the country. Headlines read "Kill the Kaiser!"

Undaunted, German U-boats torpedoed two American ships (the *Illinois* and the *City of Memphis*) on March 16, 1917, and Wilson asked Congress to declare war. "It is a fearful thing to lead this great peaceful people into war, into the most terrible and disastrous of all wars, civilization itself seeming to be in the balance," Wilson said. "The world must be made safe for democracy" was the sentiment he declared, and most of the nation rallied behind him. Only limited antiwar activism prevailed, particularly in small towns in the Midwest and South. The United States officially declared war on Germany on April 6, 1917.

The United States Deploys its Forces

General John Pershing, having led the force that took on Mexican revolutionary Pancho Villa in New Mexico, was given command of American expeditionary forces in Europe. But unlike its allies, the United States had no large standing army to send overseas, nor was the nation equipped with planes, ships, and other military might. Major efforts outfitted the newly drafted troops, and unlike the Civil War, no one could buy his way out of military service in this conflict. Thus, the first American troops arrived in France in June 1917, approximately 200,000

Yankees in training. They were ill prepared for the fierce warfare they encountered, but they had rest and enthusiasm on their side, and they truly believed they could win. Americans began learning about poison gas, hand grenades, and demolition. Trench warfare provided basic protection against enemy fire, but not nearly enough. Enemy soldiers raided the trenches, killing unsuspecting soldiers, and the mud and dampness wreaked havoc on the soldiers' health. Penicillin and other antibiotics didn't exist, so even minor cuts were potentially lethal.

The Germans had failed to destroy the British navy through submarine warfare. In addition, the Germans began sustaining heavy losses in its U-boat fleet, around the same time the Allies' ship-building efforts were increased.

Liberty Memorial (Kansas City)

Liberty Memorial Monument is expected to open by Veterans Day 2001 as a national World War I symbol, ensuring that the American sons and daughters who defended liberty, fought in European trenches, and sacrificed for their country will never be forgotten.

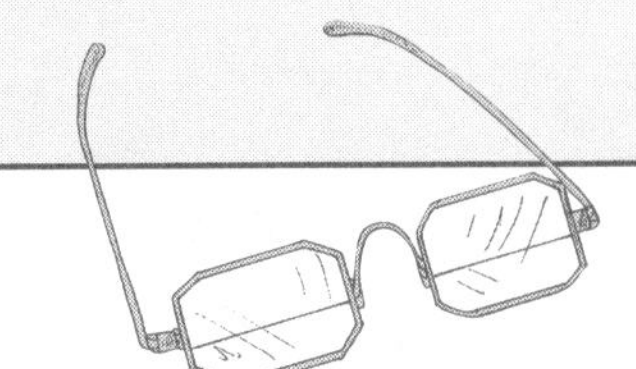

Germany Makes Peace on Its Eastern Front

In December 1917, Russia signed a peace agreement with the Austro-German negotiators, essentially ending eastern-front fighting. The Russian Revolution had occurred after Czar Nicholas II abdicated in March. Withdrawal from the Great War was a cardinal point in Bolshevik policy.

In January 1918, President Wilson proposed his peace plan, but the war continued. In May, Allied victory came in the tiny French village of Cantigny as Americans, in their first offensive of the war, took the town in less than an hour, aiding their British and French counterparts. The Germans launched a major offensive along the Chemin des Dames Ridge, and the Americans defeated the Germans at Belleau Wood, a small hunting ground, in June. In fact, U.S. artillery hit Belleau with everything it had, ravaging the area with shells and fire.

The European forces seemed weary. Originally wanting to keep American troops together, General Pershing gave in to pressure and allowed his troops to hold up the French line at various points in the conflict. Troops were now arriving daily with the confidence needed to finish the war.

On September 26, 1918, American and French troops launched the Meuse–Argonne offensive in an effort to cut off the Germans

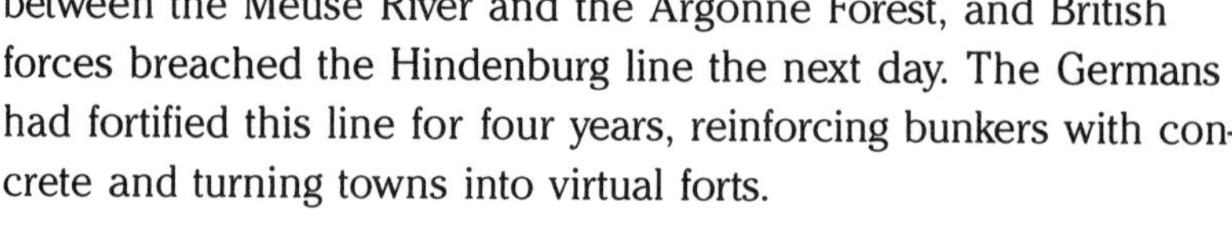
between the Meuse River and the Argonne Forest, and British forces breached the Hindenburg line the next day. The Germans had fortified this line for four years, reinforcing bunkers with concrete and turning towns into virtual forts.

Red Scare

The Red Scare resulted in America's obsession with Communism following the Bolshevik Revolution in 1917. U.S. Attorney General A. Mitchell Palmer ordered the detainment of Americans and immigrants in a dozen cities as they were suspected of Communist ties.

Victory at Hand

However, the fresh supply of Allied troops, combined with overhead fighting power, overwhelmed the Germans. It took much forward movement and military strategy on land, in the air, and through naval blockade, but the Hindenburg line was broken on October 5, sealing Allied supremacy. The Allies were gaining on the enemy. By November 1918, the American Expeditionary Forces numbered nearly two million. On November 11, 1918, Germany and the Allies reached an armistice agreement, thus ending years of heavy fighting and world rancor.

Many of those who'd survived the war died of influenza, as a worldwide epidemic struck. But victory was at hand. From January through June of 1919, the Allies discussed the treaty, which came to be known as the Treaty of Versailles. Members of the Big Four—Georges Clemenceau of France, Vittorio Orlando of Italy, David Lloyd George of Britain, and Woodrow Wilson of the United States—met in the Hall of Mirrors at the French palace.

The End of the War

The Treaty of Versailles changed the map of Europe. One provision was the formation of a League of Nations, based on President Wilson's ideas to achieve lasting peace and world justice. However, for the League of Nations to truly effect peace, it required all members' assistance. If some withheld that cooperation, the League had no way of enforcing its will.

The Allies gave Germany the ultimatum to either sign the agreement or return to battle. As a result, protests broke out in Germany and Hungary, but Germany was strong-armed into signing the treaty. Although the Treaty of Versailles solved some of Europe's problems, it created others, as the Allies had come to Versailles looking to extract the cost of the war from the Central Powers.

Over time, the League of Nations would observe the world stage as Germany rekindled the flames of another conflict. Even worse, the United States Senate didn't ratify the treaty, and the United States didn't join the League of Nations—this alone guaranteed the League's failure.

Checklist: Woodrow Wilson's Fourteen Points

The Fourteen Points was the name given to the proposals of President Woodrow Wilson to establish a lasting peace following the Allied victory in the Great War (World War I). Wilson outlined these points in his address to a joint session of Congress in January 1918, giving further evidence of his moral leadership. In order to secure support for his plan to create an association of nations, the president abandoned his insistence on accepting the full program. It was perhaps no surprise that Wilson's plan was ridiculed to some extent, with Clemenceau commenting that "the good Lord had only ten" points to make while Wilson insisted on more. To summarize, Wilson's fourteen points included:

1. Abolition of secret diplomacy by open covenants, openly arrived at
2. Freedom of the seas in peace and war, except as the seas may be closed in whole or part by international action for enforcement of international covenants
3. Removal of international trade barriers wherever possible and establishment of an equality of trade conditions among the nations consenting to the peace
4. Reduction of armaments consistent with public safety
5. Adjustment of colonial disputes consistent with the interests of both the controlling government and the colonial population
6. Evacuation of Russian territory, with the proviso of self-determination
7. Evacuation and restoration of Belgium
8. Evacuation and restoration of French territory, including Alsace-Lorraine

9. Readjustment of Italian frontiers along clearly recognizable lines of nationality
10. Autonomy for the peoples of Austria-Hungary
11. Evacuation and restoration of territory to Serbia, Montenegro, and Romania, granting of seaports to Serbia, and readjustment and international guarantee of the national ambitions of the Balkan nations
12. Self-determination for non-Turkish peoples under Turkish control and internationalization of the Dardanelles
13. An independent Poland, with access to the sea
14. Creation of a general association of nations under specific covenants to give mutual guarantees of political independence and territorial integrity

The 1920s: Life in These United States

As the new decade began, Warren G. Harding took over the presidency after campaigning to return America to normalcy. On November 2, 1920, radio station KDKA in Pittsburgh broadcast the presidential election results. This spawned not only a new industry, but also a new way to disseminate news about the nation, its leaders, and its current events. Harding was the first president to address the nation using this new medium.

In keeping with his promise, Harding was a hands-off president who delegated much authority. Unfortunately, his trusted advisors sullied the administration with numerous scandals (Teapot Dome being the greatest). But before Harding could be impeached for any wrongdoing, he died in office in 1923, amid speculation of foul play. Calvin Coolidge took the oath of office and restored trust in the executive branch. Great prosperity prevailed; Coolidge felt no need to interfere with the economy. This attitude encouraged speculation in the stock market, and as often occurs in boom times, many lived beyond their means.

The Roaring Twenties

The Roaring Twenties received this distinction because of the outrageousness of the times. Prohibition restricted many people's lifestyles, tempting them to disobey the law. Illegal "speakeasy" bars flourished along with gangsters and organized crime.

The mindsets of many also changed. Cultural influences originated at the movies, in the work of well-known writers, and on Broadway. The 1920s served as the golden era for New York theater, which in prior decades had consisted of farces, melodramas, and musicals, but nothing of much literary merit. The Roaring Twenties spawned playwrights such as Eugene O'Neill and Noel Coward. Their creativity was welcomed. Also, a new style of music hit the nation with its African-American folk rhythms combined with popular and European music. W. C. Handy, a black musician, was unable to attract a music publisher for his song "St. Louis Blues," so he published it himself in 1914. Forever after, his sound was known as jazz.

The Jazz Era, which many say first took hold in New Orleans, flourished with talented musicians such as Louis Armstrong. As African-Americans migrated north for better industrial jobs, it caught hold in Chicago and in Harlem, a section of New York City that was undergoing its own renaissance.

The Radio

After KDKA broadcast the election results, radio took hold. Prior to World War I, amateur operators in dozens of cities regularly transmitted music and speech, but the war ended all that. As peace fell on the nation, the activity resurfaced, and radio as an industry blossomed. In 1925, WSM Radio in Nashville, Tennessee, began airing barn dance music, which would later become known as the Grand Ole Opry. In 1927, Congress expanded the Radio Act of 1912 to reflect this new industry, no longer run by amateurs but by commercial enterprises. Later, in 1934, it would be revised again with the

From Slavery to Great Service

George Washington Carver was born a slave, but worked his way through high school. He graduated in 1894 from Iowa State and joined the faculty while furthering his studies. In 1896, he became director of the Department of Agricultural Research at Tuskegee Normal and Industrial Institute. There, he began experimenting with peanuts, work that included the creation of peanut butter. Carver developed many industrial uses for peanuts, sweet potatoes, and soybeans, including plastic materials, lubricants, drugs, inks, and cosmetics. His discoveries benefited farmers, earned him prestigious awards, and revived the agricultural economy, proving that a black American could accomplish great things.

Prohibition

For years the Anti-Saloon League of America (ASL) had urged saloonkeepers to give up their businesses. By 1900, millions of men and women regarded drinking alcoholic beverages as the most dangerous threat to families and society that existed. State chapters of the ASL sprang up, and the issue came frequently to the ballot box. By 1916, twenty-three of the forty-eight states had adopted antisaloon laws.

On December 22, 1917, Congress submitted to the states the Eighteenth Amendment, which prohibited "the manufacture, sale, or transportation of intoxicating liquors." By January 1919, ratification was complete. The Volstead Act made enforcement of the Eighteenth Amendment possible.

creation of the Federal Communications Commission (FCC) to consider license applications and renewals for radio stations. The FCC also set guidelines for obscenity and false claims in advertising.

A Test of the Constitution

The 1925 trial of a biology teacher named John Scopes, who had been arrested for teaching theories of evolution that contradicted the Biblical version of creation, was another famous broadcasting moment. In his state of Tennessee, the law banned teaching any information that conflicted with the Biblical account. Those who could not travel to the town of Dayton, Tennessee, could listen to the live broadcast. The American Civil Liberties Union (ACLU) named defense lawyer Clarence Darrow to represent Scopes in the carnival-like atmosphere that the trial created.

Prosecutor William Jennings Bryan led the battle for the fundamentalists. Whether Scopes received a fair trial (a prayer opened each court session, and expert evolutionists were banned from taking the stand) is unclear. Scopes was found guilty, but was fined only $100. The Tennessee Supreme Court later overturned the local court's decision, citing a technicality. Although it never reached the U.S. Supreme Court, the Scopes trial served to showcase many freedoms in the Bill of Rights—the freedoms of speech, religion, and the separation of church and state.

Immigration Policies Are Tightened

The 1924 Immigration Act became another controversial political issue stemming from the Red Scare, for it set quotas on the number of immigrants allowed into the United States. Many in the mass wave of immigration originated from southern and eastern European countries. The American labor unions became concerned that continued immigration would threaten their jobs. Congress responded by passing the act, which limited immigration to 2 percent of each nationality present in the United States in the year

1880. This year was chosen mainly because at that time there were very few people of Far Eastern and East European descent present in the United States, thus severely limiting further influx.

This was a turning point for the country. No longer were the huddled masses ensured a home in America, land of the free. Years later, the Immigration Act of 1965 put an end to national quotas for immigration, making individual talents and skills or close relationships with U.S. citizens a better basis for admittance.

Women's Suffrage and the Advancement of Women's Causes

Women's rights in the 1800s were very limited—husbands had the legal right to exercise total authority over their wives. Married women couldn't retain their own wages, control their own property, or even keep custody of their children if they sought a divorce. During the late nineteenth century, states began the gradual recognition of women's rights. In the prosperous postwar era, women stashed conservative clothing in their closets and wore dresses that clung to their bodies and skirts above the knee. Such fashionable women became known as "flappers." They cut their hair shorter in a "bobbed" style and enjoyed a new sense of freedom not granted to prior generations of young ladies. These women were the first to smoke and the first to dance "wildly" with the Charleston, popular at that time. Women also began to enter careers beyond the limits of nursing or teaching, for typewriting skills yielded further job prospects for millions of women—far more than worked around the turn of the century.

Emma Willard, self-taught in algebra, geometry, geography, and history, tutored young ladies and petitioned the New York legislature to open a girl's school. She didn't stop there as her strides led to female teachers, more competitive salaries, and financing for women's education.

Though Oberlin College in Ohio had been the first in America to admit women in 1837, Mount Holyoke Female Seminary in South

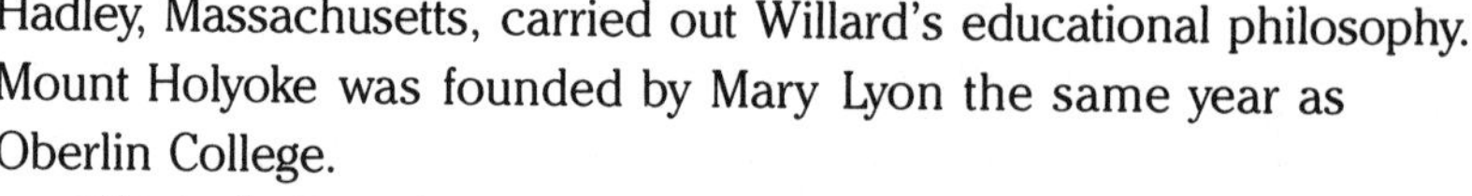

Hadley, Massachusetts, carried out Willard's educational philosophy. Mount Holyoke was founded by Mary Lyon the same year as Oberlin College.

Famous Women

Other women who had tremendous impact throughout American history included Frances Perkins, the first female cabinet member as Secretary of Labor during Franklin D. Roosevelt's administration; Jeannette Rankin, the first woman to serve in Congress; and Shirley Chisholm, the first African-American woman to serve in Congress.

Elizabeth Cady Stanton began crusading as an abolitionist, but her work furthered women's rights as well. Stanton joined Lucretia Coffin Mott, Lucy Stone, and Susan B. Anthony in speaking out in favor of a woman's right to vote, a right once granted by some colonies in Colonial America but lost years later. Carrie Chapman Catt proved to be a talented organizer and served as president of the National American Woman Suffrage Association. These women reformers became known as suffragettes, and the American suffragist movement scored its major achievement following the victory in World War I. In 1919, Congress approved the Nineteenth Amendment providing that "the right of citizens of the United States to vote shall not be denied or abridged by the United States or by any State on account of sex." The amendment was ratified August 18, 1920.

Another important effort benefiting women was Margaret Sanger's crusade for contraceptives and the newly coined phrase "birth control." As a nurse in some of the poorer sections of New York City, Sanger saw women overburdened with more children than they could care for. She believed that oversized families spawned poverty, and that in any case, women should have rights over their own bodies. Sanger opened the country's first birth control clinic in Brooklyn in 1916, but those who viewed her activities and the information she disseminated as obscene thwarted her efforts. But Sanger wasn't deterred easily, and in 1952, she persuaded a friend to back research that ultimately led to "the Pill," or oral contraceptives. However, not until 1965 did the U.S. Supreme Court invalidate Connecticut's law banning the dissemination of birth control information and prescriptions.

With Pen in Hand

Long before computers made life easier for authors, well-known writers chronicled the times—times of change and struggles. The popularity of Washington Irving and James Fenimore Cooper proved in the 1800s that Americans craved quality literature. Irving's *The Sketch Book* contained stories such as "Rip Van Winkle" and "The Legend of Sleepy Hollow." Its subsequent publication in London made Irving the first internationally recognized American writer. Cooper, using the image of the noble savage in such books as *Last of the Mohicans* and *Deerslayer,* won readers across the ocean as well.

Early American literature had begun in New England, but with the success of Irving and Cooper, New York became the literary center of America. However, a few writers known as the Concord Group, mostly followers of Ralph Waldo Emerson and his Transcendentalist philosophy, put New England back on the literary map. Emerson and other Transcendentalists maintained steadfast opposition to the overemphasis on material progress. Henry David Thoreau embraced much of this in his work, especially in his most famous book, *Walden*, describing the two years that he spent living as a virtual recluse in a simple cabin on the banks of Walden Pond, near Concord, Massachusetts.

Other Major Literary Contributors

Four other titans of American literature—novelists Nathaniel Hawthorne and Herman Melville, poet Walt Whitman, and poet/short-story writer Edgar Allan Poe—defined the craft of writing. Hawthorne penned his novel *The House of the Seven Gables* and was renowned for his masterpiece, *The Scarlet Letter.* The younger Herman Melville wrote about the South Seas and crafted his famous work *Moby Dick.* Edgar Allan Poe, a desperate man with bouts of alcoholism, depression, and unemployment, wrote some of his best work (including the mysterious and the macabre) just to survive. These included the detective story "The Murders in the Rue Morgue," but it was the publication of *The Raven and Other Poems* that set him apart as an internationally acclaimed poet. Walt Whitman wrote in rhythmic free verse about controversial subjects, but in many cases espoused democratic ideals. He self-published *Leaves of Grass* in 1855 as a collection of twelve long poems.

Mark Twain (whose real name was Samuel Clemens) of Missouri came to public notice with *The Adventures of Tom*

Not So Fleeting Fame

On May 21, 1927, Charles Lindbergh became famous for the first solo transatlantic flight from New York to Paris, which took thirty-three hours and thirty minutes. Lindbergh was awarded the Congressional Medal of Honor and in 1954, he earned a Pulitzer Prize for his book bearing the same name as his plane, *The Spirit of St. Louis*.

Babe Ruth, born George Herman Ruth in Baltimore, Maryland, made his mark in baseball, a sport synonymous with Americana. He joined the Boston Red Sox in 1914, playing as a left-handed pitcher, but soon he became a great all-around player. Nicknamed "Babe" as well as "The Bambino," he later played for the New York Yankees. By 1925, he was earning more than the president.

Sawyer, The Adventures of Huckleberry Finn, and his autobiographical *Life on the Mississippi.* Henry James wrote largely about characters visiting or traveling abroad. His early novels, written in the early 1900s, were considered to be his finest, including *The Wings of the Dove, The Ambassadors,* and *The Golden Bowl.*

Emily Dickinson was not as noticed in life, but after her death she became to be regarded as one of America's finest poets. She, too, stemmed from New England. Shortly before World War I, new poets emerged, such as Carl Sandburg and Robert Frost, who each had powerful and conversational styles. After traveling to Britain, the California-born Frost returned to teach English at Amherst College in Massachusetts and was later dubbed "the voice of New England." One of his best-known poems was titled "The Road Less Traveled."

The Lost Generation

In the postwar prosperity, some writers yearned to return to the simpler life with basic values. These were known as the Lost Generation. Ernest Hemingway was one of them, and his novels *The Sun Also Rises* and *A Farewell to Arms* both appeared in the late 1920s. Later works included *For Whom the Bell Tolls* and *The Old Man and the Sea.* In 1954, Hemingway received the Nobel Prize for literature, but sadly, he succumbed to severe depression and alcoholism, and committed suicide in 1961. T. S. Eliot, another of the Lost Generation, was awarded the Nobel Prize for Literature in 1948. F. Scott Fitzgerald, who wrote *The Great Gatsby,* and poet Edna St. Vincent Millay also saw their stars rise in the 1920s and 1930s.

As the years went by, other famous writers and their works became well-respected. Sinclair Lewis chronicled the career of a corrupt evangelist in *Elmer Gantry* and became the first American writer to win the Nobel Prize, which he was awarded in 1933. Pearl S. Buck was the first woman to win the Nobel Prize for Literature, in 1938. *The Good Earth,* a novel about a northern Chinese peasant family, is considered to be her masterwork.

John Steinbeck wrote *The Grapes of Wrath* about Oklahoma farmers driven to California by the Dust Bowl drought, and Margaret

Visit Boston's Literary Heritage

Want to see the houses and hangouts of the New England literary set? Follow the Literary Trail, which starts in Boston as an organized tour featuring information about our nation's seminal writers, mostly nineteenth-century Bostonians. The tour was modeled after the highly popular Freedom Trail, a walking tour of revolutionary sites (see Chapter 3 for details).

You'll start at the Omni Parker House that once hosted the famous Saturday Club of intellectual exchanges and endless chatter among the likes of Emerson, Hawthorne, Longfellow, Oliver Wendell Holmes, and Charles Dickens, who first read *A Christmas Carol* here. Then the tour passes the Boston Athenaeum, a two-century-old independent library and author/artist haven. The Old Corner Bookstore first nurtured many of America's literary elite, and the neighborhoods of Beacon Hill and Back Bay were once home to Louisa May Alcott, Julia Ward Howe, Annie Fields, and Sylvia Plath.

The Boston Public Library first opened in 1854. The tour visits the library's new home in Copley Square, a beautiful 1895 building inspired by the Italian Renaissance.

Crossing into Cambridge, pass through Harvard Square. The printing press of Harvard College, founded in 1636, was the first in the colonies. You'll ride down Brattle Street, finding your way to the Longfellow National Historic Site, learning about popular poets such as Henry Wadsworth Longfellow.

The Concord Museum exhibits include the entire study of Ralph Waldo Emerson. Wayside was the home of the Alcotts, the Hawthornes, and the Lothrops. Orchard House was home to Transcendentalist teacher Amos Bronson Alcott, his wife Abigail May, and their daughters (including Louisa May Alcott, who penned the beloved *Little Women*).

You'll pass the jail where Henry Thoreau spent a night in 1846 for refusing to pay taxes to a government that supported slavery and made war on Mexico, and then you'll drive past Walden Pond where he built a simple house in 1845 in order to escape to and learn from nature. Call (617) 574-5950 or visit *www.lit-trail.org* for more information.

Mitchell wrote of the South during the Civil War in *Gone with the Wind.* William Faulkner earned the Nobel Prize in 1949 for his work as a novelist. That same year, Arthur Miller made it big as a playwright with *Death of a Salesman.* Tennessee Williams, another playwright, is best known for two works—*A Streetcar Named Desire* and *The Glass Menagerie.*

The Boom That Went Bust

The era of prosperity and fun ended with a thud at the New York Stock Exchange (NYSE). The NYSE began in 1792 when a group of stock and bond brokers gathered in downtown New York City to trade stocks, bonds, and other instruments of finance. Two years later, the trading moved indoors on the corner of Wall and Water Streets. Then in 1817, the exchange moved closer to its present Wall Street location. It drew up a more formal constitution and soon became the country's center of finance. In 1863, it became known as the NYSE.

Throughout the 1920s, Americans speculated in stocks in record numbers. When they didn't have the disposable cash, they invested their life savings as well as borrowed money. Those who were highly leveraged lost everything when market jitters began on October 24, 1929. The massive selling spree of millions of shares collapsed businesses and sent investors and brokers scrambling. On October 29, 1929, the market hit bottom. On this "Black Tuesday," the single worst day for the NYSE, hotel clerks reportedly asked patrons checking in if they required a room for sleeping or jumping. It was largely thought that Black Tuesday caused the Great Depression, but truly the economy was growing at a rate that was far too fast to sustain. Another cause was increased industrialization and wealth remaining in the hands of a few. Too many products chased consumers who couldn't possibly purchase all of them. Workers lost their jobs when industry cut back, and the spiraling effect began.

12 THE GREAT DEPRESSION

The 1929 stock market crash plunged the country into despair. There had been other economic downturns and depressions, but never before had the D been capitalized. Again, although the stock crash was one reason for the Great Depression, it was by no means the only cause. During Prohibition, bootlegging made money for organized crime figures and even more respectable businessmen (such as Joseph P. Kennedy), but it did little for the national economy. For nearly a century, single-crop farming had ruined the soil and contributed to cycles of drought and flooding in America's farm belt. Throughout these events, three presidents—popularly known as the "do-nothing presidents"—avoided any government intervention, preferring to let business and its leaders take care of their own affairs.

The Do-Nothing Presidents

These three presidents were Warren G. Harding, Calvin Coolidge, and Herbert Hoover, who had been elected in 1928. Hindsight, of course, gives us the best perspective: Hoover was probably not the best person for the challenging job, though he certainly seemed to be at the time. The once-orphaned Hoover was a self-made businessman and a millionaire, and plenty of voters saw him as the quintessential American success story. Why, Hoover had even distributed food as Wilson's national food administrator in World War I. But as the effects of the Depression deepened, many unfairly blamed Hoover and lost faith in his policies of economic isolationism.

Clearly, Hoover failed to grasp the enormity of the problem. When in March 1930 he claimed that the worst was just about over, the unemployment rate rose, more businesses failed, banks closed, and many people defaulted on their mortgages and lost their homes. Congress tried to respond to the economic crisis with the Smoot-Hawley Tariff of 1930 that raised tariff rates to record levels. Although hesitant to put his name on the legislation, President Hoover signed it anyway. The intention was to increase sales of U.S. products by raising the cost of imported goods, but the measure was a miserable failure. An international trade war broke out, drastically reducing sales of U.S.-made goods overseas. It plunged foreign countries into what was now a worldwide depression.

Other nations, such as Great Britain, were reaching out to the poor with payments to the unemployed and the elderly. Most Americans began to believe that their own government owed them some form of assistance. But President Hoover, though sympathetic, held fast to his principle of individual responsibility.

The Crisis Deepens

By 1932, approximately 12 million people were out of work compared to 4 million two years before. Soup and bread lines were common sights. Schools had to close when they couldn't afford their operating costs, thus creating unemployment for teachers and an educational void for many children. The president's lack of government assistance caused his name to be given to the wretched shantytowns called "Hoovervilles," while those who covered themselves from the elements with newspaper were said to use "Hoover blankets." The president once hailed for his humanitarian gestures was now ridiculed for his lack of effort to ease the plight.

The organized march on Washington, D.C., in May 1932 made matters worse. Thousands of World War I veterans, once promised a bonus from the army, walked, rode the rails, or made their way in some fashion to the nation's capital to demand the payment, which they needed immediately, not in the mid-1940s when the payments were to occur. Congress turned them down, and some members of the "Bonus Army" disbanded while others persevered. That July, Hoover lost patience with the contingent of former soldiers and ordered the standing U.S. Army to drive them away with tear gas. As a result, the future heroes of our nation's next substantial war were positioned against veterans of another great military struggle. Once again, Hoover seemed insensitive.

Hope at Hand

Facing the 1932 election, the Republicans didn't want to take the blame for the Depression, and so they renominated Hoover as their candidate. The Democrats chose Franklin Delano Roosevelt, who had first earned a seat in Congress from New York in 1910 as a liberal Democrat. The cousin of former president Theodore Roosevelt, he had been struck by the crippling disease polio in 1921, and sidelined his political aspirations while he threw himself into rehabilitation. Roosevelt bought property in Warm Springs, Georgia, where he worked to improve his health and the health of others, mostly children whom he flew to the resort-like atmosphere for their own rehabilitation. Though he made progress with his recovery, Roosevelt would forever be confined to a wheelchair (though with radio as the popular medium, most Americans were not aware of this).

FDR's polio struggle transformed this wealthy New Yorker into a champion of the poor and downtrodden. At several important junctures he broke from his own capitalist class to side with labor or others with interests contrary to those of the wealthy. That transformation served him well. Roosevelt's campaign slogan stated "Happy Days Are Here Again," and he won the election. Like Lincoln, he inherited huge challenges during a national crisis. Some say the nation was on the verge of revolution. Sensing the sentiment, Roosevelt quickly outlined his prescription and made clear his dedication to the task. In his inaugural address, Roosevelt reassured the nation when he said, "The only thing we have to fear is fear itself." He also pledged that he would ask Congress for broad executive power "to wage a war against the emergency, as great as the power that would be given to me if we were in fact to be invaded by a foreign foe."

The New Deal

FDR implemented sweeping changes through government programs aimed at alleviating the misery of the Great Depression. On inauguration day, many states had declared bank holidays in order to keep the remaining banks solvent. They feared the runs on the banking system that had already occurred with depositors lining up to withdraw their money.

Two days later, on March 6, President Roosevelt called a halt to banking operations, and three days later Congress, which had been called to special session, passed the Emergency Banking Act. Federal auditors examined bank books, and the president's first "fireside chat" renewed trust in the banking system. As the president explained, unsound banks would be closed. Approximately 12,000 banks were back in business.

Roosevelt followed up with massive reform as Congress established the Federal Deposit Insurance Corporation (FDIC) in 1933, which guaranteed individual deposits up to $5,000 (that amount has increased over time). The new law, just as the president had intended, gave investors the confidence that if the bank failed, they wouldn't lose all their funds. Two acts, one in 1933 and another the following year, brought forth detailed regulations for the securities market, enforced by the newly created Securities and Exchange Commission (SEC). Joseph P. Kennedy became the commission's first chairman.

Off the Wagon Again

In November 1933, the Twenty-first Amendment repealed Prohibition. Most Americans heralded its passage (though the state of Utah was the last to ratify it). In the decade prior, Prohibition had only led to bootlegging, smuggling, and an increase in organized crime. But during the 1930s, when Americans yearned for escapes from their misery, gambling had also caught on, with horse racing and other forms of betting.

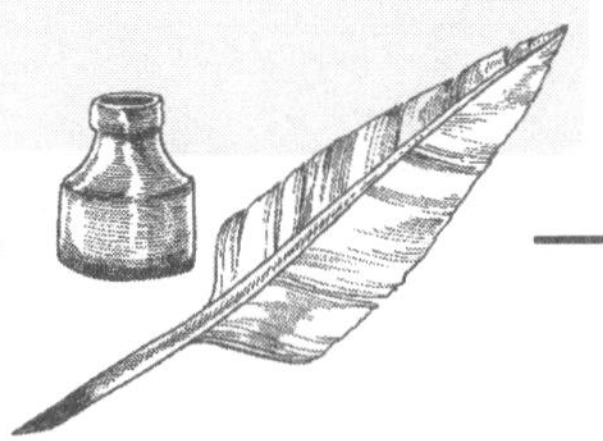

Acronyms for the People

As the administration unveiled its New Deal programs, it appeared as an alphabet soup of projects, for many of the initiatives were identified by acronyms. For instance, the Federal Housing Administration (FHA) offered loan guarantees for home purchases. The Civilian Conservation Corps (CCC) aided the unemployed by giving jobs to men between eighteen and twenty-five and putting them to work in rural camps built by the War Department (today's Department of Defense). These young men planted trees, built dams, and provided other services that conserved the environment. The Federal Emergency Relief Administration (FERA) was created in 1933 and led by Roosevelt's trusted advisor Harry Hopkins. The FERA made initial cash payments to the unemployed, but also put people to work in jobs that didn't compete with private enterprise. The Agricultural Adjustment Act was a complex farm bill that paid farmers to take land out of cultivation. At a time when the needy

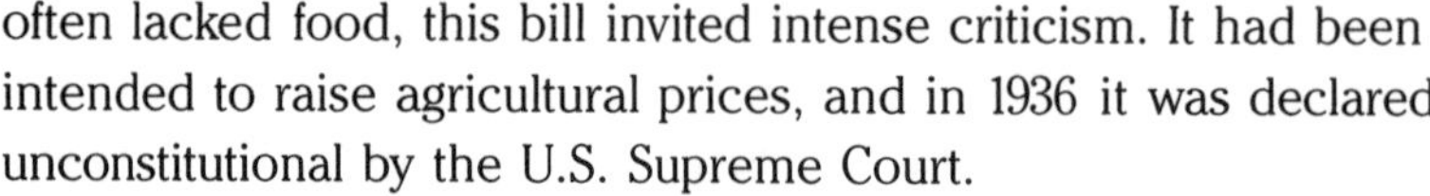

often lacked food, this bill invited intense criticism. It had been intended to raise agricultural prices, and in 1936 it was declared unconstitutional by the U.S. Supreme Court.

The Tennessee Valley Authority

The Tennessee Valley Authority (TVA) was particularly innovative, building dams in seven southeastern states to generate electricity and manage flood control programs. Power came to thousands in rural regions where electricity had not previously been delivered. Perhaps the cornerstone of the New Deal was the National Industrial Recovery Act passed in 1933 to establish the National Recovery Administration (NRA). It was supposed to encourage good business by establishing codes of fair competition. Workers were to be guaranteed such things as minimum wages, maximum hours, and the right to collective bargaining.

Unfortunately, the NRA didn't work as its supporters had anticipated. Code-making got way out of hand, resulting in hundreds of codes for various industries. Its director, the former army officer Hugh S. Johnson, resigned after failing to win over the American people, and in 1935, the Supreme Court declared the NRA unconstitutional.

The New Deal and the Nation

The New Deal seemed to be off to a rousing start, for in the first hundred days of the new administration there was a flurry of legislation to get the country moving forward again. Public works projects put thousands on the job, creating infrastructure such as the Lincoln Tunnel connecting New York with New Jersey, as well as the Golden Gate Bridge in San Francisco. Whatever political opposition the president faced was taken care of in 1934 when Democrats swept the midterm elections, increasing their majorities in both the Senate and the House.

Even with this progress, the work of restoring the economy was by no means finished. Other New Deal measures included the Wealth Tax, which raised individual income tax rates for some, as well as the federal Fair Labor Standards Act of 1938, mandating

Social Security

One of the most profound New Deal programs stemmed from passage of the Social Security Act of August 1935. This legislation consisted of three core components—a retirement fund for the elderly, unemployment insurance, and welfare grants for local distribution (which included aid for dependent children). Social Security was developed in the United States later than in several European countries, which had instituted such programs before World War I.

maximum hours and minimum wages for most workers. In addition, the Works Progress Administration (WPA) provided government funding not only for building construction, but also for artists and writers. As a result, murals were painted, plays performed, photographs taken, and folk music sung. Through the Federal Writers Project, state-by-state guidebooks were created while the Federal Theater Project staged free performances.

Though the New Deal failed to stimulate comprehensive economic recovery, it set the nation on its course with increased controls over the money supply and Federal Reserve policies. Even more importantly, it gave everyone a better understanding of the economic consequences of taxation, debt, and spending. This knowledge helped the federal government to limit the impact of later recessions. A number of the agencies created then still exist today, and the New Deal no doubt brought many more members into the Democratic Party.

A New Deal

Roosevelt's Brain Trust was instrumental in the passage of his unprecedented array of social programs. The individuals forming this advisory group consisted of government outsiders, including professors, lawyers, and economic experts. The enduring legacy of the New Deal was government's increased involvement in the lives of its citizens.

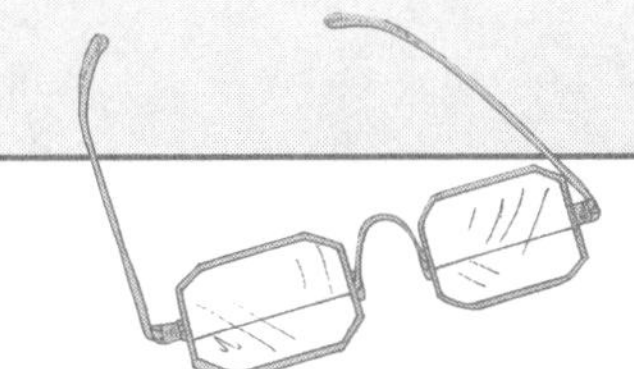

The Newsworthy and Notable

- John L. Lewis rose to power in the organized labor movement. In 1935, he founded the Committee for Industrial Organization (CIO) that broke with the American Federation of Labor (AFL) to become the most radical labor organization in the country.
- Huey Long, governor of Louisiana, became one of the most controversial politicians. Nicknamed "Kingfish," he improved roads and expanded services in his state by taxing corporations and the rich. In 1931, he resigned as governor to enter the U.S. Senate, where he developed the Share-Our-Wealth program, promising to make "every man a king." Long had planned to run for president in 1936, but was gunned down a year earlier at the height of his political influence.
- Jesse Owens captured headlines with his four-medal performance at the Summer Olympics in 1936. Owens, a U.S. sprinter, won the two sprint events as well as the long jump. Berlin, Germany, hosted that year's games.

> **Labor Relations**
>
> In 1935, Congress passed the National Labor Relations Act, known as the Wagner Act (for Robert Wagner, its sponsor). This law guaranteed workers the right to organize and bargain through unions. Frances Perkins, the first female cabinet member, served as secretary of labor during this time.

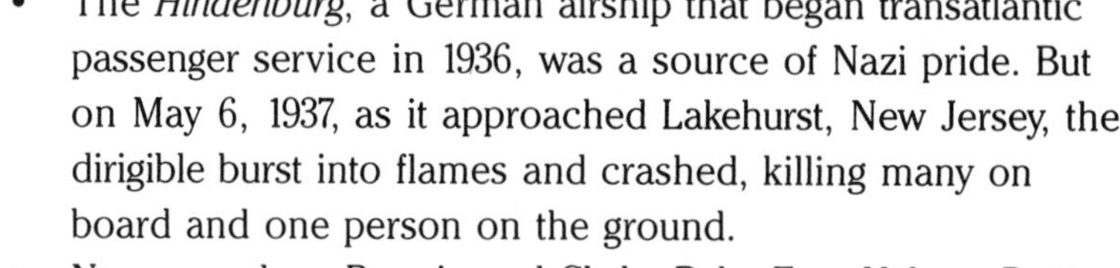

- The *Hindenburg*, a German airship that began transatlantic passenger service in 1936, was a source of Nazi pride. But on May 6, 1937, as it approached Lakehurst, New Jersey, the dirigible burst into flames and crashed, killing many on board and one person on the ground.
- Names such as Bonnie and Clyde, Baby Face Nelson, Pretty Boy Floyd, and John Dillinger fascinated the public. Though they were all gangsters who lived and died by the gun, people couldn't learn enough about them, even attending their funerals in record numbers. Dillinger, for instance, was wanted by J. Edgar Hoover and the Bureau of Investigation (today's Federal Bureau of Investigation or FBI). One of his most famous acts was his 1933 escape from jail using a mock gun carved from wood. A year later, he coerced a plastic surgeon to alter his face and fingerprints, but the "feds" caught up with Dillinger, shooting him outside a movie theater.
- Amelia Earhart was the first woman to fly across the Atlantic. She challenged herself and set several other records. But in 1937, she took off on an around-the-world trip with a navigator, never to return. Her plane simply vanished, and despite a massive search, no trace of her was found.
- Eleanor Roosevelt was an outspoken first lady who broadened liberalism as well as her own social consciousness during her tenure in the White House.
- Musicians of the times, including Count Basie, Duke Ellington, Ella Fitzgerald, and Louis Armstrong, had hit songs during the 1930s. Oddly enough, the same establishments who spun their records most likely would not have served these African-Americans on account of segregation. Shunning prejudiced attitudes, Benny Goodman toured with a racially integrated band.

Entertainment as Escapism

Radio continued to capture Americans who desperately needed an escape. Popular programs of the day included *The Jack Benny*

Show, *Fibber McGee and Molly*, *Edgar Bergen and Charlie McCarthy*, and *The Shadow*. Orson Welles popularized *The Shadow*. In 1938, he produced a radio broadcast based on H. G. Wells's science fiction classic *War of the Worlds*, in which Martians invaded a New Jersey town (in the novel, the Martians invaded several English towns). Orson Welles pulled off the production with such realism the night before Halloween that some spooked listeners panicked, believing the broadcast was indeed an actual news report of an invasion from outer space!

The sounds of Frank Sinatra and Benny Goodman could be heard on the radio, which entertained audiences through the Big Band era and throughout the Swing craze. Gossip columnist Walter Winchell and several leading evangelists also found use for the radio as a platform.

Charlie Chaplin and Mary Pickford had appeared in early silent movies, but now the technology continued to evolve with the invention of Technicolor (a three-color process) on the big screen. Alfred Hitchcock thrillers were all the rage, and so was the comedy of Laurel and Hardy and movies starring Jimmy Stewart, Clark Gable, Mae West, and the young Shirley Temple. Clark Gable played opposite Vivien Leigh in the Hollywood blockbuster *Gone With the Wind* in 1939. Gable immortalized himself when he uttered the shocking words, "Frankly my dear, I don't give a damn." The Marx Brothers, silly comedians who distracted people from harsh realities, were quite popular as well. The antics of Groucho, Chico, Harpo, Gummo, and Zeppo poked fun at the rich. Movie theaters provided not only entertainment, but information as well, since many learned their current events from the newsreels that chronicled headlines and images from around the world.

Emerging Skyscrapers

William Le Baron Jenney, American architect and engineer, pioneered the use of metal-frame construction for large buildings. He used cast-iron columns encased in masonry to support steel beams bearing floor weights. Freed from bearing the load, outside walls

Visit the Empire State Building and World Trade Center

For your best views of Manhattan, tour the observation decks of the Empire State Building in midtown, or the World Trade Center in the financial district. At the Empire State Building you can visit the observation deck eighty-six floors up (yes, there's an elevator, but if you prefer, check out the annual foot race up the eighty-six flights of stairs!). Walk outdoors in the protected space to get a great view in all four directions, or continue up to the glass-enclosed observatory on the 102nd floor. On a clear day, the view extends to parts of New Jersey and Pennsylvania. Check out the different colors illuminating the skyscraper at night—colors that change seasonally. During Fourth of July celebrations, it's colored in red, white, and blue.

The twin towers of the World Trade Center were completed in 1973. One World Trade Center offers dining at the Windows on the World restaurant, and Two World Trade Center offers you indoor and outdoor observation decks. Take the one-minute elevator climb up 107 floors for a view that can extend sixty miles on a beautiful day (ask about visibility before heading up). You'll most likely see the Statue of Liberty, Ellis Island, and New York Harbor. You can also learn from the murals and displays about the city's rich history.

Both the Empire State Building and World Trade Center offer simulated rides—the Skyride and the Helicopter Ride, respectively. At the World Trade Center, there's a 750-building model of Manhattan, restaurants, and a souvenir stand. To contact the Empire State Building, call (212) 736-3100; contact the World Trade Center at (212) 748-1006.

could be filled with windows. Jenney's revolutionary construction method spurred the emergence of skyscrapers.

Finished in 1902, the Flatiron Building at 5th Avenue and 23rd Street was Manhattan's first skyscraper, standing approximately 312 feet tall. In 1930, architect William Van Allen added the Art Deco Chrysler Building to the skyline. Inspired by cubist art and machine forms, he made the building rise in a series of narrowing arches to the stainless steel spire. His building competed for stature with The Bank of the Manhattan Company at 40 Wall Street (927 feet). Determined to win the height fight, Van Allen secretly had the spire launched through the finished crest, making his building taller by 121 feet. Its finished height measured 1,048 feet. But in 1931, the Empire State Building was completed on Fifth Avenue, between 33rd and 34th Street, making it the tallest building in the world at that time (1,250 feet), 202 feet taller than the Chrysler Building. The structure's two-year completion was amazing not only because of its height, but also given the Great Depression. Indeed, the next challenge was to attract tenants. American architects in the firm of Shreve, Harmon and Lamb streamlined the design. The skyscraper featured prominently in the 1933 movie *King Kong*, where the creature climbed the Empire State Building (actually, he climbed a model used for the sequence).

Even though it no longer holds the distinction of the tallest building, with its elegant Art Deco design the Empire State Building is regarded as the quintessential American skyscraper. In 1966, a new project promised to reach greater heights. The World Trade Center opened at an even more astonishing 1,377 feet. It will forever be remembered for the terrorist attack in 1993, when a bomb detonated in an underground parking garage, killing six and injuring hundreds in the first attack of its kind on American soil.

13

The World War II Era

The world at the end of the 1930s was becoming a darker place, as if a large cloud loomed above. As each year went by, it seemed that additional ramifications of the Treaty of Versailles unveiled themselves. For instance, the treaty had stripped the German military of its weapons and replaced the Kaiser with a democratic government, when there had never really been a model for that in Germany. The treaty had given part of German territory to Poland, an area known as the Polish corridor. The League of Nations lacked the ability to act decisively, for it required unanimous opinion (always hard to obtain, but particularly tough with feuding nations). In addition, when financial markets around the world collapsed, the German mark was devalued. The Russian Revolution popularized the ideas of Communism and other antidemocratic philosophies. As if that wasn't enough, Fascist parties were gaining influence in many countries, but particularly in Italy.

The Seeds of German and Italian Discontent

In Germany, the National Socialist (Nazi) Party was attracting attention. A rather bitter group of German World War I veterans, the first Nazis blamed their defeat on the Communists and German Jews. By 1932, the Nazi Party wielded considerable power in the German parliament (called the Reichstag). German President Paul von Hindenberg was growing weak in his advanced years. Adolf Hitler, known for his racial hatred and contempt for democracy, took advantage of the situation and won a following that placed him in a position to ascend to power. Hitler gained the chancellorship in January of 1933 and became dictator three months later. Before von Hindenberg's death, Hitler had already ordered the killings of high-ranking Germans whom he saw as a threat to his power. Books that contained thoughts contrary to the Nazi beliefs were burned.

Defying the Treaty of Versailles, Germany had left the League of Nations the year before. The country also began its rearmament, again defying the treaty. Most Allies, along with the League of Nations, stood idly by as the new dictator sent troops to the demilitarized zone. All but Italy, that is. Benito Mussolini, a Fascist and another bully in Europe's yard, invaded Ethiopia (in Africa). Fascism favored antidemocratic ideals where the individual only had worth in serving the state. Any opposition was quickly quashed.

Trouble in Spain

Almost simultaneously, the Spanish Civil War erupted. Factions, one led by Generalissimo Francisco Franco, struggled from 1936 to 1939. Hitler and Mussolini aided Franco as if they were practicing for larger conflicts to come. Again, countries including the United States remained neutral, though Soviet dictator Joseph Stalin provided military aid to Franco's opposition in Spain.

The World Makes Concessions

Nazi Germany and Fascist Italy made their alliance formal in 1936 with the Rome–Berlin Axis. Meanwhile, the Empire of Japan aligned with Germany against Communism, and Italy followed suit. In 1938, Hitler invaded Austria, annexing it to his Third Reich. Not satisfied, he went after the Sudetenland in Czechoslovakia, demanding its annexation. The Treaty of Versailles had formed Czechoslovakia at the conclusion of World War I. France and Britain, based on the terms of a treaty, should have defended the Sudetenland, but to pacify Hitler and avoid conflict they didn't oppose his aggression. In fact, British Prime Minister Neville Chamberlain returned to Britain in 1938 with Hitler's signature on the Munich Pact, guaranteeing what Chamberlain called "peace in our time."

Proving he couldn't be trusted, one year later Hitler seized the rest of Czechoslovakia, followed by a portion of Lithuania. During this same period, Mussolini took Albania. When Germany rolled tanks into the Polish Corridor with massive force on September 1, 1939, France and Britain could no longer watch from the sidelines. They'd had enough. World War II had erupted.

What British and French leaders didn't know, unfortunately, was that within a few years, nearly every European country would be brought to its knees by Nazi Germany. The Germans invited the Soviets into Poland from the east early that September, and by September 6, the Polish government fled Warsaw. Dividing Poland between Germany and Russia made it look as if there were an alliance between the two countries. Indeed, the Soviet Union and Germany had signed a nonaggression pact in 1939. However, Hitler had long desired to conquer European Russia. The pact simply bought him some time.

France Digs In

The French held fast to the Maginot Line, a series of strong fortifications built in the 1930s along the Franco-German frontier to ensure that Germans stayed on their side. The line ran from Switzerland to the Belgium–Luxemborg border and into the south of France. At one end lay the Ardennes Forest.

Putting their trust in Germany that this line would be honored, the French had not crossed it either. Believing Hitler's army would attack through Belgium over the open plains, France and Britain mobilized to meet the German troops east of Brussels. Germany, however, chose to invade France through the dense forests of the Ardennes, cutting off the British and French armies in Belgium. Hitler's strategy was to push through the Ardennes toward Boulogne, Calais, and Dunkirk. The British, aiding their French allies, had to escape across the English Channel to avoid capture. But unlike the French, who gave in to German terms, the British vowed to fight on. Chamberlain, who had led Great Britain into its war effort, was forced to resign in May 1940. Sir Winston Churchill succeeded him and proved to be one of President Roosevelt's closest confidants during the crises ahead.

Having escaped to London across the Channel, French General Charles de Gaulle put together a Free French government in exile while Jean Moulin held together the resistance movement within France. Moulin was arrested in

The Tide of Hitler's Anti-Semitism

Adolf Hitler was maniacal in his obsession with creating a pure master race that had no traces of Jewish influence, and no place for the handicapped, the independent thinker, and certainly the Jew. In 1935, Hitler's Nuremberg Decrees forbade Jews from marrying non-Jews. They could not hold government positions, and they were barred from practicing law or medicine. Furthermore, they could no longer attend German universities. In essence, their civil rights were stripped away because of their lineage. This forced many German Jewish families to emigrate. Those who felt that Nazism wouldn't endure and chose to stay, made a fatal error in judgment. Hitler's police force (called the Gestapo, a branch of the *Schutzstaffel,* or SS for short) began rounding up Jews and other supposed undesirables, who were then sent to forced labor camps. Those able to work were used to build roads or provide other manual labor, but the rest were exterminated in camps such as Auschwitz in Poland. Gas chambers, disguised as showers, killed thousands. It wasn't immediately apparent that Hitler was systematically murdering Jews, particularly in Russia where mass graves were dug by the victims before Nazi soldiers mowed them down with machine gun fire. But in time, Nazi atrocities were unveiled to the world's horror.

So that the nation and the world would never forget this atrocious time, the U.S. Holocaust Memorial Museum opened in 1993 in Washington, D.C. It's disturbing but compelling to see this documentation of the horrors Hitler inflicted on the Jewish people. Because of the graphic nature of the exhibits, artifacts, and photographs, touring the museum isn't recommended for children. Research facilities, a small café, and a museum/book shop are also available in the five-story building. Free tour tickets are available the day of your visit, or in advance by calling PROTIX at (800) 400-9973. For more information, contact the museum by phone at (202) 488-0400 or at *www.ushmm.org*.

1943 by the Gestapo (Geheime Staatspolizei, or secret state police). His torture by German captors led to his death.

The Popular American President

In 1940, FDR made history, for never before had a president served longer than two terms or eight years. President Roosevelt's leadership was pulling the nation out of its economic depths, and the public rewarded him with a third term. Seeing Europe embroiled in conflict, Roosevelt tried his best to remain neutral, though he viewed the world stage cautiously. When France fell in 1940, he did whatever he could within his neutral status to aid the beleaguered British. But no one could deny the prudence of appropriating funds for American warships and airplanes. Congress passed the first-ever peacetime draft. Still, isolationists believed that the oceans on either side of the American continent would protect it from war. Many of them, including the prominent Charles Lindbergh, spoke out in an organization called America First, filled with isolationists who wished to prevent U.S. entry into the growing conflict.

That sentiment changed dramatically on what would otherwise have been a restful Sunday morning. On December 7, 1941, Japanese dive bombers and torpedo planes launched a surprise early morning attack on the U.S. naval base at Pearl Harbor, Hawaii (then a territory). The air raid sank most of the American Pacific fleet of ships and destroyed aircraft on the ground. It also killed more than 2,300 servicemen and nearly 100 civilians. President Roosevelt, reflecting the mood of an outraged nation, called on Congress the next day with these remarks:

"Yesterday, December 7, 1941—a date which will live in infamy—the United States of America was suddenly and deliberately attacked by naval and air forces of the Empire of Japan.

"The United States was at peace with that nation and, at the solicitation of Japan, was still in conversation with the Government and its Emperor looking toward the maintenance of peace in the Pacific . . . As Commander-in-Chief of the Army and Navy, I have directed that all measures be taken for our defense . . . With confidence in our armed forces—with the unbounding determination of our people—we will gain the inevitable triumph—so help us God.

"I ask that the Congress declare that since the unprovoked and dastardly attack by Japan on Sunday, December Seventh, a state of war has existed between the United States and the Japanese empire."

War Across Two Oceans

Japan had sought to become a dominant force in Asia in order to increase its influence and acquire the raw materials it lacked. The small island believed that it had to expand and seize other parts of Asia such as China and the Pacific islands. Nationalism had grown in Japan during the 1930s just as it had in Germany. Loyalty toward Emperor Hirohito was drilled into young children, who revered the man not only as a leader, but as a god. When Japan attacked China, it found itself fighting not one but two governments—the Chinese Nationalists, led by Chiang Kai-shek, as well as the Chinese Communists with their leader Mao Tse-tung. America preferred the Nationalists, yet was determined to remain neutral.

The Attack on Pearl Harbor

Relations between the United States and the Japanese had weakened prior to the Pearl Harbor attack. In fact, our government officials felt a Japanese attack was fairly imminent, but strongly suspected that it would occur in the South Pacific islands (such as the Philippines). As the Japanese attacked Oahu on that peaceful Sunday, the new radar technology had detected blips on the screen, but most believed they were U.S. aircraft. The attack crippled nearly all of the U.S. battleships, with the *Arizona* exploding into a blaze five stories high. Four-fifths of her crew died instantly. The only vessels to escape the onslaught were two aircraft carriers, which had been at sea—the *Lexington* and the *Enterprise*. These two ships would soon have surprises of their own for the Japanese.

Three days after the Hawaiian attack, Germany and Italy declared war on the United States. Suddenly thrust into the Second

Visit Pearl Harbor and the *Arizona*

The USS *Arizona* Memorial was established to honor the servicemen who perished during the surprise attack on December 7, 1941. More than 1,000 sailors went down with the sunken ship and remain buried at sea.

Architect Alfred Preis designed the floating white memorial, built in 1962. It's 184 feet long and constructed over the site of the *Arizona*'s sinking. The hull lies about forty feet beneath the memorial and can be seen from above. Only the mast rises above the water. Reading the names of the men who died—engraved on a marble wall within the memorial—is a sobering experience. For more information about the memorial visit *www.nps.gov/usar*.

A Presidential Legacy

When Franklin Roosevelt asked the National Archives to take custody of his papers and historical material, he said, "To bring together the records of the past and to house them in buildings where they will be preserved for the use of men and women in the future, a Nation must believe in three things: It must believe in the past; it must believe in the future; it must, above all, believe in the capacity of its own people so to learn from the past that they can gain in judgment in creating their own future."

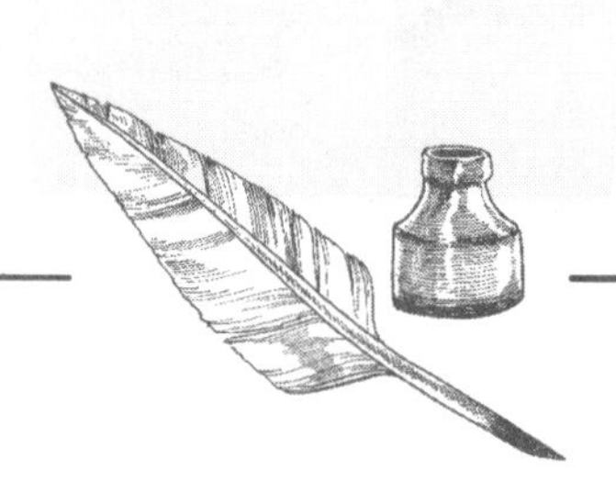

World War, Americans found themselves immersed in the war effort with emotions running high. During the early months of 1942, more than 100,000 Japanese-Americans (though they were U.S. citizens) found themselves relocated into internment camps. Anti-Japanese sentiment crossed to hysteria as these citizens were forced to leave their homes and jobs to live under the harsh conditions of the camps. It's reported that President Roosevelt opposed this relocation measure, but that he bowed to public pressure. After he was re-elected in 1944, Roosevelt ordered the camps closed.

Europe in Distress

In Europe, the British had already taken a pounding and France was now occupied. At the beginning of the war, the Royal Air Force in Great Britain was besieged by German air attacks as Hitler attempted to control British airspace for his planned invasion. Terrified Londoners had crowded into underground subways for protection from the nightly bombing. Hitler later abandoned his invasion plans, but torpedoed supply ships, attempting to starve the island nation into surrender. At this juncture, FDR did everything in his power to help the beleaguered British. He loaned them fifty or sixty destroyers for their own protection, even though the United States (at the time) was maintaining its position of neutrality.

As if the Western European conflicts weren't enough, Hitler had his eye on expanding into western Russia, as well as Yugoslavia. Leningrad proved to be a stronghold, however. Its people would not surrender, despite a three-year blockage.

War also raged through Africa, but it was fought mostly by Italy, Germany, and Britain, along with a few American forces. When Allied forces made their way onto the Mediterranean shores of Morocco and Algeria, they hoped to cut off German lines. But the landings were politically tricky because under terms of the French–German armistice, the North African French colonies were now in the hands of the Vichy French government (a puppet government while the Free French worked in the Resistance). Defending the colonies would have poised them against Allied soldiers. But as hoped, the Allies met with only slight resistance coming ashore.

MAJOR WWII BATTLES

SOUTH PACIFIC

- *Battle of the Coral Sea.* This battle between American and Japanese forces was a turning point as it effectively checked the Japanese advance to the south. Admiral Nimitz, privy to decoded enemy messages of the Japanese, tried to thwart their plans to cut off Australia. The *Lexington* was sunk and the *Yorktown* damaged. The Japanese retired from this battle with heavy losses.
- *Battle of Midway.* Attempting to destroy the remaining U.S. Pacific fleet at this important naval outpost, the Japanese hadn't counted on American naval reconnaissance planes observing their armada from a distance. In June 1942, U.S. carriers ambushed Japanese carriers descending on the Midway Islands. Four Japanese carriers sank. The U.S. victory here dashed any Japanese hopes to invade Hawaii. Coming on the heals of the Battle of the Coral Sea, it gave the United States supremacy at sea in the South Pacific.
- *Battle of Guadalcanal.* Guadalcanal, the largest island of the Solomon Islands not far from Australia, was the site of heavy fighting as the Japanese occupied the Solomons in January 1942. On August 7, U.S. Marines launched the first of their amphibious assaults on the enemy, fighting in the jungles until February 1943, when they secured the island.
- *Battle for Saipan.* In early 1944, American forces pounded Japanese garrisons, then in June landed Army and Marine troops, who fought a three-week campaign. Victory here was crucial, as it would put the island of Japan within range of U.S. bombers. The island could accommodate bases for long-range bombers, but an invasion of Japan would have to wait until Germany was defeated.
- *Battles in the Philippine Seas.* General MacArthur had promised the Filipino people in 1942 that he'd return to liberate the Philippine Islands, for which Japan fought aggressively. If the United States took them back, Japan's oil supply in the East Indies would be in great jeopardy.

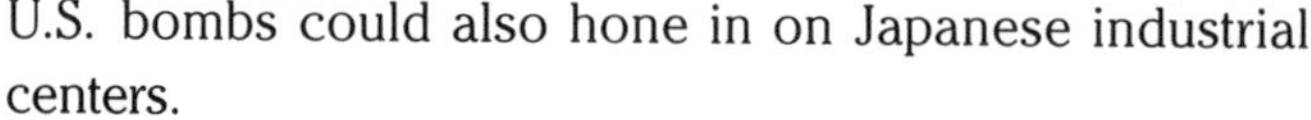

U.S. bombs could also hone in on Japanese industrial centers.

General MacArthur's troops landed on Biak Island on May 27, 1944. From there U.S. planes could target the Japanese fleet in the Philippines. The fighting took place in the air and beneath the sea. Several Japanese battleships and three aircraft carriers fell victim to U.S. submarines, including one prize—the *Shokaku*, which had participated in the Pearl Harbor raid. The invasion of the Philippines brought the Japanese navy out in force for the last time. During the three-day Battle for Leyte Gulf in October, the Japanese lost twenty-six ships, including an enormous battleship, while the Americans only lost seven ships. MacArthur's pledge was fulfilled.

- *Iwo Jima.* Though a tiny volcanic island merely five miles long, its airstrips were vital for American short-range aircraft targeting Japan. Air strikes preceded the U.S. Marines' landing on February 19, 1945. The brutal struggle was unlike anything Europe had seen. More than 6,000 U.S. Marines lost their lives capturing the island from the Japanese (whose losses were estimated at 20,000). The campaign concluded on March 16 of that year.
- *Okinawa.* The landing on this island only 350 miles from Japan was a massive amphibious assault on April 1, 1945. The U.S. Navy, protecting the landings, came under kamikaze (suicide air raid) assault. It was a savage land battle with eighty-two days of fighting that killed General Simon Buckner.

Did You Know?

When soldiers dropped from parachutes during the D-day invasion, they were so scattered about on land that in order to identify one another as Allied forces they used clicker devices that made the sound of a cricket. This way, they could remain fairly quiet before facing enemy forces.

Africa

- *Kasserine Pass.* After U.S. and British forces landed in North Africa, they suffered defeats in Tunisia around 1942. The Kasserine Pass was an important gateway to Algeria. Fortunately, the Germans were low on supplies, and their general called off further fighting. German and Italian forces surrendered in North Africa in May 1943, allowing the Allies to focus on the European continent.

EUROPE

- *The Invasion of Sicily.* Surprising Hitler and Mussolini, the Allies struck Sicily in early July 1943. By now, the Italian army had lost the will to fight. Mussolini was arrested but later rescued by Hitler, who poured in fresh troops to maintain control of the Italian peninsula. After U.S. and British troops stormed ashore, and after air strikes and naval bombardments, the Allies took all of Italy south of Naples. The muddy, miserable fighting was reminiscent of World War I trench warfare. Though the Italians surrendered in September 1943, fighting within Italy would continue. The Allies liberated Rome on June 5, 1944. Fresh Allied troops trained to fight in the mountainous terrain replaced those sent back to England. It took them until spring 1945 to break into the plains of northern Italy.
- *Normandy Invasion.* When it became apparent that Germany and the United States were waging war against one another, it also became clear that a French invasion to liberate Europe was pivotal to any plan for defeating Hitler. But the Germans felt certain that the Allies would cross the English Channel at its narrowest point (Calais). The Allies played on this misconception, deceiving the Germans with a fake buildup precisely at Calais.

  Dubbed Operation Overlord (a name coined by Winston Churchill), the invasion of France would take place in Normandy on what the Allies termed D-day. Amphibious forces from the United States, Canada, and Britain would storm five beaches code-named Utah (American), Omaha (American), Juno (Canadian), Sword (British), and Gold (British). Three airborne divisions would also be dropped to protect the invading troops.

  The mission called for just the right weather conditions to be successful. Severe wind and rain postponed the crossing by one day. General Eisenhower okayed the invasion to begin on June 6 when the weather cooperated. Though he dreaded a disaster such as the British had experienced in evacuating Dunkirk, Eisenhower knew he had to

Eisenhower's Message to the Troops

Many of the troops in Operation Overlord saved the message from Eisenhower in their wallets (and had it framed upon their return). It read, "You are about to embark upon the Great Crusade, toward which we have striven these many months. The eyes of the world are upon you. The hopes and prayers of liberty-loving people everywhere march with you . . . I have full confidence in your courage, devotion to duty and skill in battle. We will accept nothing less than victory!"

move forward with the plan. Supposing the invasion collapsed, Eisenhower had drafted a speech that he carried with him stating, "Our landings . . . have failed . . . The troops, the Air and Navy did all that bravery and devotion to duty could do. If any blame or fault attaches to the attempt, it is mine alone."

Though this was not to be the anticipated landing site, the Germans had still booby-trapped the French landscape, making it difficult to land gliders, or bring boats ashore. The worst fighting came at Omaha, as the Americans had landed in the midst of a German defense area. The tide had risen and fallen, the terrain was difficult, and many of the landing maps were inaccurate. At least 5,000 men perished, but soon Omaha Beach and the surrounding areas were secured. Not long after, forces forged out into the Normandy countryside and began making their way toward Paris.

- *Liberation of France.* The Allies knew they'd best not linger on the beaches, for Hitler had promised swift retaliation if they tried to invade France. As the Normandy beaches were secured, it was no longer necessary to use artificial harbors (called Mulberries) because Cherbourg was a genuine port, allowing replacements and supplies ashore. Fighting at Caen left that ancient town a pile of rubble, but on August 25, the Allies marched triumphantly through the streets of Paris.
- *The Ardennes.* The Allies were closing in on the German frontier, but Hitler surprised them with an attack through the Ardennes forest. Hitler reasoned that if the Germans cut off Allied supplies at Antwerp, Belgium, it would prevent their moving into his homeland. Dressed in G.I. uniforms, German troops fooled the weary Allies, who couldn't combat the raids with aircraft because of poor weather.
- *Battle of the Bulge.* After the Normandy invasion, Allied forces swept through France but stalled along the German border that September. From intelligence reports, the Allies realized that the Germans were within striking distance of Antwerp. A particularly harsh winter also hindered defense efforts. In December 1944, General George Patton pushed

his troops through Bastogne, Belgium, in forty-eight hours, a feat others swore he couldn't manage. Germany's Panzer Division proved as stubborn as the U.S. general. Their aim was to lay siege to Antwerp, but their advance was halted near the Meuse. The Allied success took weeks to accomplish, with the help of air power pushing the Germans back to their own lines in January. Heavy German casualties contributed to their final collapse the following spring.

- *Battle of Stalingrad.* In late 1942 through early 1943, this battle nearly destroyed most of the men and military might of Germany and Russia. Stalingrad was a strategically located industrial center and a vital German target. After heavy fighting, the Germans could no longer sustain their losses, and the Soviets were able to prevail. There ended the German advance into the USSR, though much of Stalingrad was destroyed. Thus, the Soviets moved the Germans west while the other Allied armies drove the Germans east, pushing them back to the Rhine.
- *Crossing the Rhine.* The Germans had hoped to stop the Allies as they crossed the Rhine, but American forces used the Ludendorff Bridge, which the Germans had failed to destroy. The Red Army pushed toward Berlin as Germans scuttled to protect their women, children, and property. The Soviets reached Berlin on April 22, but with Hitler's orders that even children mount a defense, it took another ten days for the city of Berlin to surrender. Anyone refusing to obey and fight was publicly executed by Hitler's SS squads (the secret state police).

While Hitler Slept

So confident were the Germans that the invasion would occur at Calais that General Rommel left France to return to his homeland for his wife's birthday. It was the worst move the German general would ever make. After giving strict orders that his sleep was not to be interrupted, Hitler slept through the great invasion. Furthermore, even after D-day the German high command still believed it was a ruse and that the real invasion would occur at Calais.

HITLER'S DEMISE

As Allied troops battled to liberate Caen in July 1944, Hitler's officers tried to act on their belief that the Führer was insane as they plotted to assassinate him. One staff member was poised to take over to form a new government. But a heavy desk saved Hitler when the conspirators' bomb exploded during a meeting. When the

V-E Day

After the Americans and Soviets converged in Germany in April 1945, Berlin fell to the Allies at the month's end. As his last significant act before his suicide, Hitler named Grand Admiral Karl Doenitz to succeed him as chief of state. Though loyal to the Führer, Doenitz had no other course but to surrender. General Alfred Jodl, Doenitz's representative, signed the surrender document at Eisenhower's headquarters in Reims on May 7. Forces elsewhere in Europe had already thrown down their arms. The full and unconditional surrender took effect at one minute past midnight after a second signing in Berlin with Soviet participation. May 8, 1945, would forever after be known as V-E Day, short for Victory in Europe.

coup failed, those responsible knew what Hitler's retaliation would be like. Indeed, some were executed, but others took poison first. Among those committing suicide was General Erwin Rommel.

On April 30, 1945, Hitler and his new wife Eva Braun, realizing that Berlin was finally falling, committed suicide in the bunker where they had lived for the past six months. The Nazis burned their bodies. Hitler's Third Reich was literally reduced to ashes.

Life on the Home Front

Once President Roosevelt asked for a declaration of war, the country rallied together to support the war effort. The increased industrialization certainly stimulated the sluggish economy, which was climbing out of the Great Depression. As military production rose, and with men conscripted into the armed services, women took jobs or volunteered in staffing weapon factories. This quickly earned females the moniker "Rosie the Riveter."

With so many raw materials needed for the war, rationing became a way of life. The emergency Office of Price Administration (OPA) was created to oversee the rationing of, among other things, automobiles and tires, leather shoes, farm machinery, typewriters, bicycles, gasoline, home heating oil, coal, coffee, sugar, and meat. In fact, the government instituted a thirty-five-mile-per-hour speed limit aimed at conserving tires and gasoline. Speeders were not looked on too kindly and were viewed as unlawful and unpatriotic. Rationing was undertaken in conjunction with price and rent controls as well.

Rationing Forces Creative Measures

Women, accustomed to wearing nylon or silk stockings, had to do without these. Some disguised their legs with a black line down the back to give the appearance of a seamed stocking! Of course, where there is limited supply and great demand, the illegal or black market flourishes. Ration coupons, stamps, and certificates were used for items in short supply.

In addition, many families planted victory gardens in their back yards to supplement their diets, allowing commercial farms to supply food for the troops. The war provided the impetus some farmers needed to experiment with crop rotation and better fertilizers. Everyone, it seemed, became frugal, industrious, and resourceful, not because they wanted to, but because they had to.

Mail and packages between loved ones in the states and the troops overseas were government inspected. At times, portions of letters were cut out for fear critical information would fall into enemy hands. Citizens back home also purchased war bonds to help finance the effort. For many of the young recruits, their experience in World War II would serve as the defining moment of their lives.

In 1944, Congress passed the Servicemen's Readjustment Act, better known as the "G.I. Bill." This was essentially a benefits package for returning veterans that spawned a postwar baby and housing boom. It established veterans' hospitals around the country where vets could obtain rehabilitation and medical care and provided low-interest mortgages, college tuition, and trade-school funds.

Discussions at Yalta

Roosevelt, Churchill, and Stalin met at the Soviet Black Sea port of Yalta to formulate Allied military strategy and declare an end to German militarism and Nazism. In addition, they expressed determination that war criminals would be brought to swift and just punishment.

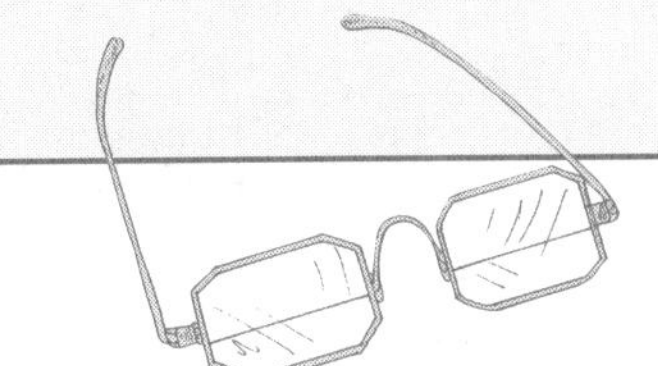

Roosevelt's Death

As if exhausted by his efforts overseeing the war, Franklin Delano Roosevelt died of natural causes at his home in Warm Springs, Georgia, in April 1945. The only president to be elected four times was mourned by the entire country, if not the world. Sadly, the man whose administration was plagued by the actions of Hitler and the Japanese died before any surrender or victory. Vice President Harry S. Truman was sworn in as the nation's thirty-third president on April 12, 1945.

Building the Bomb

In 1932, British scientist James Chadwick discovered an atomic particle, the neutron, which could penetrate the nucleus of an atom and cause it to separate. The divided atom would release more neutrons, causing other atoms to split. As the chain reaction progressed and built up, an enormous amount of energy would be released.

During the first days of World War II, leading physicists such as Albert Einstein suspected that Germany was already at work to create a massive weapon of annihilation, better known as the atomic or A-bomb. They pooled together, and in 1939 Einstein wrote the president to tell him of their suspicions. Fortunately, the president heeded the warning.

In 1942, many prominent scientists began developing the A-bomb in a small Tennessee community (as well as in research sites such as Los Alamos, New Mexico). The undertaking was termed the Manhattan Project because some of the work took place at Columbia University. Physicists Enrico Fermi and J. Robert Oppenheimer worked on the Manhattan Project as did chemist Harold Urey. U.S. Army engineer General Leslie Groves headed the project that at one time involved approximately 600,000 people.

Oak Ridge, Tennessee (near Knoxville), originally called Clinton Engineer Works, was founded in 1942 by the U.S. government to produce the uranium for the Manhattan Project. By the end of the war, the town's population had grown to more than 80,000.

Birth of the U.N.

Leaders at the Yalta Conference called for a conference of nations to promote world peace and cooperation following the war. Thus, the United Nations (U.N.), with its home in New York City, was created to foster better relations and encourage respect for human rights. Member nations pledged to settle differences peacefully.

The Bomb Put to Use

After V-E Day, the war in the Pacific theater still raged on. American bombing raids on Japan's industrial centers met with limited success. Radar, still in its infancy, proved too unreliable to use in designating targets. Even B-29 bombing raids aimed at residential and civilian targets didn't convince the Japanese to surrender, and the raids were proving to be costly as well.

With the Manhattan Project, U.S. scientists proved they could use the explosive power of nuclear fission rather than TNT to wreak mass destruction. Oppenheimer and his team tested the A-bomb near Alamogordo, New Mexico, on July 16, 1945. No one knew whether it would work until a tremendous blast

rushed across the desert. Oppenheimer's team informed President Truman that it had indeed worked.

Although the bomb had originally been created for possible use against Hitler's Third Reich, Truman now faced a crucial decision—whether to use the A-bomb against the Japanese in order to end the war. Truman didn't want to risk the lives of American servicemen in a potential invasion of Japan, and it's said he had little to no hesitation in using this powerful new weapon. At Potsdam (outside Berlin in July 1945), Churchill agreed that Truman should use the A-bomb.

At 8:15 A.M. on August 6, 1945, an American B-29 bomber named the *Enola Gay* ferried the bomb to Hiroshima, the Japanese city chosen for the drop. There, it exploded about 2,000 feet above the ground, producing a fireball hotter than the surface of the sun and leveling several square miles. Atomic radiation and searing heat vaporized everything in its range.

Japan Brought to its Knees

Surprisingly, Japan didn't ask for terms of surrender following the attack. So on August 9, another B-29 bomber dropped yet another A-bomb on Nagasaki, causing almost as much destruction. Meanwhile, the Soviet Union had declared war on Japan on August 8, destroying its army in China and taking over most of occupied Manchuria. The Red Army was continuing its move into Korea as Japan finally surrendered to the Allies on August 15, 1945. This wasn't an unconditional surrender, as the Allies agreed that the Japanese could keep their emperor. The formal signing took place on September 2 in Tokyo Bay aboard the battleship *Missouri* with an American delegation headed by General MacArthur, who then became the military governor of Allied-occupied Japan.

The Nuremberg Trials

In October 1945, twenty-four individuals were indicted by a tribunal of French, British, Russian, and American judges for war crimes and atrocities committed during World War II. These charges included the instigation of war, the extermination of ethnic and religious groups,

Einstein's War Efforts

Albert Einstein, best known for his theory of relativity, decried Germany's involvement in World War I, but his public stance provoked anti-Semitic attacks that ultimately led him to leave Europe for the United States (where he took up teaching). In 1939, he collaborated with several physicists in writing to President Roosevelt and warning him of possible German attempts at making an unbelievably destructive weapon—the atomic bomb. This lent urgency to American efforts to build the A-bomb, but Einstein played no role in the work and had no knowledge of what would be called the Manhattan Project.

the murder and mistreatment of prisoners of war, and deportation of hundreds of thousands to slave labor in lands Germany occupied. A number of high-ranking members of the Nazi party were charged. The trial began on November 20, 1945. Much of the evidence that Allies discovered after the war was used by the prosecution.

Twelve defendants were sentenced to death by hanging, seven received lengthy prison sentences ranging from ten years to life, and three were acquitted. At the conclusion of the first trial, twelve additional trials occurred in which approximately 185 others were indicted, including doctors who performed medical experiments in concentration camps as well as SS officials.

Germany Divided

After the war, parts of Germany occupied by France, Great Britain, and the United States were allowed to merge, forming the Federal Republic of Germany (FRG), commonly called West Germany. The eastern part of Germany occupied by the Soviets became the German Democratic Republic (GDR), better known as East Germany.

Berlin, the capital of pre-war Germany, had suffered much damage and was situated in East Germany. Subsequently it was divided into four parts—each controlled by the United States, Britain, France, and the Soviet Union. In 1945, West Berlin (controlled by the United States, Britain, and France) became a Western-ruled island until East Germany fell in 1990. This division symbolized the collapse of the German Empire and represented the tension evidenced in the Cold War between communist and free nations in the decades ahead. However, it wasn't until 1961 that a physical barrier—the Berlin Wall—was erected to block free access in both directions. From the time the wall was built until it was torn down in October 1990, following Germany's reunification, about eighty people died attempting to cross from East to West Berlin.

The Woman Behind Computer Advances

While computers were still large and complex in the 1940s, Grace Hopper, educated at Vassar College and Yale University, volunteered for duty with the Naval Office Computation Project. In 1945, she was sent to Harvard to assist Howard Aiken in building a computer. There, she created the first computer language and the compiler necessary to translate it into a form that the computer could work with. In 1959, Hopper joined a Pentagon team trying to create a language for commercial use. This work ultimately led to the development of COBOL, a widely recognized computer language.

THE MARSHALL PLAN

Europe lay in ruins after the six-year-long war. Without a prosperous European continent, the United States might have suffered another severe economic depression. In addition, America feared that with little infrastructure and many on the verge of starvation, ravaged countries might fall into the hands of socialists or communists.

The U.S. program of financial assistance to help rebuild these devastated countries was called the European Recovery Program. Today, it's better known as the Marshall Plan after U.S. Secretary of State George Marshall. Leaders in 1947 met in Paris, but when the Soviets realized that the United States wanted their cooperation with the capitalist societies of Western Europe, they left the meeting to establish their own plan to integrate Communist states in Eastern Europe. With more than $13 billion in U.S. aid to Western Europe, there was clearly an economic curtain dividing it from the Soviet-backed lands. The largest amounts of aid went to Great Britain, France, Italy, and West Germany, respectively.

Truman Doctrine

Truman believed the United States had to assist Greece and Turkey when Communist rebels threatened their security. His policy of containing communism whenever possible became known as the Truman Doctrine.

14

The Fifties and Sixties

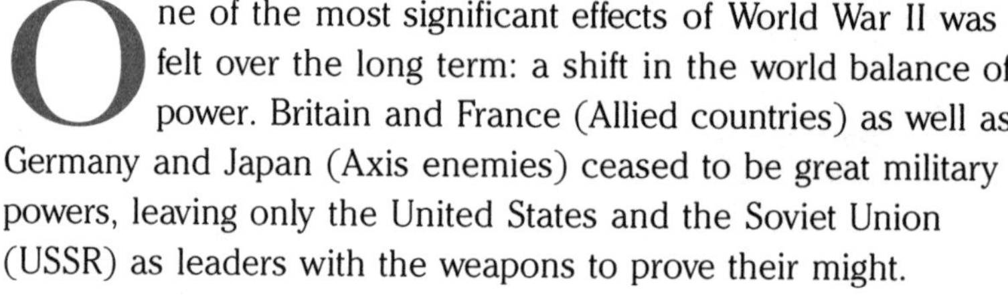

One of the most significant effects of World War II was felt over the long term: a shift in the world balance of power. Britain and France (Allied countries) as well as Germany and Japan (Axis enemies) ceased to be great military powers, leaving only the United States and the Soviet Union (USSR) as leaders with the weapons to prove their might.

Chuck Yeager

Test pilot and U.S. Air Force officer Chuck Yeager was the first aviator to fly faster than the speed of sound, maneuvering his plane (the *Glamorous Glennis*) through the shock waves produced as the plane neared the speed of Mach 1. Read more about it in *Yeager,* his autobiography published in 1985.

Prelude to the Cold War

During the 1940s, President Truman ordered the investigation of applicants for government jobs for fear of communist infiltration. Both the Central Intelligence Agency and the National Security Council were created to focus on new security and intelligence issues.

Yet Truman faced criticism that he hadn't gone far enough. In 1948, American writer and editor Whittaker Chambers testified before Representative Richard Nixon and the House Un-American Activities Committee that he'd been a Communist in the 1920s and 1930s, and that he'd transmitted secret information to Soviet agents. He charged that Alger Hiss, a member of the State Department, was a Communist and that Hiss turned over classified documents to him. Although Hiss denied the charges, Chambers produced document copies implicating Hiss in the matter. After a probe by the Department of Justice, Hiss was indicted for perjury. His first jury failed to reach a verdict, but his second trial in January 1950 handed him a conviction.

The Spread of Communism

Communism was taking hold in China as well, where the Nationalist government of Chiang Kai-shek (which the United States had supported) could no longer withstand the onslaught of Communist forces led by Mao Tse-tung (now often spelled Mao Zedong). By the end of 1949, government troops had been defeated, forcing Chiang into exile on Taiwan. Elated by victory, Mao formed the People's Republic of China. Truman's critics charged that the administration failed to support the anti-Communist movement in China to its fullest ability. It didn't make anyone less nervous when Truman also announced that the Soviet Union had developed its own atomic bomb. Soon, fallout shelters were built and stocked with provisions in the event of atomic attack.

In 1952, the United States conducted tests on a weapon of even greater magnitude. In fact, the hydrogen or H-bomb was 500 times more powerful than the atomic bomb dropped on Hiroshima. This thermonuclear device was powered by a fusion reaction rather than the fission reaction of the A-bomb.

Things Start to Get Out of Hand

Many opposed the H-bomb's development, including well-known scientists, but it was thought that the Soviets would produce their own. Although it was terrifying, this new superbomb equipped the United States with a powerful deterrent—or, heaven forbid, weapon—in any future conflict.

In 1957, the Soviet Union successfully launched the first man-made object placed in orbit, which they called Sputnik. This event also fueled fears that the USSR was gaining important ground in the sciences, overtaking the United States. Congress passed the National Defense Education Act the following year to enable scholarships and laboratories for science students, who had to sign an oath vowing they had no Communist sympathies.

McCarthyism

Communist fear festered within government ranks. In February 1950, Wisconsin Senator Joseph R. McCarthy charged that the State Department knowingly employed more than 200 Communists. He later revised his claim to a much lower number, and after an investigation, all of his charges were proved to be false. But McCarthy, as chairman of the Senate Subcommittee on Governmental Operations, continued to accuse others of Communist sympathies, often without any evidence. He launched investigations of the Voice of America as well as the U.S. Army Signal Corps. J. Edgar Hoover, Federal

Wiping Out Polio

Until 1955, parents dreaded one of summer's greatest risks—polio. With the knowledge that killed-virus vaccines could conquer some diseases, Dr. Jonas Salk led research at the University of Pittsburgh that brought forth a polio vaccine. After extensive testing, the Food and Drug Administration approved it that year.

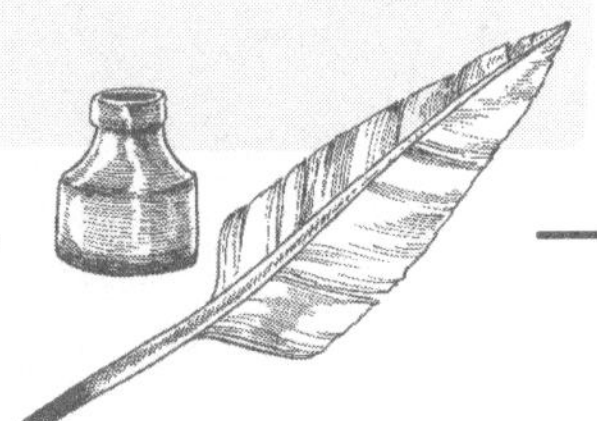

The McCarren Act

Congress passed the McCarren Act in 1950, forcing the registration of all Communist organizations and allowing the government to intern Communists during national emergencies. It also prohibited those people from doing any defense work and prohibited entry into the United States to members of "totalitarian" organizations or governments.

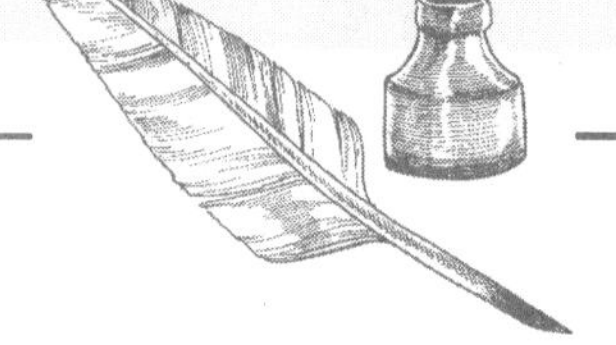

Bureau of Investigation (FBI) Director, assisted McCarthy in hunting Communist spies and sympathizers, often using the power of his bureau.

Such behavior became known as McCarthyism, meaning any unfounded accusation of subversive activities. Not only were government officials accused and interrogated, but also film directors, military officers, and others from all walks of life were brought before Senate hearings to name those they knew with Communist ties. As a result, many reputations were ruined and careers left in shambles. A few of the accused even committed suicide.

U.S. Senator Margaret Chase Smith, lambasting her Senate colleagues, said, "Freedom of speech is not what it used to be in America." President Truman warned of the fear and hysteria wrought by Senator McCarthy, for the senator even accused the U.S. Army of Communist infiltration. By 1954, his Senate colleagues censured McCarthy for abusing his powers. A known alcoholic, Joseph McCarthy died of liver damage a few years later.

The Korean War

As World War II was raging, the Allied powers had agreed that once Japan was defeated, Korea would become an independent state. After Japan's surrender, General Douglas MacArthur's plan called for the creation of an artificial line at the 38th parallel in Korea. The line essentially split the country in half. The Japanese forces above the parallel surrendered to the Soviet Union, and those to the south to the Americans.

In June 1950, the Communist government of North Korea launched a full-scale military invasion of neighboring South Korea, a capitalist country. Of course, the Soviet Union was modeling the North Korean government on its own example of Communism.

The United Nations (U.N.) Security Council voted 9–0 to hold North Korea accountable for the attack. The resolution sent a peacekeeping force, virtually all of which was made up of U.S. troops. The Soviet Union was a permanent member of the Security Council, but it had been boycotting meetings because other members refused to recognize the Communist government in China as the rightful government of the Chinese people.

The Korean "Police Action"

Not wanting to call these actions involvement in a war, President Truman termed the conflict a police action and put General MacArthur in command of the U.N. forces, a post he would hold until his replacement in April 1951. MacArthur held his position on the southeastern portion of the peninsula, and American bombing missions crippled North Korean supply lines.

In one of his boldest military operations, General MacArthur planned for a large amphibious landing on the west coast of South Korea at Inchon. Once ashore, American troops would push back the enemy and recapture the capital of Seoul. Concurrently, the Eighth Army would break out of the Pusan Perimeter and head toward Seoul as well. Despite skepticism, MacArthur pushed for his plan. American forces hit the beaches in September, taking the capital on September 27, 1950. Many thought the war was over with the U.N. goals having been achieved. The Communists were contained behind the 38th parallel.

South Korea Pushes North

The Americans had done so well, however, that the South Koreans believed they could push farther to expel Communism from Korea completely. Others in Washington didn't concur, knowing how strongly China and the Soviet Union felt that North Korea served as a buffer state. Syngman Rhee, president of South Korea, was determined to fight regardless of American sentiment. His troops crossed the 38th parallel and attacked the North Koreans. When they did, President Truman immediately committed U.N. forces (with the majority of

them being U.S. soldiers) to follow Rhee. The next month, Truman and MacArthur met on Wake Island, hoping to discuss the final phase of the Korean War, which they anticipated ending by Thanksgiving.

A little too arrogant and confident, MacArthur advanced his men too close to the Chinese border, in violation of his instructions. MacArthur had seriously underestimated the Chinese forces, leaving the Americans vulnerable. By November, it was evident that China was invading on a much larger scale. MacArthur outwardly opposed some of the restraints on his command, but Washington officials feared that the Soviet Union would view the Korean conflict as a global struggle, sparking another world war. President Truman's anxiety over this eventually led to his replacing MacArthur with General Matthew Ridgway. General MacArthur faced a Senate hearing for his insubordination to the commander in chief—threatening the Chinese with a powerful U.S./U.N. attack without clearing it first with Truman.

Fighting Ends

Back home, General Dwight D. Eisenhower and his running mate Richard Nixon won the presidential election in 1952. Though peace negotiations had begun in 1951, the new administration inherited the war, and fighting continued for two more years until an armistice was signed on July 27, 1953. In the final analysis, the war cost everyone in lives and materials and left no country satisfied—certainly not the United States. Americans had to accept something less than victory in this, the first limited U.S. war. But limited warfare certainly beat nuclear annihilation.

The Cold War continued. After Joseph Stalin died, Nikita Khrushchev exposed the brutal crimes that Stalin had committed against his own people. He'd ruled with terror, executing millions of Soviet citizens. These revelations softened the tensions with the West, but only slightly. The United States committed more funds to NATO (the North Atlantic Treaty Organization), and it stepped up aid to another capitalist government in danger of Communist takeover in South Vietnam.

Everyone Liked Ike

Obviously, the American people liked Ike, the nickname given to Eisenhower as a teenager. Why, he won a war for them with his strategy to storm the beaches of France on D-day. Truman's demeanor was feisty compared to Ike's relaxed attitude. So it shouldn't have come as a surprise that as America was embroiled in yet another war, citizens would elect the Republican Eisenhower, after a long reign by Democrats.

Eisenhower kept his campaign promise to end the Korean conflict. He ran the government much as he ran things in the army, by appointing people to office who would take charge under his supervision. With the United States and Soviet Union as contentious superpowers, President Eisenhower cut back defense spending on traditional weapons while boosting nuclear deterrents. He came to office in the midst of McCarthyism and was president when Julius and Ethel Rosenberg, a couple convicted of passing atomic secrets to the Soviets, were executed in 1953.

On the lighter side, America prospered. With the G.I. Bill providing affordable mortgages to returning veterans, many began the slow migration to the suburbs. It seemed prosperity followed the frugality of the 1940s. Consumer goods were plentiful. The baby boom was in full swing, and so was Ike. Since golf was his favorite pastime, the sport caught on with Americans, establishing a nationwide trend. On sunny days, the president practiced his shots on the White House lawn.

With the automobile freeing Americans to move about the nation, Congress passed the Interstate Highway Act of 1956, making good roads a convenient way of life. People were no longer as isolated, and they certainly knew more about the nation and their neighbors, with the influences of radio, television, movie theaters, and drive-ins, and the handy 45-rpm vinyl records.

Two New States

The year 1959 brought America two new states. Alaska was admitted as the forty-ninth and most northerly state in January, followed by the volcanic islands in the Pacific—Hawaii—as the fiftieth state in August.

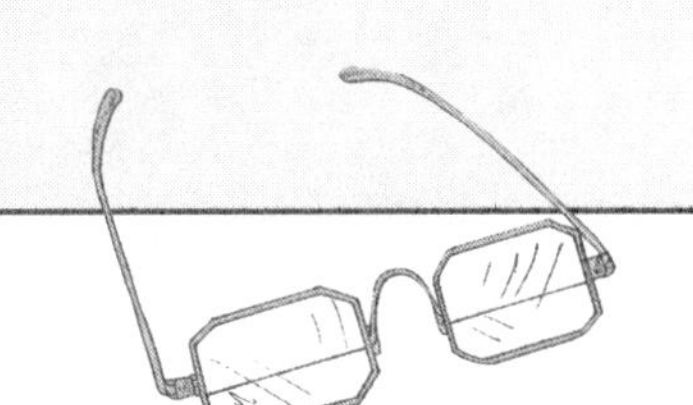

Civil Rights Strides

During the 1950s, a very prominent case took center stage, advancing the interests of African-Americans. There were laws in

seventeen states (mostly southern) that established racial segregation in public schools. Other states segregated children by district. All justified the practice by using the "separate but equal" standard, according to a Supreme Court decision (*Plessy v. Ferguson*) in 1896. But in 1954, the NAACP challenged this doctrine at the elementary school level. Thurgood Marshall and other NAACP lawyers argued before the Supreme Court that children in all-white schools received a better education than those in all-black schools. It was not an easy decision, but Chief Justice Earl Warren used his considerable influence among the two dissenting justices in order to reach a unanimous decision that May.

That case, *Brown v. Board of Education of Topeka, Kansas,* outlawed racial segregation in public schools. As fate would have it, Marshall argued thirty-two cases before the high Court, winning twenty-nine of them. In 1967, he became the first African-American appointed to the Supreme Court.

Some southern states, however, defied the ruling. In 1957, President Eisenhower used federal troops to protect African-American students attempting to attend a previously all-white public high school in Little Rock, Arkansas.

Another landmark moment that propelled civil rights forward involved a weary seamstress named Rosa Parks who boarded a bus in Montgomery, Alabama, at the end of her work day. Although the forward section was traditionally reserved for white passengers, Parks sat down there. When asked to give up her seat for a white person and move to the back of the bus, she declined. Arrested and jailed, she became a symbol for the struggle to attain racial equality as the African-American community rallied around this refined, mild-mannered woman. Local black ministers, led by Dr. Martin Luther King Jr., organized a boycott of the bus system. For over a year, African-Americans in Montgomery used car pools, walked to work, or rode horses to get around. Only when the Supreme Court ordered the city to stop segregating black passengers in 1956 did the boycott end.

Music That Changed America

Memphis record producer Sam Phillips often boasted that with "a white boy who could sing black," he could make a million dollars. In July 1954, Phillips found his ticket to riches and stardom as nineteen-year-old Elvis Presley recorded his first song for Phillips's Sun Records. Singing the rhythm-and-blues style teenagers coveted at the time, Presley was more acceptable to the racially-conscious country because he was white, though parents derided him for his sexual style as he shook his hips. Soon, Presley became known not only as "Elvis the Pelvis," but as the king of rock 'n' roll.

Truly, rock 'n' roll music provided an escape from Cold War anxieties. Teenagers had more disposable income than previous generations of youth. As music became more portable with transistor radios, teens could listen to whatever they chose. And from 1964 through 1969, teens listened to a British band called the Beatles. Thirty Beatles songs achieved top-ten status in *Billboard* magazine charts. The band, which formed in 1959, was comprised of four musicians born in Liverpool, England. George Harrison and John Lennon played guitar, Paul McCartney was the bassist, and Peter Best (replaced by Ringo Starr in 1962) played drums.

Although their musical style started fresh with early songs such as "I Want to Hold Your Hand," it moved to more innovative and experimental works, culminating in the 1967 release of their album *Sgt. Pepper's Lonely Hearts Club Band*. This was a concept album, with songs centered around a common theme, and it was also admired for its haunting harmony and lyrics. Lennon and McCartney penned many songs for the band. In 1970, the Beatles split up to pursue their own musical interests. Speculation about a proposed reunion continued for years until the 1980 murder of John Lennon outside his Dakota apartment building in Manhattan. The group was inducted into the Rock and Roll Hall of Fame in 1988.

A Wall Goes Up

The migration of East Germans escaping into the West threatened the stability of East Germany. On the night of August 19, 1961, the Berlin Wall was erected as a barricade. President Kennedy saw this as a poignant symbol depicting the difference between Communism and the Free World. "Let them come to Berlin . . . " he said. "Democracy may not be perfect but at least we don't have to build walls to keep our people in."

THE 1960 ELECTION

As Americans approached the 1960 presidential election, life was good. Americans reveled in their music and the stardom of movie icons such as Marilyn Monroe and Marlon Brando, and they enjoyed the new medium of television.

Many assumed that since Eisenhower had been a popular president, Vice President Richard Nixon would easily win the 1960 election as the Republican nominee. To beat Nixon, Democrats selected a dashing senator from Massachusetts who was certainly groomed if not destined for the presidency. John F. Kennedy (known by his famous initials JFK) had a successful and wealthy father (Joseph P. Kennedy, who had served in the New Deal) and maternal grandfather (John F. Fitzgerald, also known as Honey Fitz, who had been the mayor of Boston many years before).

Although Kennedy had the intellect, connections, charm, and World War II heroism (the rescue of his PT-109 crew off the Solomon Islands was well known), he faced certain challenge as the first Irish Catholic to seek executive office. Choosing a southern running mate—Lyndon B. Johnson of Texas—balanced the Democratic ticket.

In a series of debates, the first ever to be televised, the candidates squared off. Their race remained close, but most agreed that Kennedy seemed much more poised on camera, pointing up Nixon's haggard appearance. That finesse paid off at the polls, where Kennedy edged ahead in a very narrow defeat of Richard Nixon. In fact, Kennedy garnered 49.7 percent of the popular vote to Nixon's 49.6, though he clearly won the electoral votes needed (303 to Nixon's 219).

At forty-three, Kennedy was the youngest president ever elected (Theodore Roosevelt was slightly younger when he became president, but he had not been elected). In his dynamic inaugural address, Kennedy challenged his fellow Americans with "Ask not what your country can do for you—ask what you can do for your country." He energized the nation with his idea of a new frontier, and subsequently inspired a generation to public service, particularly with the Peace Corps, which rallied professional and skilled Americans to work in developing nations.

These initiatives served Kennedy's clear vision of volunteerism, freedom, and equality for all—as well as technological achievement, as he pledged that the United States would land a man on the moon by the end of the decade. With his stylish wife Jacqueline and the couple's young children, Kennedy rose to near-royal status in the public's eye.

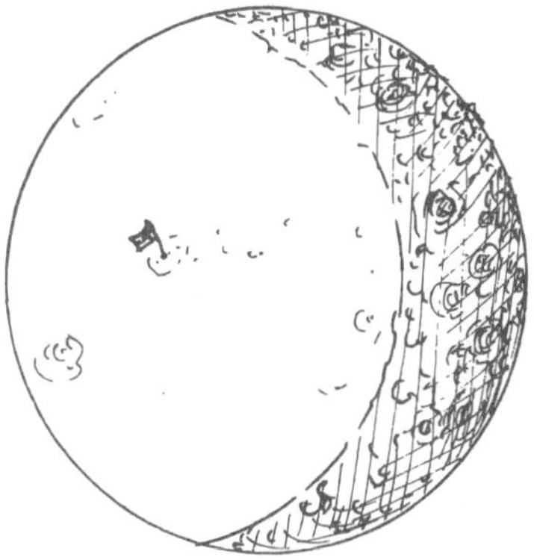

THE SPACE RACE

The Soviet launch of Sputnik in the 1950s and cosmonaut Yuri Gagarin's outer space journey in 1961 shifted everyone's attention to mastering space technology before the Russians did. NASA had already been created, but Kennedy poured funding into the agency for research and space exploration. Project Mercury recruited seven brave pilots to become the first astronauts, and soon launched Alan Shephard as the first American in space, followed by John Glenn's 1962 achievement as the first American to orbit the earth. The Telstar 1 satellite became the first telephone and television satellite as well.

The Apollo program carried on this tradition of achievement. On July 21, 1969, Neil Armstrong and "Buzz" Aldrin realized Kennedy's dream. Crewman Michael Collins watched as his fellow astronauts landed on and explored the lunar surface. "That's one small step for a man, one giant leap for mankind," said Armstrong as he set foot on the moon, to a television audience watching in amazement at this great human achievement. Thanks to the science invested in the moon quest, Americans benefited from new medical advances and technological inventions that might have taken years to discover without Kennedy's push to claim the lunar surface.

Ten more astronauts explored the moon before the Apollo program ended in 1972. Space exploration turned to sending unmanned missions to other planets, a joint Soviet-American venture in space, and the manned Space Shuttle missions.

The Bay of Pigs and the Cuban Missile Crisis

In January 1959, following a coup on the Caribbean island of Cuba, President Fulgencio Batista fled to the Dominican Republic. For much of the 1950s he had run a police state that favored the wealthy. Fidel Castro led the Cuban rebels—known as "the bearded ones"—along with his second-in-command Ernesto "Che" Guevara. Triumphant, they took Havana, the capital, making Castro the Cuban leader.

The United States broke diplomatic relations with Cuba in early 1961, and Castro turned to the Soviet Union for assistance. This brought the threat of Communism within ninety miles of U.S. shores, and it was an unsettling factor for both the outgoing Eisenhower and incoming Kennedy administration.

On April 19, 1961, approximately 1,500 Cuban exiles returned to the island to mount an invasion they hoped would incite an uprising and topple the Castro regime. Although no U.S. forces were deployed, U.S. support of what became known as the Bay of Pigs incident was undeniable. The CIA had trained antirevolutionary exiles under the Eisenhower administration, and Kennedy approved the invasion. Armed with U.S. weapons, the exiles landed at the Bahia de Cochinos (Bay of Pigs) on Cuba's southern coast. Castro's army quickly discovered them, killing about ninety and taking the rest as prisoners. The invasion was not only a failure, but also an embarrassment for the Kennedy administration, which was blamed for not fully supporting it and for allowing it to occur in the first place. Although the captured Cuban exiles were later let off with ransom, the entire incident set the world stage for increased tensions between the superpowers.

This unease culminated the next year when U.S. reconnaissance missions flying over Cuba photographed Soviet-managed construction work and spotted a ballistic missile in October 1962. Castro, certain that the United States would try another invasion, had agreed to Soviet missiles for his island's protection.

Without alarming the nation, President Kennedy consulted his top advisors to discuss options—an invasion, air strikes, a blockade, or diplomacy. Kennedy demanded the immediate dismantling and removal of the missiles, and chose a naval blockade to prevent new missiles from arriving on the Caribbean island. The United States would intercept and inspect any ships believed to be carrying weapons, and members of the Organization of American States supported this action.

For several tense days during the Cuban Missile Crisis, Kennedy and Khrushchev communicated through diplomatic channels. The world held its breath for fear of nuclear war between the superpowers. The crisis was solved after the Soviets agreed to remove the missiles and allow U.S. on-site inspection in return for the guarantee not to invade the island nation. Kennedy accepted, agreed to remove U.S. missiles from Turkey, and suspended the blockade, but Cuba refused to permit the promised inspection, out of anger at Soviet submission. Aerial photography did reveal that the missile bases were being dismantled. The entire incident revealed the young president's grace under extreme pressure. Kennedy had needed to redress the humiliation of the Bay of Pigs.

Shots Heard Worldwide

As Kennedy faced an uncertain re-election campaign he began to pool support from those who could help. That meant traveling where his base was dwindling. Texas, home to Vice President Lyndon Johnson, was one of those areas. On November 22, 1963, Mrs. Kennedy, the vice president, and Mrs. Johnson, along with Texas Governor John B. Connally and his wife, accompanied President Kennedy on a visit to Dallas, Texas. En route to a downtown luncheon, the president chose to ride in an open convertible through the motorcade route with his wife sitting beside him.

As the motorcade approached an underpass, shots rang out in rapid succession. President Kennedy slumped into his seat. One bullet passed through the president's neck and struck Governor Connally in the back. To everyone's horror, the next shot hit Kennedy in the head. Rushed to Parkland Hospital, the president never regained consciousness. Governor Connally survived surgery,

A Lone Gunman?

Those who are fascinated by the Kennedy murder conspiracies can choose from several videos on the subject. Director Oliver Stone brought *JFK* to the screen in 1991, portraying a broad-based conspiracy among the government, military, and intelligence communities. The film's release provoked much discussion about assassination theories and the director's dramatic license in interpreting the case. In addition, *Ruby* (released in 1992) speculated on the motives of Jack Ruby, Oswald's convicted assassin, portraying him as a lowlife influenced by the mob and serving as an FBI informant. MPI Home Video has a two-tape edition called *The Men Who Killed Kennedy* outlining many of the assassination theories.

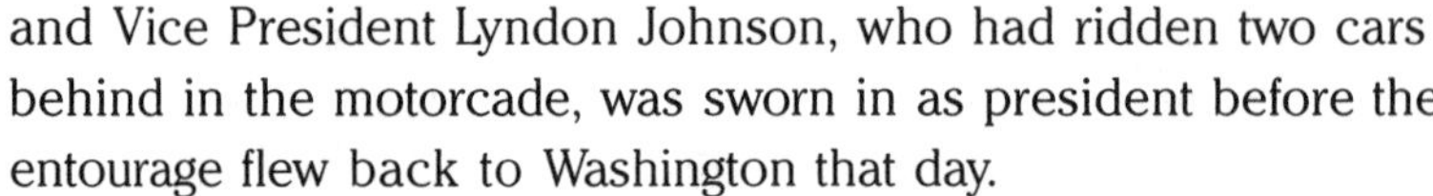

and Vice President Lyndon Johnson, who had ridden two cars behind in the motorcade, was sworn in as president before the entourage flew back to Washington that day.

Suspect Apprehended

Hours later, Dallas police arrested the suspect Lee Harvey Oswald, an employee in a warehouse building along the motorcade route, who was also charged with shooting a police officer the same afternoon. Oswald's background check quickly revealed he'd suffered a troubled youth, defected to the Soviet Union (where he was denied citizenship), and had obvious Communist leanings.

Two days later, as the nation mourned the slain president and prepared for a state funeral, Oswald was himself assassinated while being transferred from one jail to another. Dallas nightclub owner Jack Ruby sprang from a group of reporters to shoot the suspect, who also died at Parkland Hospital. Chief Justice Earl Warren headed a special commission to investigate Kennedy's death and concluded in 1964 that Oswald had acted alone. In 1979, a committee from the U.S. House of Representatives acknowledged the likelihood that a second assassin had been involved, but to this day, the Kennedy assassination is the subject of conspiracy theories and much debate. Jack Ruby was convicted of Oswald's death and later died in prison.

National Mourning

On November 24, 1963, the nation mourned as the president's body was carried by horse-drawn carriage from the White House to the Rotunda of the Capitol. Hundreds of thousands filed past the coffin to pay their respects. A state funeral took place the next day. Foreign dignitaries and heads of state attended. Citizens lined the streets of Washington, D.C., as the funeral cortege made its way to Arlington National Cemetery. One poignant moment the nation would not soon forget was the sight of the slain president's three-year-old son John Jr., saluting his father's casket. At Arlington, Mrs. Kennedy lit an eternal flame that still burns today. Jacqueline Kennedy Onassis was buried decades later next to her late husband.

Kennedy Space Center

Following the president's death and cognizant of his quest for space exploration, NASA renamed its space center on a promontory in eastern Florida, known as Cape Canaveral, the John F. Kennedy Space Center. Today, visitors can watch satellite and space flight launches, view an IMAX presentation, take tours, and learn about America's space program. For more information, visit the Web page at *www.ksc.nasa.gov*.

Voices of Civil Rights Activists

Freedom Rides across the South were common in the decades-old struggle for civil rights in a segregated society. James Meredith made headlines when he tried to enroll in the all-white University of Mississippi and the governor personally blocked his attempts despite federal law. This being the early 1960s, President Kennedy had sent in federal marshals. Alabama Governor George Wallace blocked the University of Alabama, and once again, Kennedy sent in the National Guard. Such incidents incited the president to propose a bill on desegregation, and his successor would push through significant civil rights legislation.

Several African-American leaders' voices rose up amid the chaos of the 1960s. Angela Davis promoted the concept that being black is beautiful. Malcolm X, assassinated in 1965, gave voice to the Black Power movement, urging blacks to reject white culture in favor of their own heritage. Although at first he preached violence as a means of expression, he later devoted himself to peace. The Black Panther activists also staged antiwar protests and stood for the black cause.

The Rise of Martin Luther King Jr.

The most noted of the leaders was the Reverend Martin Luther King Jr., who had organized the bus boycotts during Rosa Parks's struggle in the 1950s. As a clergyman, he used his vision of nonviolent confrontation to challenge segregation and the racial divide, and in doing so, he convinced other Americans to join his cause.

King, along with other black leaders, organized the August 1963 March on Washington. During this march he delivered his famous "I Have A Dream" speech, where he said:

" . . . Now is the time to make real the promises of democracy. Now is the time to rise from the dark and desolate valley of segregation to the sunlit path of racial justice. Now is the time to open the doors of opportunity to all of God's children . . . I have a dream that one day this nation will rise up and live out the true meaning of its creed: 'We hold these truths to be self-evident; that all men are created equal.' I have a dream that one day on the red hills of Georgia the sons of former slaves and the sons of former slave owners will be able to sit down together at the table of brotherhood . . . I have a dream that my four little children will one day live in a nation where they will not be judged by the color of their skin but by the content of their character. I have a dream today . . .

"When we let freedom ring, when we let it ring from every village and every hamlet, from every state and every city, we will be able to speed up that day when all of God's children, black men and white men, Jews and Gentiles, Protestants and Catholics, will be able to join hands and sing in the words of the old Negro spiritual, 'Free at last! Free at last! Thank God Almighty, we are free at last!'"

King's speech showed not only his articulate and passionate delivery, but also his moral character, and it gave momentum to his followers and their cause. As a result of his work, he was awarded the Nobel Peace Prize in 1964.

A Hero Falls

Continuing his work to speak out for equality, King made another speech in Memphis, Tennessee, on April 3, 1968, where he said, "We've got some difficult days ahead, but it really doesn't matter to me now, because I've been to the mountaintop." The next evening, on April 4, Martin Luther King Jr. was gunned down by an assassin as he stood on the balcony of his Memphis motel.

Robert F. Kennedy, brother of the slain president and now a presidential contender himself, informed a crowd of people in Indianapolis of King's death, refusing to cancel his remarks in light of the danger of further violence. Kennedy told those gathered that he understood their anguish, as he'd lost a brother to an assassin's bullet, and he added, "What we need in the United States is not division; what we need in the United States is not hatred; what we need in the United States is not violence or lawlessness, but love and wisdom, and compassion toward one another, and a feeling of justice

Martin Luther King Jr.

towards those who still suffer within our country, whether they be white or they be black . . . Let us dedicate ourselves to what the Greeks wrote so many years ago: to tame the savageness of man and to make gentle the life of this world. Let us dedicate ourselves to that, and say a prayer for our country and for our people."

While the crowd listened intently and followed Robert Kennedy's advice, others around the country engaged in a week of looting, rioting, and burning.

SEEDS OF THE VIETNAM WAR

By 1884, France had annexed Vietnam, placing it under colonial rule. In 1921, however, Ho Chi Minh created a nationalist party seeking independence from France. During World War II, the Japanese wrested control temporarily from the French, and as Japanese forces surrendered, Ho Chi Minh launched a full-scale revolt, taking Hanoi, the capital.

France refused to allow the independence movement, and by 1946 re-established rule, fearing (along with the United States) that all of Asia could become Communist as China fell to Mao Tse-tung. President Truman sent military supplies and funds for the French war in Vietnam, aiming to stem Communist imperialism. A cease-fire in July 1954 established a buffer zone between North and South Vietnam. The Communists, led by Ho Chi Minh, controlled the North while Ngo Dinh Diem stepped in as interim premier in the south.

Having seen enough war through the Korean conflict, Eisenhower was content to leave the area to itself, but as his successor took office, Communist forces were becoming more aggressive, carrying out attacks against South Vietnam. South Korea sent military advisors and aid to assist South Vietnam. Diem's regime, however, was corrupt, complicating matters for the United States as Vietcong Communists within South Vietnam killed Diem's authorities. General Maxwell Taylor, one of Kennedy's top advisors, suggested that sending a few thousand soldiers would quickly take care of the situation, and after Vice President Johnson returned from a

fact-finding mission, he concurred that the United States needed to act against the Communist threat in southeast Asia. Kennedy withdrew support of Diem's regime. Shortly thereafter, the Vietnamese overthrew Diem, who was later murdered.

Following Kennedy's own assassination, President Johnson was wary of committing U.S. forces, but when North Vietnamese torpedo boats allegedly attacked U.S. naval destroyers in the Gulf of Tonkin, Johnson ordered immediate retaliation. Later investigation cast doubt on whether the North Vietnamese really attacked or whether radar blips confused naval personnel. But this occurred only after Congress passed the Gulf of Tonkin Resolution, authorizing Johnson to wage war in Indochina with whatever force he desired. By the end of 1964, approximately 20,000 troops had already been sent to the region.

The Least Popular War Waged On

The United States began a bombing campaign, code-named Operation Rolling Thunder, to stem the stream of supplies from Communist North Vietnam. The operation met with little success. Missions were halted, then stepped up against Hanoi and Haiphong. Relentless aid streamed in to North Vietnam from the Soviet Union and China. But Johnson ignored the real source, as the threat of war between the superpowers was too daunting.

In 1965, when it became clear that mere bombing wasn't enough, the United States sent ground combat troops. Helicopter-borne troops surprised villages harboring suspected Communist supporters. Troops often destroyed such villages, forcing the Vietnamese to find new homes. Fighting became more brutal, as the Vietcong and the North Vietnamese were experts at mine warfare. The resulting explosions often caused the loss of a limb or even death.

The War Gets Uglier

Though the South Vietnamese elected a new president, the conflict dragged on. In 1968, U.S. troops massacred Vietnamese civilians at My Lai in the aftermath of the Tet Offensive in Saigon (where Vietcong soldiers attacked the U.S. embassy as well as multiple military targets throughout all of Vietnam). And at home, protest raged. Too many were dying for a cause not clearly defined or valued. The objections to the war were so profound that they convinced President Lyndon Johnson not to seek re-election in 1968. War protests at the Democratic National Convention in Chicago that year provoked riot police, and at Kent State University in Ohio in 1970, National Guardsmen fired into a crowd of students, killing four and wounding eleven.

Peace negotiations opened in Paris in May 1968, and after Nixon won election, he began a gradual withdrawal of forces, which had reached a high of 550,000. South Vietnamese forces with U.S. helicopter support attacked Communist bases in Cambodia in 1970. Nixon continued to withdraw troops while the conflict lingered. Congress withdrew the Gulf of Tonkin Resolution on December 31, 1970, and peace came in 1973. The last U.S. combat troops left South Vietnam that March, and many prisoners of war were freed. In spite of the truce, skirmishes continued in South Vietnam, Cambodia, and Laos. The North Vietnamese troops entered Saigon as remaining Americans and South Vietnamese troops evacuated. South Vietnam's president announced an unconditional surrender in April 1975.

Vietnam Memories

Visitors to Washington, D.C., can visit the Vietnam Memorial just a short walk from the Reflecting Pool and the Lincoln Memorial. Designed by Maya Ying Lin and known as "the Wall," it is a moving tribute to Vietnam veterans, listing the names of more than 58,000 Americans who perished in the war. For information on the memorial, call (202) 426-6841 or go to *www.nps.gov/vive/home.htm*.

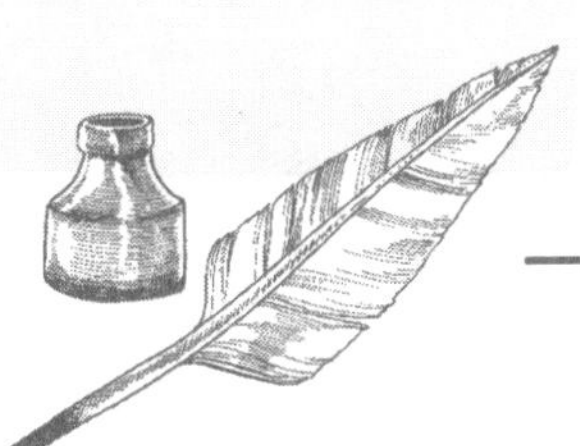

LBJ and the 1968 Elections

Lyndon Johnson's dream was to make America a "Great Society." Coming to office under tragic circumstances, he declared a war on poverty and introduced extensive social legislation, vowing shortly after Kennedy's death that equal rights for Americans needed to become law. The legislation was probably passed more quickly in Kennedy's memory, but turmoil took its toll despite its passage. Race riots flared up in many cities, such as the Watts Riots in Los Angeles. Protests regarding the Vietnam War also escalated to the point that Johnson refused to seek a presidential nomination.

With Johnson out of the running, Robert F. Kennedy, who had left his post as attorney general to become a senator representing

the state of New York, sought the Democratic nomination. Kennedy was a champion of the downtrodden, particularly concerned about problems in urban ghettos and Appalachia. After winning the essential California primary, he gave his victory speech and exited through a hotel kitchen where a Jordanian immigrant named Sirhan Sirhan waited with a gun. Severely wounded, Kennedy died in a Los Angeles hospital the next day, June 6, 1968. His funeral service was held in New York City's St. Patrick's Cathedral, and he is buried not far from the grave of his brother at Arlington National Cemetery.

Vice President Hubert Humphrey won the nomination that summer and was set to run against Richard Nixon, once vice president in the Eisenhower administration. Having been defeated for the high office in 1960, Nixon, who had once pledged to the media that they wouldn't have him to kick around again, returned to politics, vowing to end the Vietnam War. Meanwhile, Governor George Wallace of Alabama mounted a third-party campaign. Nixon, who had named Maryland Governor Spiro T. Agnew as his running mate, gained a comfortable majority of the electoral votes (though he won by a slim margin of the popular vote).

The Counterculture of the 1960s

The 1960s were known as a decade of enormous social change. In many respects, the unpopular and misunderstood Vietnam War served as the catalyst for a counterculture movement where young people openly questioned the status quo and decisions made by older generations. The birth control pill gained popularity as well, leading to a sexual revolution and a change in lifestyle for many.

Those who dropped out of traditional society were called "hippies" and gravitated to areas such as the Haight–Ashbury section of San Francisco. They became known as "flower children" and believed that life was found in nature. Their utopia was the wild rock concert held at Woodstock in 1969. Youth also experimented with mind-altering, illegal drugs such as LSD. The movement found

Visit the White House

The official residence of the president of the United States sits at 1600 Pennsylvania Avenue in Washington, D.C. First occupied in 1800, it became known as the White House in 1901 when Theodore Roosevelt had the name engraved on his stationery. It's been renovated several times since architect James Hoban designed the main building. Jefferson added the east and west colonnades; Theodore Roosevelt added the east and west wings for additional space and offices. By 1902, the home clearly showed 100 years of steady use and underwent a restoration. The changes made in Truman's administration would be termed more of an overhaul, as major structural changes using more modern materials took years to complete. At this time Truman added a south balcony.

Inward appearances varied with the different occupants. The most memorable restoration of the interior came under the auspices of First Lady Jacqueline Kennedy, who firmly believed the White House should represent the national treasures found in historical art and antiques, many of which had been warehoused or placed in storage. Mrs. Kennedy focused on the first floor formal rooms (those open to the public on tours), and she gave all of America a glimpse in her highly acclaimed 1962 televised tour of her restoration.

The private residence of the president and his family occupies the second floor. The third floor is used for guests and staff, and the ground floor also contains rooms that are not open to the public. For tickets to tour the White House, you can contact your representative or senator in Congress. You'll see the East Room, the largest room, which had once been used to hang laundry and provide refuge for Union troops. It's also been the site of large receptions, as well as somber occasions such as when presidents lay in state. In the oval Blue Room, the president receives guests at state dinners, and in the Red Room, the first lady greets visitors. The Green Room is used for informal receptions, and the State Dining Room hosts formal dinners. In her work, Mrs. Kennedy established a permanent art collection for the Executive Mansion, and in 1964, President Johnson issued an executive order establishing the Committee for the Preservation of the White House.

If you can't make it to Washington, but would still like a glimpse of the treasures found inside, there are plenty of books published in conjunction with the White House Historical Association as well as the videos *Within These Walls: A Visit to the White House* and *Upon These Grounds: Exploring the White House Gardens*. There is also a virtual tour CD-ROM titled *The White House Is Our House*. Contact the Historical Association at (202) 737-8292.

its expression in alternative newspapers such as the *Chicago Seed* and the *Village Voice* that promoted radical ideas. People such as Abby Hoffman and Jerry Rubin led the counterculture, and musicians such as the Beatles also contributed. They were disciples of transcendental meditation (Eastern religions caught on in force during the decade), and after John Lennon married Yoko Ono, the unconventional pair decided to host a "bed-in for peace" for their honeymoon. They stayed in the presidential suite of a large Amsterdam hotel for seven days, protesting the war.

Sixties Sensations

From movies such as the debut of James Bond 007 in *Dr. No* early in the decade to the rise of Motown recording stars, Americans enjoyed a vast array of entertainment. Barry Gordy, an African-American who made Motown Records of Detroit, Michigan, the most profitable minority business of its time, also built the fortunes and fame of artists such as Stevie Wonder, the Temptations, the Four Tops, Smoky Robinson and the Miracles, and Diana Ross and the Supremes. Successful musicians such as these showed by example that blacks could achieve stardom. Their achievements helped break down the racial divide in America.

As the 1960s continued, folk music carried with it songs of protest with a sense of growing militancy against the war in Vietnam. Peter, Paul, and Mary, Joan Baez, and Bob Dylan caught on with their music and their message. But there was also more traditional music. In 1966, *The Sound of Music* won an Academy Award for best film, and with it the voice of Julie Andrews, fresh from her recent success with *Mary Poppins.*

More Sixties Pop Culture

In sports, U.S. boxer Cassius Clay (who would later be known as Muhammad Ali) won the world heavyweight title. Andy Warhol startled the art world with pop art, a whole new style evident in images of Campbell's soup cans. And in the 1960s, being fashionable meant wearing false eyelashes, Vidal Sassoon hairstyles, and mini dresses or skirts as model Twiggy depicted so well. Knee- or thigh-length boots completed the fashion ensemble.

Television no doubt captured America's attention in this decade, turning the world into a virtual global village. Dramatic series sponsored by soap manufacturers became known as soap operas for all to follow. Comedies and talk shows aired at night, and the networks broadcast events such as man's landing on the moon. Space exploration of the fictional variety could be seen with the starship *Enterprise*, launched in 1966 with characters Captain James Kirk and Mr. Spock. Sporting events were increasingly broadcast, and cartoons came on the television as well.

Two lasting icons for children's television began in the 1960s. When Fred Rogers began working at NBC in the 1950s, he knew there had to be a way to make a difference using this new medium. So when educational television began in his home area of Pittsburgh, Pennsylvania, Rogers left a promising career to begin his life's work. *Mister Rogers' Neighborhood* began airing in the United States in 1968. The next year, *Sesame Street*, funded by the Children's Television Workshop, began as an hour for preschool children in deprived areas. It quickly took hold with characters such as Big Bird, Cookie Monster, and Kermit the Frog, helping children everywhere learn their letters, numbers, and social skills.

What Time Is It?

In 1966, Congress passed the Uniform Time Act. Though states weren't obligated to observe daylight saving time, those that did had to make the time adjustments the last Sunday in April and end the last Sunday in October. In 1974, Congress adjusted the plan to ten months, and in 1975, to eight months. Officials calculated that the country saved 10,000 barrels of oil for each day of the time change. President Ronald Reagan signed yet another change in 1986, moving the start date to the first Sunday in April. Today, daylight saving time is observed across the United States except in Hawaii, Arizona, and several counties in southeast Indiana.

15

Watergate Rocks the Nation

The 1970s saw continued efforts to end the war in Vietnam and return veterans to U.S. soil. Richard Nixon had won the 1968 election on his campaign promise to end the war, though he was helped by the opposing party's disarray. As the years passed, President Nixon would show another side of himself that remained fairly well hidden. An increasing sense of paranoia pervaded the presidency. He became resentful of the antiwar movement, using his powers as president and government agencies at his disposal to intimidate those he saw as enemies. And as time wore on, his list of enemies seemed to grow substantially larger.

Foreign Relations

Nixon's initiatives in foreign affairs dated back to the Eisenhower administration. As vice president, while escorting Soviet Premier Nikita Khrushchev through a model U.S. kitchen, he debated the merits of the two countries' political systems in what was termed the "kitchen debate." During his presidency, Nixon might have been slow to proceed with Vietnamese peace, but he was more adept at foreign affairs. He was the first president to meet with Communist leaders in Moscow and Beijing, signing trade agreements with both countries and a treaty with the USSR to limit the deployment of antiballistic missile systems. His secretary of state, Henry Kissinger, was an especially skilled diplomat, helping to establish strategic détente with both the Soviet Union and China.

Domestic Turmoil

At home, Nixon became an impetuous leader obsessed with his re-election campaign. Inflation was under better control and the country's international relations had also improved. But the war continued, and so did Nixon's distrust of his perceived enemies—particularly what he saw as the liberal media. The president was outraged when Daniel Ellsberg, a former serviceman turned civilian, put together a compendium of material that came to be known as

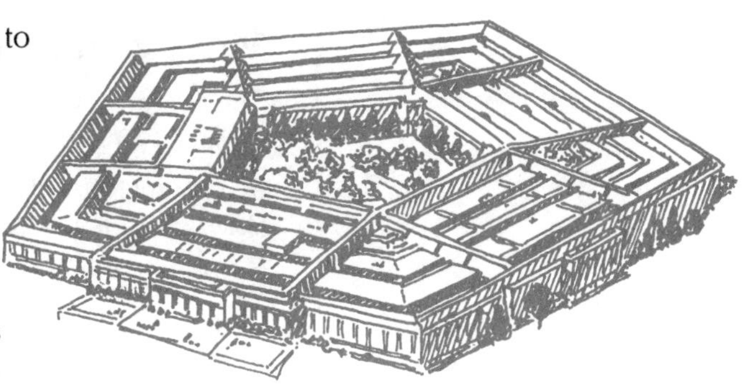

"the Pentagon Papers." The papers were related to the Vietnam War, essentially disclosing that the war's objectives were not achieved and that the United States had planned to oust another country's head of state. Ellsberg contacted the *New York Times*, and the papers began to be published. Nixon sought an injunction to prevent the publication, but in the end it was denied by the Supreme Court.

It was also revealed that a White House team had placed illegal wiretaps on Ellsberg's telephone and had broken into his psychiatrist's office in an attempt to discredit him. Ellsberg was never convicted of a crime.

In the election of 1972, Richard Nixon won easily over his Democratic opponent, South Dakota Senator George McGovern. Later it came out that White House operatives had dug up information regarding McGovern's first vice presidential pick, making Thomas Eagleton out to be mentally ill. McGovern replaced Eagleton on the ticket with Sargent Shriver, a Kennedy in-law and the first director of the Peace Corps. History would prove that Nixon had the election sewn up and that his efforts to increase his lead actually led to his own destruction.

In an unrelated scandal, Vice President Spiro Agnew resigned in October 1973 after his financial misconduct was revealed. President Nixon nominated Gerald R. Ford, a Michigan congressman, to succeed Agnew as vice president.

Nixon's popularity suffered when the economy endured severe inflation, due in some measure to a U.S.–USSR agreement under which the Soviet Union could purchase huge quantities of grain. This devalued the U.S. dollar again. Nixon then cut government funding to many social programs in order to be more fiscally conservative, but this further strained relations with Congress. When two young and eager journalists with the *Washington Post* investigated the arrest of five men connected with Nixon's re-election committee, hardly anyone paid attention. But the pair followed a convoluted trail that would change history.

WATERGATE

The five men arrested breaking into the Democratic National Committee (DNC) offices at Watergate apartment and office complex in Washington, D.C., included Charles Colson, G. Gordon Liddy, and Howard Hunt Jr. Collectively, the group was known as the White House plumbers, given the name for their ability to plug White House information leaks. As history would record, however, their duties extended to spying and other odd jobs. The arrest was the result of a piece of tape left over a door lock that had tipped off security.

The DNC office break in targeted the Democratic party leader Larry O'Brien, who had connections dating back to the 1960 election that Nixon had lost to Kennedy. The two *Washington Post* journalists assigned to cover this story—dubbed a "third-rate burglary" by the White House—were Bob Woodward and Carl Bernstein. As they gathered clues, often from sources who demanded anonymity, the two pieced together a trail of money and cover-ups that led back to the Committee to Re-elect the President (CREEP) and to the Oval Office. U.S. District Court Judge John Sirica remained persistent in his questioning, which also helped crack the case. During the 1973 trial, they learned that this group had attempted to steal documents and placed wiretaps on telephones.

A Senate committee on Watergate (the name applied to the scandal) convened, as did an investigation by special prosecutor Archibald Cox. This investigation truly shed light on the espionage conducted against Nixon's political rivals. With each revelation, it seemed as if one more official in the Nixon administration was forced out or resigned. The president's own counsel, John Dean, testified that there was a cancer on the presidency. Dean confessed to everything, and one by one, Nixon's inner circle was implicated in the Watergate scandal. When it was disclosed that the president routinely taped Oval Office conversations, investigators had the tool they needed to chip away at the deception and reveal the truth. Yet President Nixon, claiming executive privilege, refused to hand over the tapes. He viewed them as his personal property. When

he did finally surrender them, they were extensively edited versions, one with an eighteen and a half minute gap. In the end, Nixon only bought himself some time as pressure mounted to release the tapes in unaltered form.

The president saw many resignations of key advisors and staff. When Nixon ordered the firing of special investigator Cox over the tape matter, he saw yet another of his attorneys general leave the administration. The greatest exodus of staff became known as the Saturday Night Massacre. It outraged the public and diminished everyone's trust in the president.

The Fall of a President

In October 1973, the House Judiciary Committee began considering impeachment proceedings against Nixon, who was stalling with subpoenaed material. The appointment of yet another special investigator, this time Leon Jaworski, did little to quell the outcry. On July 24, 1974, the U.S. Supreme Court ruled in an appeal, *United States v. Nixon,* that the president could not use his claim of executive privilege in refusing to hand over tapes. Not even the president was above the law. The House voted to introduce three impeachment articles that same month with the charges of obstructing justice, abusing presidential power, and refusing to obey subpoenas by the House of Representatives.

On August 5, bowing to pressure, Nixon released tapes that clearly showed his involvement in the Watergate cover-up as early as June 1972. The tape that did the most damage, recorded on June 23, became known as "the smoking gun," for the president could be heard discussing payoffs and other illegal actions.

What little support remained to President Nixon quickly eroded. House impeachment and Senate conviction seemed certain. After a visit from Republican leader Barry Goldwater and others, Nixon announced that he would resign from office. On August 9, 1974, he flew away from the White House in a helicopter, and shortly thereafter, Vice President Gerald R. Ford was sworn in as president, inheriting a nation in shock and dismay at the problems in their government.

Entertainment 1970s Style

Box-office successes included action films such as *Rocky, Jaws,* and *Star Wars.* The Watergate hearings, broadcast live, preempted many daytime programs, annoying fans of popular shows and furthering the sense of cynicism that pervaded the decade. Director Norman Lear brought about a real change in prime-time television when *All in the Family* hit the air in 1971. The show openly dealt with feminism, racism, and the sexual revolution in America. *Happy Days* revived interest in the 1950s with "the Fonz," decked out in a leather jacket, surrounded by girls. In 1977, Americans watched the ten-part miniseries *Roots,* based on a novel by Alex Haley, which traced the story of a slave family from its origins in Africa.

AFTERMATH OF WATERGATE

Richard Nixon never did admit guilt over the Watergate affair, and historians believe that if it were not for the man's suspicion, smear campaigns, and illicit activities, his presidency would have been remembered for its foreign policy strides rather than for scandal. Almost everyone agreed that the surreptitious behavior was unwarranted, as Nixon would have won election without the covert activities that tried to guarantee victory.

In September 1974, President Ford issued a pardon to Nixon for all federal crimes he may have committed during his administration. It was an unpopular decision and may have cost Ford re-election in 1976. Yet it spared the nation a great deal of lingering turmoil.

In the wake of Watergate, citizens remained distrustful, and government officials and politicians had to earn back that trust. Reflecting national skepticism, journalists began digging into the farther recesses of a candidate's behavior, and journalism schools were inundated with wanna-be Woodward and Bernstein–type journalism students. Almost everyone associated with Watergate went on to pen memoirs or accounts of the political saga, including John Dean with his book *Blind Ambition*. In his retirement, former president Richard Nixon wrote books on political affairs, including *No More Vietnams* (1985), *In the Arena* (1990), and *Beyond Peace* (1994). Nixon traveled and gradually regained some respect for his foreign policy expertise. He died of a stroke in 1994 and was buried next to his wife Pat on the grounds of his presidential library.

Jonestown Tragedy

In the 1970s, quasi-religions and cults became popular, sometimes with tragic outcomes. In 1978, Jim Jones convinced followers to move to Guyana and commit mass suicide. More than 900 members of the People's Temple perished.

SINGLE-TERM PRESIDENTS

Some would say that Gerald Ford's presidency existed in the shadows of disadvantage. He was never elected, even as a vice-presidential candidate. Though he'd served twenty-five years in the House of Representatives, he was barely known on the national scene. And though he offered amnesty to Vietnam draft dodgers and in regard to Watergate proclaimed that "Our long national nightmare is over," he was no doubt hurt by the pardon extended to his predecessor and by veterans' resentment toward forgiving those who dodged military service. When the hit TV show *Saturday*

Night Live started spoofing his missteps (literal ones, as Ford tripped and fell in front of TV cameras a few times), his credibility suffered. People were stunned that he was the target of two failed assassination attempts, but his popularity suffered when he failed to turn around a troubled economy. When New York City almost went bankrupt, it turned to Washington for help. At first Ford denied the request, but pressure mounted from other states feeling the fallout of New York's troubled economy. The cumulative effects of all these factors made it possible for another virtual unknown to hit the political circuit in 1976—Jimmy Carter.

President Carter

Carter, with his genuine toothy smile, was a peanut farmer and former Navy man who had studied nuclear physics. Overcoming the question of "Jimmy who?" he touted his outsider status to a public tired of scandal-ridden politics. It didn't hurt that Carter was a born-again Christian who positioned himself as a better remedy for an ailing economy. When he ran against incumbent Gerald Ford, he won the 1976 presidential election.

But President Carter's administration inherited record inflation at a time when people's wages were not keeping pace and jobs were being lost (a condition termed "stagflation"). Unemployment in large manufacturing towns such as Detroit, Cleveland, and Pittsburgh became a problem. Carter's biggest obstacle in turning around the economy became the energy crisis. Crude oil prices had continued to rise, leading to a shortage of gasoline, rationing, and long lines at the pumps. Japanese automobiles flooded the market, appealing to Americans in search of better fuel efficiency. Essentially, Carter's status as an outsider helped him to win the office, yet he struggled without an inside track to promote his ideas and legislation. In addition, his micromanagement style may have gotten in the way of his success.

One area in which Carter certainly excelled was hosting President Sadat of Egypt and Prime Minister Begin of Israel in talks

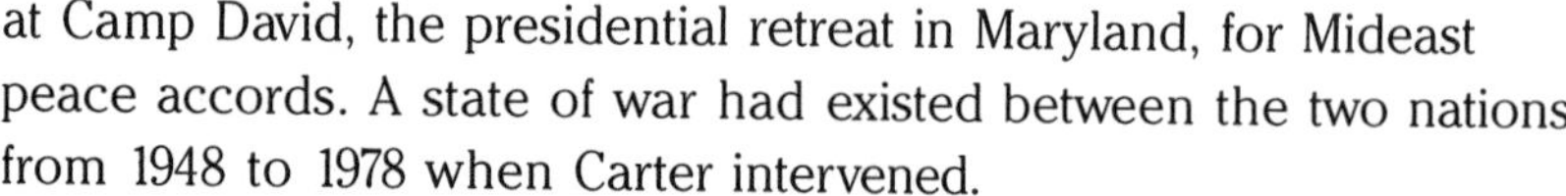

at Camp David, the presidential retreat in Maryland, for Mideast peace accords. A state of war had existed between the two nations from 1948 to 1978 when Carter intervened.

Unfortunately, that foreign policy flair didn't extend to the nation of Iran. Years before, the CIA had used covert aid to help restore Mohammad Reza Pahlavi as the shah of Iran, in order to protect its interest in this volatile region. But the shah's regime lost its religious roots and became corrupt and autocratic. Conservative Muslims led by the Ayatollah Ruhollah Khomeini opposed the Iranian government, inciting a revolution that deposed the shah and sent him and his family into exile. When the shah sought asylum in the United States, the Ayatollah demanded his return and that of billions of dollars the shah had allegedly hidden abroad. Tensions grew. On November 4, 1979, a mob of Islamic students attacked the U.S. embassy in Tehran, taking sixty-six members of the staff as hostages. Though thirteen were soon released, the other fifty-three remained hostages for 444 days. Negotiations did not secure their return, nor did a failed U.S. commando raid the following April. Carter ordered an airborne rescue attempt in April 1980 that failed miserably. On day 445 of the Iranian hostage crisis, the hostages were released, but only as Jimmy Carter's presidency ended at noon that day.

Don't Call Me Miss or Mrs.

Gloria Steinem, a writer and political activist, founded the magazine *Ms.* in 1971 when women's magazines began covering crucial topics such as health and sexuality, law, work, and the arts as opposed to merely recipes and sewing. She espoused a belief that when women felt liberated, men would become whole people as well. Women everywhere began insisting on the title Ms. as opposed to Miss or Mrs., asserting that their male counterparts had no courtesy title that revealed their marital status. As for Ms. Steinem herself, she chose to marry for the first time in her sixties.

Women's Rights

During both the Ford and Carter administrations, the women's liberation movement surged forward. During the late 1960s, abortion became the topic of debate in the political arena. "Pro-choice" advocates believed that only a woman and her doctor should decide whether to end a pregnancy. They argued that life begins when the fetus can survive on its own outside the mother's womb. "Pro-life" advocates argued that life begins at conception and that states should prohibit the procedure. Many women had illegal abortions, risking their health and their lives. In 1973, however, the U.S. Supreme Court ruled in the case of *Roe v. Wade* that every woman had a legal right to end a pregnancy during the first trimester.

Religious and conservative groups led the outcry against the high court's decision. They also categorized women who supported the proposed Equal Rights Amendment (ERA) as immoral and antifamily. They sent an underlying message that played on hidden fears that if the ERA passed, America would see same-sex marriages and unisex bathrooms. Yet women who felt they could rise only so far (to the "glass ceiling") in a male-dominated corporate world argued for equal pay for equal work. Betty Friedan, Gloria Steinem, Bella Abzug, and Shirley Chisholm, among others, argued for agendas including child-care centers and equal opportunities in employment, education, and in the military, as well as abortion rights.

By August 1974, the Equal Rights Amendment had been ratified by thirty-three of the required thirty-eight states. A congressional mandate had set March 1979 as the deadline for ratification, and by June 1978, only three additional states had approved the ERA. Even when given an extension for approval, the amendment failed to be ratified. Yet many states do now guarantee equality of the sexes in their state constitutions.

Other Activism and Social Change

The 1970s saw an increase in all kinds of activism. Gay liberation occurred all over the country, but particularly in areas such as New York's Greenwich Village and San Francisco. The music scene saw the success of the Village People, a group of gay men who hit the pop music charts.

Ralph Nader brought consumerism to the forefront, making him an instant enemy of corporate America, whose products he questioned. There is little doubt that Nader's efforts raised the quality of goods. Cesar Chavez, who organized farm workers in the 1960s, continued his struggles for migrant workers and other Hispanics during the next decade. In addition, environmentalists brought their concerns into the spotlight. Conservationists pushed for greater environmental controls, and public service messages supporting the

anti-littering cause hit the airwaves with the well-known phrase "People start pollution, people can stop it."

In 1979, the public's concern for the environment grew when an accident occurred at Three Mile Island, the site of a pressurized-water nuclear reactor outside Harrisburg, Pennsylvania. A maintenance error and a defective valve led to the loss of coolant. The safety systems seemed to have worked properly but when the emergency cooling system was shut off, a partial core meltdown (with resulting damage) occurred, and a small amount of radioactive gas escaped from the containment building. The financial cost to the utility was substantial, but the public scare was even worse. Legislation was soon enacted requiring the Nuclear Regulatory Commission to adopt far more stringent standards for the design and construction of nuclear power plants, as well as preparation of emergency plans to protect public health and the environment. Several nuclear power plants already under construction were cancelled.

Outstanding Athletes of the 1970s

- *Hank Aaron.* Henry Louis "Hank" Aaron hit his 715th home run in 1974, breaking Babe Ruth's record that had stood for thirty-nine years. He was one of the first black players to enter major league baseball.
- *Muhammad Ali.* He first came on the scene in the 1960s as Cassius M. Clay Jr., an Olympic gold medallist and later world heavyweight champ, but was stripped of the title when convicted of draft evasion. He took a new name when he joined a Black Muslim sect, and won a Supreme Court reversal. He regained the heavyweight crown in 1974 against George Foreman.
- *Arthur Ashe Jr.* The first black man to win a major tennis tournament, Ashe began playing the game in the segregated parks of Richmond, Virginia. He won important tennis titles,

survived heart surgery, and retired from the game. Later, he developed HIV, which causes AIDS, likely acquired through blood transfusions. He became an active fundraiser prior to his death.

- *Dorothy Hamill.* Winner of the ladies' figure skating gold medal at the 1976 Winter Olympics, Hamill not only gained international popularity but brought a resurgence to figure skating, her own trademark "Hamill Camel" to her spins, and a new hairstyle that was all the rage in America.
- *Bruce Jenner.* He won the Olympic decathlon event at the 1976 Olympic Games in Montreal and was one of the first athletes to use his Olympic popularity as a springboard to wealth and celebrity off the track.
- *Billie Jean King.* In what was dubbed the "Battle of the Sexes," this female tennis star defeated her male opponent Bobby Riggs in three straight sets. King was one of the most successful tennis players in the history of Wimbledon.
- *Jack Nicklaus.* As the premier pro golfer of the 1960s and '70s, Nicklaus consistently captured major pro tournaments, including the U.S. Open, Masters, and Professional Golfers' Association (PGA) Championship.
- *Mark Spitz.* This American swimmer won seven gold medals at the 1972 Olympic Games in Munich, West Germany. He set world records in many races including the 200-meter butterfly event.
- *The Pittsburgh Steelers.* During the 1970s, this was the first NFL team to win four Super Bowls. Head coach Chuck Noll led the talented quarterback Terry Bradshaw, defensive end "Mean" Joe Greene, running back Franco Harris, and linebackers Jack Ham and Jack Lambert.

16

The End of the Millennium

In 1980, the presidential race pitted the incumbent chief executive Jimmy Carter against a newcomer to national politics, Ronald Reagan. First famous as an actor and later governor of California, Reagan charmed the public, and his conservative following in particular. The nation seemed to be searching for old-fashioned values, and citizens found them in Reagan. He became the fortieth president of the United States, and also the oldest person ever elected to the job.

The Great Communicator

Reagan was an exemplary communicator, often quoting from popular movies. Great with a script, he wasn't as talented without one. As the Carter administration failed to revive a sagging economy, Americans looked to Reagan for leadership. He'd previously tried to enter the national political arena (challenging Gerald Ford for the Republican nomination in 1976), but this time people took Ronald Reagan more seriously. In an ironic twist, Reagan briefly considered former President Ford as a potential running mate, but selected George Bush instead.

Reagan blasted Carter on the campaign trail on everything from the struggling economy to the need for a strong military. Meanwhile, the Iranian hostage crisis continued. Each day, programs such as ABC-TV's *Nightline* kept the drama alive for Americans. The Iranian stalemate humiliated the nation. When Americans went to the polls that November, they elected Ronald Reagan by a landslide. On the day Reagan was sworn in, Iran released the hostages.

Reagan Takes the Helm

Reagan brought sweeping change to the economy and social policies that had been set in place over the preceding decades. He reduced federal programs and lifted restrictions on business activities and regulations. Conservative and religious groups, businesses in search of tax breaks and eased restrictions, and defense contractors wanting a piece of Reagan's new military buildup supported the president's agenda. So did those who believed the

USSR was the proverbial U.S. enemy. TV evangelist Jerry Falwell had a very public pulpit with his Moral Majority, pressing for prayer in public schools and restrictions on abortion, gay rights, and women's rights.

On March 31, 1981, Reagan's presidency was almost cut short by an assassination attempt. His attacker, John W. Hinckley, was an unstable drifter acting out a fantasy to gain the attention of actress Jodie Foster. Foster had starred in the movie *Taxi Driver*, which partly dealt with political assassination. Hinckley was found not guilty by reason of insanity and committed to a mental hospital. Reagan recovered from the shooting. The public's concern and support made it a bit easier for the new president to push through his legislative agenda.

Reaganomics

The recession that had begun during the previous decade lingered, but during the 1980s, economic recovery began. Inflation was low, but with interest rates at record highs, many wealthy citizens prospered as a result of "Reaganomics." This was an era of conspicuous consumption by "yuppies," young urban professionals. With the good came the bad, however. Government spending and a burgeoning civil service produced a record national debt, which future generations would have to contend with. In October 1987, Wall Street investors panicked, causing stocks to plummet 508 points, even more sharply than they'd done in 1929. However, the nation did not slump into a depression, but recovered from "Black Monday."

Still, thousands of manufacturing jobs were eliminated in the new economy and replaced with lower-paying positions in service industries. Poverty became more of a problem with many social services cut to help those who most needed assistance. The emphasis was clearly on the supply side of economics, with the hope that money would trickle down from the top.

Known as the "Teflon president" because none of his mistakes seemed to stick, Reagan won re-election in 1984 against his Democratic opponent, Walter Mondale, who had named

Must-Have MTV

What do we mean by the MTV Generation? The phrase was coined to describe an entire generation introduced to a brand-new art form, unveiled in 1981 when the cable channel MTV began showing music videos. VJs (the equivalent of disc jockeys, only for videos) showcased recording artists who mastered the new medium, often propelling their careers to new heights. One such talent was Michael Jackson, youngest of the Jackson Five from the 1970s, who released his *Thriller* album in 1982 and became well known for his moonwalk dance.

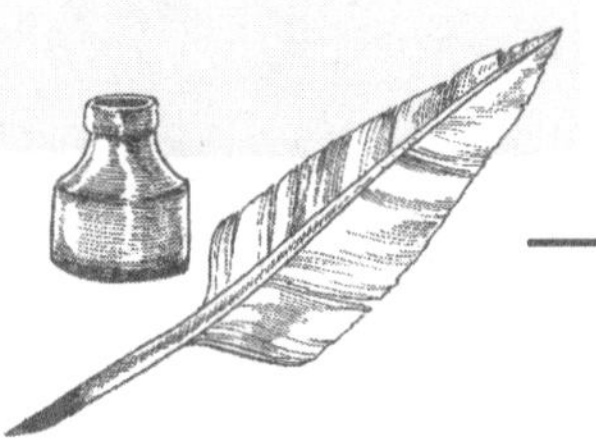

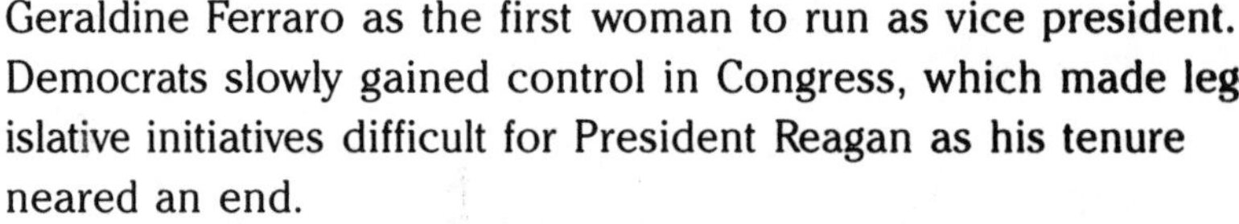

Geraldine Ferraro as the first woman to run as vice president. Democrats slowly gained control in Congress, which made legislative initiatives difficult for President Reagan as his tenure neared an end.

President Reagan did appoint three new justices to the Supreme Court, including Sandra Day O'Connor, the first woman to serve on the high bench. If détente (peaceful coexistence) had been stressed in the prior decade, in the 1980s it was de-emphasized in favor of fighting Communist influences. This fighting occurred in Central America and in the Caribbean. The United States cut off aid to Nicaragua in order to support an anti-Sandinista guerilla movement known as the Contras. Nicaragua signed an aid pact with the Soviet Union, and Reagan focused on sending money, weapons, and military training to the Contras, as well as arms and advisors to El Salvador. In 1983, U.S. troops invaded Grenada, a Caribbean island, after rebels overthrew the government there. Reagan supported anti-Marxist regimes in Afghanistan and Angola. Unlike Vietnam, the fighting brought few casualties. In the Middle East, the president wasn't as lucky: U.S. Marines were attacked in their Beirut headquarters after Reagan sent them into Lebanon to strengthen the Christian government. Even after the president pulled the marines out of the territory, radical Muslims kidnapped many westerners.

The country's military buildup took care of keeping the Soviets in check. The military boasted of its Strategic Defense Initiative technology, often called "Star Wars," which was supposed to permit the United States to intercept enemy missiles before they hit their targets. Reagan had insisted on the technology, though many felt it was too expensive. Some called it a hoax to make the Soviets believe the United States had a strategic advantage. The U.S. rearmament brought much protest from Mikhail Gorbachev, the Soviet leader, during summit meetings. However, the two superpower leaders agreed to eliminate land-based nuclear missiles of intermediate and shorter range. These were admittedly only a small fraction of both nations' nuclear arsenals, but nonetheless it was progress in the arms race.

Indelible Images

As the Iron Curtain collapsed, two images captured the moment—the enthusiastic tearing down of the Berlin Wall and the toppling of the life-size Lenin Monument.

Communism Crumbles

The Communist empire as generations had known it, and feared it, unexpectedly began to unravel during the tenure of Mikhail Gorbachev. He initiated a campaign called *perestroika* (Russian for "restructuring"), reforming and revitalizing the Soviet system that had been in place for decades. Gorbachev first mentioned his ideas in a speech before the Central Committee of the Communist Party in 1985, and his policy of *glasnost* ("openness") became the subject of public debate. Works previously banned were now published; the Soviet media was also less restricted.

Unfortunately, the Soviet economy was still hurting, and *perestroika* introduced a market-based system, encouraging private ownership, which had always been shunned by previous Communist regimes. *Perestroika* was far more than economic reform. The broader use of the term meant social, political, and most definitely historic change. Soviet citizens, for instance, would have a greater say in who would run their government.

Yet this sweeping change was not automatically welcomed. Youth, often better educated and largely dissatisfied with the traditional system, embraced the concepts, but the less educated, older generations opposed them. Under the new Soviet system, prices soared, as did unemployment. When people could get to the stores through the long lines, they often found nothing of value. Unable to navigate the change as the Soviet economy continued its decline, Gorbachev watched as the USSR collapsed in 1991 and Russia remained under the leadership of elected President Boris Yeltsin. Communist governments in Central and Eastern Europe also collapsed as a result.

THE IRAN–CONTRA SCANDAL

Reagan's administration became embroiled in controversy, damaging his reputation as an honest communicator. In November 1986, word leaked to newspapers that the United States had secretly sold weapons to Iran, diverting approximately $30 million in profits from these sales to help the Contras fight the leftist Sandinista government in Nicaragua. If indeed arms had been swapped for hostages, it would embarrass the administration, for once the arms were in Iranian control, others could use them to capture additional hostages. But the matter was even more complex.

Initially, Reagan denied the allegations that arms had been swapped to win the release of U.S. hostages held by Lebanese terrorists (who supported Iran). Administration sources blamed the diversion of profits on Lieutenant Colonel Oliver North, a National Security Council staff member who directed the secret operations against Nicaragua. North had set up covert support for the Contras, including airplanes and secret bank accounts. He had reported his activities initially to his superior, National Security Advisor Robert C. McFarlane, and subsequently to McFarlane's successor, Admiral John Poindexter. Congressional hearings focused on whether and how Reagan was personally involved in the matter, and particularly whether his administration violated the Boland Amendment (passed in 1984) forbidding U.S. military aid to the Contras. North denied the administration's claims that he'd acted independently. To complicate matters for the White House, North had a certain All-American patriotic fervor about him that appealed to people, making his testimony all the more believable.

Admiral John Poindexter testified that he'd never told Reagan about the diversion of funds, but that the president had approved a direct arms-for-hostages deal with Iran. In the end, members of Congress admonished the administration for its incompetence in handling the secret operations and funding. But there was no overall investigation of Contras financing, for the investigative committee found no concrete evidence to suggest that Reagan had known of the diversion of funds to the Contras. It had been alleged that there were ties between the Contras and drug smugglers—this in an era where the first lady had publicly espoused a campaign for school children called "Just Say No" to drugs. Lt. Col. North was tried and convicted in 1989 of obstructing Congress and unlawfully destroying government documents, but his conviction was later reversed. Poindexter was also found guilty, and this verdict was also overturned.

Just when everyone thought the matter was put to rest, it resurfaced for George Bush when he issued pardons for many high-level government officials charged or convicted of Iran–Contra activities. Independent prosecutor Lawrence E. Walsh issued a final report on the investigation in January 1994. He found no evidence that President Reagan had broken the law, but admitted that Reagan may have known about or participated in a cover-up of the scandal.

End of the Reagan Era

Toward the end of Reagan's tenure as president, it was reported that he dozed off during cabinet meetings and spent less and less time on presidential duties. The Iran–Contra scandal had weakened his political clout, and Congress openly rejected some of his initiatives. Congress overrode a presidential veto of a civil-rights enforcement bill and refused funding for Contras military operations. But Reagan's successors, not the president himself, would have to address the government spending that had begun under the president dubbed "the Gipper." Vice President George Herbert Walker Bush won the election of 1988 against Democratic rival Michael Dukakis, the governor of Massachusetts. Bush came across as a more patriotic campaigner than his rival, and though he took some flack for his choice of Senator Dan Quayle as running mate (against Senator Lloyd Bentsen), he triumphed. Many did not see Quayle as presidential, and he became fodder for late-night comedians, further eroding public confidence.

History on Tape

The MPI Home Video Collection produces mini-series, televised documentaries, and tapes chronicling major news events of the century. *The 20th Century: A Moving Visual History* is a ten-volume series featuring a tape per decade with video footage and interviews with historians. Visit your book or video store or order a catalog by calling (800) 777-2223, or check out *www.mpimedia.com*.

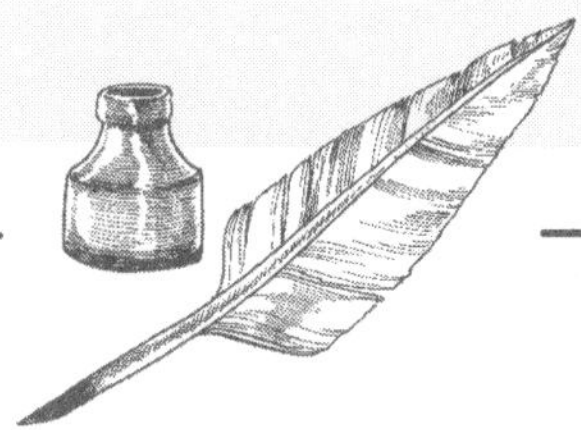

No Beating Around the Bush

George Bush believed that the former Soviet Union could become an ally, and that if the Cold War ended, American taxpayers would no longer have to finance the military might it had necessitated. Thus, Bush helped edge the Soviet leader toward democracy. As the Berlin Wall separating Communist East Berlin from capitalist West Berlin fell in November 1989, Bush showed restraint rather than gloating over the event. He talked of "a new world order" to replace the former relations between the two superpowers.

Bush gravitated toward foreign affairs rather than many domestic initiatives. In 1989, Manuel Noriega, the Panamanian president indicted in the United States for drug trafficking, nullified a presidential election that had swept him out of power, even after U.S. observers insisted he had lost. Critics pointed to the fact that Noriega had been an agent of the Central Intelligence Agency (CIA) while President Bush had been the agency's director. Bush sent troops to Panama to assist in a coup against Noriega. The invasion lasted only days and resulted in Noriega's capture and return to the mainland, where he was convicted in Miami, Florida, on drug and racketeering charges in 1992.

Tensions in Iraq, however, demanded much of Bush's attention as Iraqi leader Saddam Hussein launched an offensive on neighboring Kuwait in August 1990. The tiny nation, governed by a sheik, held 10 percent of the world's oil reserves. President Bush mounted an unprecedented global alliance against the Iraqi assault, trying to protect the largely defenseless nation, but also to prevent future Iraqi conquests. Saudi Arabia, home to another 25 percent of the world's reserves, bordered Saddam's forces. It was too close for comfort for many in the Western world. If Saddam Hussein, a headstrong leader at best, ordered another attack, he would control almost half of the world's oil.

Tensions in the Persian Gulf

President Bush favored diplomatic resolution of the tensions, but also vowed that Hussein would not succeed with his naked aggression. In a televised speech, Bush likened Hussein to Hitler. The president created a coalition under the auspices of the United Nations (U.N.), including many European, Asian, and Middle Eastern countries (some of whom had had their own tensions with one another). Bush convinced the Saudi Arabians to allow a U.S. troop presence on their soil. The U.S. Department of Defense deployed military weapons and soldiers, even some called up from the reserve forces, in the largest such undertaking since Vietnam. Bush demonstrated patience when Arab nations (such as Egypt) bowed to political pressure to resolve the tensions alone. But when this failed, the Arabs joined the U.N. coalition along with the USSR, a longtime ally of Iraq. Negotiations between Secretary of State James Baker and Iraqi foreign minister Tariq Aziz, and U.N. resolutions, continued while the president deployed the military. Despite Hussein's requests for a portion of Kuwait, Bush held firm to his demand for complete withdrawal and warned of the consequences if he was not heeded. The proverbial line in the sand was drawn with a deadline of January 15 for Hussein's withdrawal.

The United Nations Security Council had already sanctioned the use of force, if necessary, in 1990. President Bush received congressional approval for possible military action January 16, 1991. He ordered the multinational invasion of Kuwait called Operation Desert Storm to begin the next day, January 17.

Operation Desert Storm

The Allied coalition had approximately 1,700 aircraft poised to attack Iraqi forces. U.S. General Norman Schwarzkopf commanded the operation. Apache helicopter gunships and Stealth fighters went into service. Finally, the United States had a chance to use many of the weapons amassed during the Reagan–Bush era, including cruise missiles.

Though the Stealths were designed to be invisible to radar, the U.S. Air Force took no chances and jammed enemy radar.

Almighty Counselor to Many Presidents

Born William Franklin Graham, he found his calling as an evangelist at age seventeen, attending a revival meeting. As he gained ground as a preacher, he evangelized around the world, energizing people in mass rallies called the Billy Graham Crusades. He converted thousands to Christianity over the years, and as his stature rose over the course of many decades, several presidents sought his counsel. It's said he met with President George Bush before the president declared war in the Persian Gulf. In 1992, Graham announced that he suffered from Parkinson's disease and handed most of his religious crusading over to his eldest son Franklin.

Unfortunately, the jamming alerted the Iraqis that something was happening, and Hussein ordered blind firing of missiles without even knowing the target. The Allied bombing did destroy much of Iraq's communications ability. The next targets were weapons factories where it was believed Hussein had stockpiled arsenals of biological and chemical weapons.

From the start of the Allied bombing, Iraq launched missile attacks against Tel Aviv and Jerusalem, as Saddam Hussein had threatened. He unleashed his Soviet-made Scud missiles against the Israelis to antagonize the region. Trying to keep the coalition he'd organized together, Bush worked to prevent Israel from retaliating against Iraq. Otherwise, the fragile Arab–Western alliance would disintegrate. To fend off Hussein's attacks, the United States brought in newly developed Patriot missiles.

The Allies tried to avoid a ground war, as it would no doubt bring with it the risk of more casualties. In addition, Iraq had fought with Iran previously, and Iraqis had slaughtered their enemies with chemical weapons. No one welcomed the prospect of a repeat. In late January, Hussein ordered his troops to open a Kuwaiti pipeline, pouring petroleum into the Persian Gulf. The oil not only damaged the environment, but threatened the desalination plants that provided drinking water to Saudi Arabia. U.S. bombing raids managed to curtail the pipeline damage, but the oil had already done great harm to the water, beaches, and sea life.

The Ground War

On February 24, the ground war began as U.S. Marines penetrated Iraqi lines and pushed to liberate Kuwait City. Kuwaiti oil fields were already ablaze, filling the skies with thick, black smoke. Again, Saddam Hussein ignored demands to withdraw from the country. The Allied air force kept attacking Iraqi tank positions, using all of its military might, including B-52s and bombers from the nuclear strike force. With laser-guided bombs, U.S. forces destroyed tank after tank. From the sea, the USS *Missouri* shelled the beach.

Schwarzkopf wanted to avoid close fighting, so he took advantage of the trenches Iraqis had established to protect their tank units. U.S. soldiers simply bulldozed over them, giving their enemies only seconds to surrender.

As fleeing Iraqi soldiers moved back toward their border, U.S. forces dropped a string of bombs on the convoy, stalling it. On the third day of the ground war, the U.S. 7th Corps caught up with the Iraqi Republican Guard Division. Tank fighting was heavy, but the U.S. equipment was far superior to the Soviet-made tanks that Iraq used. Other defeats soon followed, and the Iraqi troops retreated.

Bush After the War

In the months after the Gulf War, President Bush enjoyed a 90 percent approval rating among Americans. As the months wore on to the 1992 election, however, it became evident that although Bush handled foreign relations well, his comprehension didn't extend to his electorate, who resented his inaction on domestic matters.

The Aftermath of the Gulf War

Critics felt the Allied effort didn't go far enough: it failed to eliminate Hussein altogether, or to press forward to take Baghdad. In his defense, Bush cited his original objective—to liberate Kuwait for its rightful government and leaders, not to remove any other leader such as Saddam Hussein. The president consulted with General Colin Powell, chairman of the Joint Chiefs of Staff, and they decided to end the war effort. Compared to other wars' casualty numbers, the Allied casualty count was relatively low: a total of 149 Allied soldiers died in the line of duty, and a little more than 500 were wounded. Iraqi casualties were much higher, with estimates ranging from 25,000 to 100,000.

Headline News

Several events made headlines at this time in mainstream America:

- *Headline News* itself was newsworthy as an offshoot of the Cable News Network (CNN), created by Ted Turner, an Atlanta businessman, in 1980. When others fled the Persian Gulf as war approached in 1991, CNN reporter Peter Arnett and others remained in Iraq and brought the air raids and Scud missile launches into people's homes as they occurred tens of thousands of miles away.

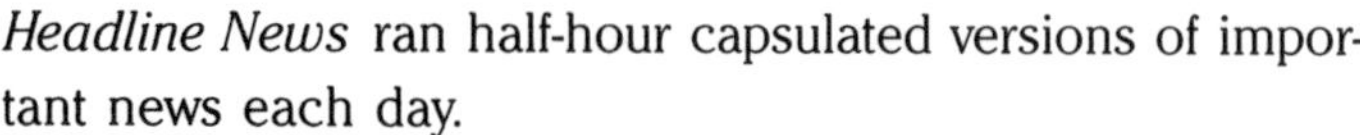

Headline News ran half-hour capsulated versions of important news each day.

- Mount St. Helens, a volcano in the Cascade Range of Washington state that had been dormant for more than 120 years, erupted May 18, 1980, with rock and debris spewing twelve miles, and volcanic ash much farther. Rumbles had been heard early in the year, but the sudden eruption measured 4.1 on the Richter scale. It blew the top off of the 9,675-foot peak, causing flooding, mudslides, and billions of dollars in property damage.
- Millions watched the royal wedding of Britain's Prince Charles and Lady Diana Spencer. Americans quickly took a liking to the young princess, following the births of her children, her rise as a fashion icon and humanitarian, her divorce, and her tragic death in an automobile accident in 1997.
- Acquired Immune Deficiency Syndrome (AIDS) came to everyone's attention in the mid-1980s as the killer virus was identified almost simultaneously at the Pasteur Institute in Paris and at the National Cancer Institute in Bethesda, Maryland. Actor Rock Hudson died of the disease in 1985; this loss and others galvanized those fighting for adequate research. As a longtime friend of Hudson's, President Reagan even had to re-evaluate his preconceptions about the dreaded disease.
- On the night of March 24, 1989, the *Exxon Valdez*, an American oil tanker, went aground on a reef in Prince William Sound, Alaska. The 987-foot tanker began leaking oil in a spill that continued for two days, making it the worst oil disaster of its kind in U.S. history. Remaining barrels of oil were transferred onto other tankers, and the cleanup moved slowly, at least at first. Approximately 1,100 miles of Alaskan shoreline was contaminated, killing birds, sea mammals, and fish. The captain of the tanker not only lost his job amid allegations of a substance-abuse problem, but faced criminal charges in the matter.

Challenger Disaster

The Space Shuttle *Challenger*, with a crew of seven astronauts featuring America's first civilian and teacher sent into space, exploded in a burst of flames only seventy-three seconds into its flight, on January 28, 1986. Mission commander Francis R. Scobee, pilot Michael J. Smith, mission specialists Ronald E. McNair, Ellison S. Onizuka, and Judith A. Resnik, and payload specialists Gregory B. Jarvis and Christa McAuliffe, who was a high school teacher from New Hampshire, all perished in the accident. The launch program was halted during the investigation until designers modified the shuttle and implemented tighter safety measures. Shuttle missions resumed on September 28, 1988, with the flight of the space shuttle *Discovery*.

- Another San Francisco earthquake, this time measuring 6.9 on the Richter scale, struck the city as baseball fans were finding their seats for the third game of the World Series, October 17, 1989. The tremor erupted along the San Andreas Fault. Although it lasted a mere fifteen seconds, it resulted in collapsed highways, dozens of deaths, and billions of dollars in property damage.

The Computer Age

In the 1980s, expanding technology ushered unprecedented numbers of Americans into the computer and information age. Thanks to the microchip, computers that used to be the size of a room could now be placed on a desktop.

It was actually in 1971 that the world's first microprocessor, containing all the main components of a computer, was developed. The chips became smaller and smaller with time, so computers became more and more affordable and convenient for business and home use. Cheap mass production brought forth handheld electronic gadgets that transformed everyday life. Calculators, once the size of a box on a desk, shrank to the size of a credit card. Much of this occurred south of San Francisco in what has become known as Silicon Valley, a mecca of high-technology start-up operations.

The Tech Leaders

At the forefront of this revolution were two young entrepreneurial spirits—Steve Jobs and Steve Wozniak—both Californians with no special programming or electronics knowledge. Working together in a garage, in 1977 they developed the first user-friendly computer, designed for mass marketing rather than big business, called the Apple II. It was followed by the Macintosh in 1984.

Jobs and Wozniak named their operation the Apple Computer Company. At the core of their success was the graphic user interface (GUI), which allowed a computer user to point and click on particular icons rather than type complicated computer codes into a machine.

Another computer whiz dropped out of Harvard with the vision that software was where the real excitement and money lay. Bill Gates, with his company Microsoft, was hired by IBM (International Business Machines) to develop an operating system for the corporation's computers, which was called MS-DOS. IBM, which had built personal computers or "PCs" in 1981 around the latest Intel microprocessor, failed to claim exclusive rights for MS-DOS, and Microsoft grew steadily in the industry. Soon, Microsoft developed its own GUI system with Windows 3.0 software. It took the computing world by storm. Gates helped other companies use reverse engineering to circumvent patent law, creating almost identical computers (or clones) of the IBM hardware. Today IBM compatibles are widely seen in stores, homes, and business, and as of this writing, Bill Gates is one of the richest men in the world. As for Apple Computer, it developed a loyal following with fans of the Macintosh but never captured the market share held by the compatibles market.

Famous Faces of the 1980s and '90s

- *Newt Gingrich.* A Republican, Gingrich was elected to the U.S. House of Representatives from Georgia after two prior unsuccessful bids for Congress. His conservative platform focused on lowering taxes. He and his cronies were known for their long-winded speeches late into the night. In 1987, Gingrich initiated ethics charges again Speaker of the House Jim Wright, eventually leading to Wright's resignation. Gingrich's passionate pursuit of shrinking the federal government (his "Contract with America") was widely publicized, enabling his fellow Republicans to gain control of both the House and the Senate in the 1994 elections. Sworn in as Speaker of the U.S. House of Representatives, Gingrich was later reprimanded in 1997 by house members for ethics violations, giving false information, and using tax-exempt donations for political activities.

- *H. Ross Perot.* Having worked early on as an IBM salesperson, Perot left to found Electronic Data Systems (EDS), a business he built serving the data processing needs of medical insurance companies. Perot came into huge profits when EDS stock traded publicly in 1968. In 1984, he sold the company, and in time launched a new enterprise, the Perot Systems Corporation. In social and political matters, Perot was self-guided and outspoken. He attempted to deliver food, medicine, and other supplies to U.S. prisoners during the Vietnam War, and in 1979 organized a commando rescue of two EDS employees jailed in Iran. But his most outrageous and nationally known move was his announcement on CNN's *Larry King Live* that he was available as a presidential contender in 1992. With his pet issues of the federal deficit and term limits for Congress, he hit the campaign trail, always offering his colorful commentary on government's problems. For example, Perot likened the burgeoning deficit to "the crazy aunt in the basement" that you never want to talk about! As a third-party candidate, he captured people's attention. Of course, as a billionaire, he could well afford to run thirty-minute "infomercials" conveying his message and economic plans. Oddly enough, he dropped out of the race in July 1992, citing personal and family reasons, only to re-enter in October. That November, he received 19 percent of the national vote, the highest percentage any independent candidate had won. Analysts deemed Perot's candidacy more detrimental to Bush than to Clinton, who won the presidency. Perot remained outspoken with his watchdog group United We Stand and his Reform Party challenging both Democrats and Republicans.

Surf the Web

To find the names, locations, and Web sites of major offices of tourism where key historic sites are centered, try the History Channel Traveler Web site at *www.historytravel.com*.

- *Oprah Winfrey*. Born and raised in the south, Oprah Winfrey rose from a troubled youth to win a full scholarship to Tennessee State University. She was the first black woman to anchor the news on a local Nashville station and moved into larger markets such as Baltimore and Chicago with news and talk shows. But she's better known for how she turned that television finesse into media might. One year after Winfrey became the host of *A.M. Chicago*, the program took the name *The Oprah Winfrey Show* and began to deal with controversial subjects. The next year, it achieved national syndication, truly showcasing Oprah's ability to emotionally connect with her guests and audience. An author appearance almost guaranteed a rise to bestseller status, and even political candidates used the program as a platform to reach the masses, especially women. Oprah formed Harpo Productions to produce her show as well as other projects. She appeared in the film *The Color Purple*, for which she won a 1986 Academy Award, as well as in miniseries and documentaries. In an era when numerous talk show hosts aired questionable content and drew ratings from outrageous guests, Oprah committed herself to a quality program, even introducing her own book club to encourage viewers to discover the healing power of reading.
- *John F. Kennedy Jr.* Born just weeks after his father won the 1960 presidential election, John F. Kennedy Jr. seemed destined for great things. Who could forget the playful romping under his father's Oval Office desk or the poignant moment when he saluted his father's coffin the same day he turned three? Although he had little memory of his father's life, John Jr. certainly lived the legacy of the famous Kennedy family. His mother Jacqueline moved him and his sister Caroline to Manhattan for added privacy, and when she later married shipping magnate Aristotle Onassis, the family spent time abroad. Throughout their childhood and despite their name and wealth, however, Jackie strove to keep her children grounded. Still, Kennedy's every move

made headlines, from failing the bar exam to being named *People* magazine's Sexiest Man Alive in 1988. After his mother's passing, he and Caroline remained close, each year presenting the Profile in Courage award at their father's presidential library.

In 1995, Kennedy launched the premiere issue of *George*, his new political magazine. His celebrity status might have helped his publishing efforts, but when he tied the knot with Carolyn Bessette in 1996, the couple kept their nuptials a secret from the roving press. Rumors that he, too, would enter the family business of politics were forever dashed when tragedy struck the Kennedy clan once more. Flying his own plane, a single-engine Piper Saratoga, en route to a cousin's wedding in Massachusetts, Kennedy, his wife, and her sister Lauren plunged into the Atlantic Ocean on July 16, 1999. The National Transportation and Safety Board (NTSB) investigated the accident, finding that Kennedy lost control of the aircraft and suffered from spatial disorientation in hazy and dark conditions. All major news magazines produced memorial editions honoring Kennedy's young life, cut so short. His ashes were buried at sea.

A Presidential Encounter

In 1963, Bill Clinton was elected as an Arkansas delegate to Boys Nation, a government study program for youth in Washington, D.C. While in the nation's capital, he shook the hand of President John F. Kennedy at a White House Rose Garden ceremony. This famous photo was displayed during the Democratic National Convention in 1992 as the party depicted Clinton as the boy from Hope, Arkansas.

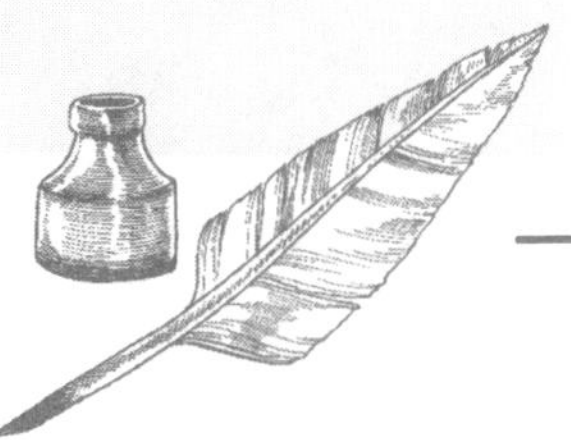

It's the Economy, Stupid

Although George Bush enjoyed a very favorable rating among Americans for his handling of the Persian Gulf Crisis, people were far less accepting of his leadership when it came to the nation's economy. The recession hit American workers and families hard, and President Bush failed to acknowledge this fact and provide solutions. That left someone else to take the lead, and Arkansas Governor William Jefferson "Bill" Clinton stepped into the spotlight, calling himself "a new kind of Democrat."

From the start, Americans appreciated this attitude of being liberal on social issues and conservative on economic matters. Clinton chose Tennessee Senator Al Gore as his running mate. Assembling

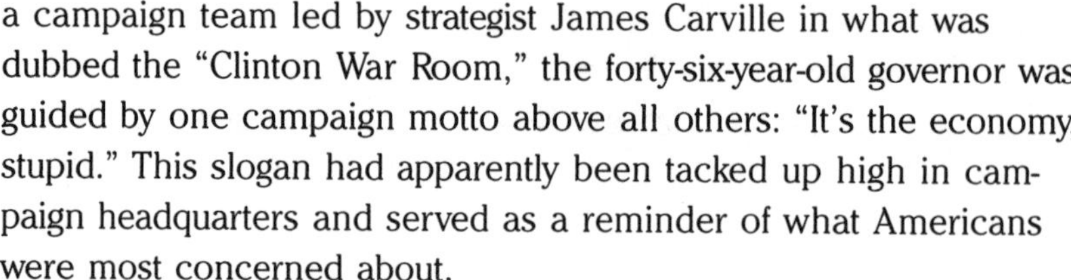

a campaign team led by strategist James Carville in what was dubbed the "Clinton War Room," the forty-six-year-old governor was guided by one campaign motto above all others: "It's the economy, stupid." This slogan had apparently been tacked up high in campaign headquarters and served as a reminder of what Americans were most concerned about.

Clinton dodged allegations of womanizing and dealt with having been in Oxford, England, as a Rhodes Scholar, while his contemporaries were drafted into Vietnam service. He jammed with musicians on late-night talk shows with his saxophone, and used other media opportunities to fullest advantage. Meanwhile, incumbent President George Bush angered people as he abandoned his "Read my lips: No new taxes!" pledge. Ross Perot, the self-made man with billions to spend on his campaign, focused the electorate on the burgeoning federal deficit. His appearance on CNN's *Larry King Live* proved the power of the electronic media in modern-day political campaigns. Had those who voted for the third-party candidate favored the president, Bush would have won in a landslide. But the new kid on the block won this election—Bill Clinton garnered 43 percent of the popular vote and a majority of the Electoral College. It seemed voters had gone for the Clinton/Gore ticket for change.

All's Fair in Love and War

He was a chief strategist for the Clinton campaign, and she was a key player in the Bush camp. Democrat James Carville and Republican Mary Matalin didn't share the same political allegiances, but did indeed date during the 1992 election, and later married. With a collaborator, they wrote *All's Fair: Love, War, and Running for President*.

Clinton's Charm and Early Accomplishments

To win election, Bill Clinton capitalized on a certain charisma he had, being the first of the baby boom generation to be elected to the presidency. He appointed more women and minorities to high government office and cabinet posts than any previous president. Among his appointments were Attorney General Janet Reno, Secretary of Agriculture Mike Espy, Secretary of Commerce Ron Brown, Secretary of Health and Human Services Donna Shalala, and two new Supreme Court justices, Stephen G. Breyer and Ruth Bader Ginsburg. Madeleine Albright became the first female secretary of state during Clinton's second term in office.

The first lady, Hillary Rodham Clinton, took an active role in her husband's administration, spearheading the effort to focus on health care, an issue voters deemed important. Clinton had promised guaranteed health insurance for every American, but the first lady's efforts were stalled by controversy over her role and opposition from those who disliked the federal government's involvement in medical care. Thus, health care reform was never truly accomplished.

Clinton remained popular among women for his advocacy of their concerns. He overturned restrictions on abortions and signed into law a family leave bill requiring companies with more than fifty workers to allow parents up to twelve weeks of unpaid leave a year to cope with family issues. Clinton tackled discrimination against homosexuals in the armed forces with a policy that would become known as "don't ask, don't tell." Thanks to his economic policies and budget packages, the federal deficit shrank. Clinton also saw the passing of the Brady Bill, named for President Reagan's press secretary, James Brady, who was shot in the attempt on Reagan's life. This bill made it more difficult for criminals to purchase handguns.

Victories and Stalemates

Clinton and Congress were successful at passing the presidential line-item veto, which allowed the president to veto individual items on appropriations bills. But this was challenged in court as being unconstitutional. Many measures were halted by the president's veto or threatened veto of Republican initiatives.

Clinton and Congress were unable to reach an agreement on the federal budget for 1996. Debate brewed over how to reform welfare, Medicare, Medicaid, and other programs. The result was two partial shutdowns of the federal government. Finally, Clinton and Congress agreed on budget concessions. Republicans got the spending cuts they wanted, but Clinton managed to maintain

> **Character Questions**
>
> From the start, it seemed that Clinton had well-organized enemies. New questions were posed regarding failed real estate dealings the first couple had been involved with in Arkansas, in the Whitewater Development Corporation. A second scandal faced the president when a woman named Paula Jones, a former Arkansas state employee, filed suit alleging sexual harassment during Clinton's tenure as governor. Contending that a sitting president shouldn't have to be distracted by such litigation, the president's attorneys tried to get the matter thrown out of court. But the U.S. Supreme Court ruled in May 1997 that a sitting president was not exempt from civil lawsuits.

educational and environmental programs that the administration deemed vital. Clinton did sign an increase in the minimum wage, as well as making it easier for workers to transfer from one employer's health insurance to another without losing coverage (even with a pre-existing condition). Clinton also overhauled the welfare program, which had been a 1992 campaign promise. In addition, the president lobbied hard for sweeping trade legislation lowering the barriers to trade with other nations. In doing so, he faced the opposition of many supporters, including trade unions, as they feared American jobs would be lost to a cheaper labor market. But Clinton maintained, despite vigorous debate among the likes of H. Ross Perot, that the North American Free Trade Agreement (NAFTA) was necessary. Clinton persuaded members of his own party to join in the largely Republican-backed legislative vote. The treaty was passed in the House of Representatives in November 1993. In foreign affairs, Clinton helped secure peace in Haiti by reinstating ousted president Jean-Bertrand Aristide.

Terrorism Strikes

Early in the Clinton administration, terrorists struck in the United States. A car bomb left in an underground parking garage exploded in the heart of New York City's financial district in February of 1993. The World Trade Center bombing killed six people, injured more than 1,000 others, and caused around $600 million worth of damage. The next year, four members of a militant Islamic group were convicted in connection with this incident. In another New York case, ten Muslim militants were convicted of conspiring that same year to bomb the United Nations headquarters, two tunnels, and other prominent New York landmarks. Their convictions were handed down in 1995.

Also in 1993, members of a heavily armed religious sect calling themselves the Branch Davidians held a fifty-one-day standoff with law-enforcement officials near Waco, Texas. When negotiations failed and the government lost patience, federal agents stormed the complex, resulting in the death of eighty Branch Davidians and four agents. Attorney General Janet Reno accepted responsibility for giving the go-ahead.

On April 19, 1995, terrorism struck in America's heartland. A blast caused by a huge car bomb blew open one whole side of the Alfred P. Murrah Federal Building in Oklahoma City, killing more than 168 people, at least fifteen of whom were children in day care. It was the worst act of terrorism on U.S. soil. Understandably, it outraged a nation, especially because the act had been committed by an American. The FBI arrested their key suspect, twenty-seven-year-old Timothy McVeigh, who harbored a far-right political agenda and alliances to paramilitary groups. Terry Nichols was also charged in the crime. Believers in this extremist group encouraged others to stockpile weapons, for they feared the government was plotting to take away their rights.

During the 1996 Summer Olympics held in Atlanta, Georgia, a pipe bomb exploded in an outdoor park. Also in 1996, the FBI finally caught up to a mail bomber, Ted Kaczynski, in the back woods of Montana. Authorities had been chasing after the "Unabomber" for twenty years.

Though Clinton had to work with a Republican Congress, he was able to pass legislation to help combat terrorism, making it easier to deport foreigners suspected of terrorist activities.

Congressman and Author Gore

As a member of Congress, Al Gore earned a reputation for his stand on environmental issues, pioneering efforts to clean up hazardous waste dumps and prevent depletion of the earth's ozone layer. He wrote *Earth in the Balance: Ecology and the Human Spirit*, published in 1992.

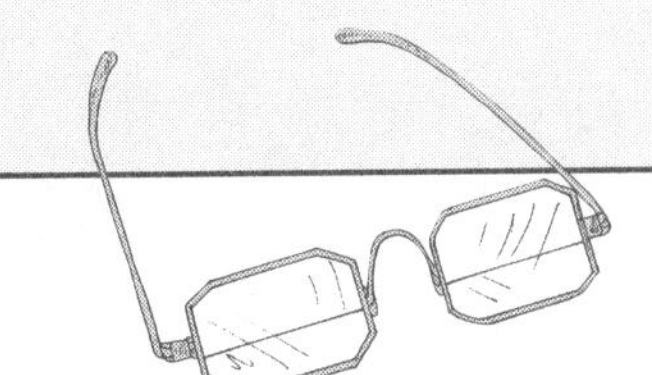

The 1996 Election

Though Clinton's popularity suffered during the first two years of his first term, it rebounded, especially after the government shutdowns and budget debates. Once again, Bill Clinton lived up to his nickname of "the comeback kid."

Approaching the election, the president proved that he could enact more moderate measures, achieving some of the goals he set initially and proving to others that he was the "new Democrat" he claimed to be. Clinton easily won a second term against Republican Senator Bob Dole despite the controversy over lingering investigations. Dole was a World War II hero, with a message that perhaps rang true to older generations—but with the economy moving along,

Americans felt prosperous and content. It appeared that Clinton's personal peccadilloes mattered less than his leadership.

Second Administration

Clinton's second term was markedly marred by scandal. In the spring of 1999, the Paula Jones case finally reached an $850,000 settlement, with Ms. Jones's attorneys collecting much of the money. In her lawsuit, Paula Jones claimed that President Clinton, then Governor Clinton, made sexual advances toward her in a Little Rock, Arkansas, hotel room in 1991. Clinton steadfastly denied the accusation. Although the case had been dismissed, it was in the appeals process at the time Clinton and Ms. Jones reached a settlement. Jones's credibility was called into question years later when she posed nude for a magazine, weakening her claim that she despised the media attention she had received.

During a deposition in the Paula Jones case, however, Clinton had testified that he had not had a relationship with a former White House intern named Monica Lewinsky. Ms. Lewinsky had begun work at the White House in June 1995, later becoming a salaried employee in the White House Office of Legislative Affairs. Unfortunately for the president, she spoke rather freely with a friend named Linda Tripp, a government civil servant, who quietly taped their assorted (and sometimes sordid) telephone conversations. Lewinsky told Tripp of her trysts with the president in the Oval Office, sometimes in gossipy, graphic detail.

Inauguration Firsts

Though Inauguration Day is steeped in tradition, there have been many "firsts" throughout the years. Herbert Hoover was the first to have his inauguration captured on "talking newsreel," while Harry Truman's was the first televised inauguration. And Bill Clinton was the first president to have his ceremony broadcast live over the Internet.

Problems Escalate

No longer an intern or government employee, Lewinsky became a magnet for the curious media. The Clinton–Lewinsky extramarital affair was exposed by Kenneth Starr, the independent counsel originally hired to investigate the Whitewater matter. But that investigation moved in convoluted directions, as some say his motives were purely political and that he had clients directly opposed to the Clinton administration. Indeed the White House called his attacks and probing "fishing expeditions."

When the independent counsel released *The Starr Report*, Americans read excerpts in newspapers and magazines and could go online to devour the steamy details of Oval Office sexual encounters. What made matters worse was that Clinton originally and very publicly denied the charges. He said, pointing a finger at his accusers, "I did not have sexual relations with that woman, Miss Lewinsky." But as the scandal unfolded and the president gave sworn testimony in August 1998, he eventually had to admit to having had an "inappropriate relationship" with her. Defending his earlier comments, he split hairs over the definition of sexual relations as he understood the term to be defined at his deposition. Overall, Americans soon became disgusted at the drama, which read worse than a trashy novel, but they couldn't let go of the sexual intrigue. The matter almost cost Bill Clinton his presidency.

Because Clinton had given false statements under oath, impeachment proceedings began in the House of Representatives (with a vote that was largely split among party lines), followed by a trial in the Senate in 1999. Clinton became known in the history books as the second president ever to be impeached. He was acquitted in his Senate trial, and so was not removed from office.

Everyone's Surfing

In the 1990s, the Information Superhighway got average Americans surfing the Net. Actually, the Internet was developed in 1969 by the defense department, military, and universities to link up computers in remote areas. But in the 1990s, almost every government agency and private enterprise started a site on the World Wide Web. "Dot.com" stocks soared in the midst of the frenzy.

What Was America Coming To?

During the 1990s, America witnessed the age of celebrity. It seemed that if you could make a name for yourself—whether it be as an Olympic champion or prime athlete, a television talk show host or box-office favorite, or even a jilted lover or victim of a horrendous crime—you could cash in on that celebrity status. A world of opportunities remained open to you. Among the favorites were teen heartthrobs such as Leonardo DiCaprio, star of the movie *Titanic*, which became the biggest box-office hit in history and grossed more than $1 billion. Basketball player Michael Jordan excelled not only on the court but in commercials as well, appearing as the spokesperson for dozens of companies. Musicians such as Madonna took control

of their careers, and their hits catapulted to the top of the record charts.

There were some tragic events as well. Throughout the decade, schools increasingly became the scene for angry assaults, mostly at the hands of troubled youth. In towns such as Paducah, Kentucky; Pearl, Mississippi; Edinboro, Pennsylvania; and Springfield, Oregon teenage boys targeted classmates, teachers, even their own parents in some cases with gunfire. The worst of these incidents occurred in April 1999 as two young men tossed homemade bombs and fired bullets throughout Columbine High School in Littleton, Colorado. The rampage left twelve young people and one teacher dead, with many others injured, both physically and psychologically.

"All of us are struggling to understand exactly what happened and why," said President Clinton of the Colorado incident. Legislators, educators, and parents called on the entertainment industry to become more responsible with their material aimed at children. It became overwhelmingly clear that many troubled youth had easy access to weapons, found potentially lethal information such as how to make pipe bombs on the Internet, and enjoyed violent themes in the music they listened to or the films they viewed.

Millennium Madness

As the year 2000 approached, everyone wondered if the turn of the century would bring with it massive infrastructure problems. Computers and computer software, the mainstay of most business, government, military, and nonprofit operations, had to be retooled for the new century. People feared that when the clock struck midnight, computer systems would fail to recognize the "00" and create havoc worldwide. Banking establishments, utilities, government, and other entities spent millions of dollars during the later part of the 1990s preparing for "Y2K." Consumers reacted either nonchalantly or in a quasi-hysterical mode, stocking up on canned goods and batteries and fresh water supplies, withdrawing money in advance from automated teller machines, and filling their bathtubs with water

he Newseum

o
their
r
eum
e
nes
s
tors
rters
those
.
e of
tage
from
first
ol-
Vall
born
n will
mo-
ed into

In the Interactive Newsroom, you can test your skill as an investigative reporter, make tough front-page calls that editors routinely face, and ponder the ethical choices journalists encounter in newsrooms every day. Along the 126-foot-long Video News Wall, you can experience breaking news where technology has made its global reach possible. The News Gallery features real-time news feeds, Associated Press headlines and photos, and the daily front pages from newspapers around the world. Journalism books, framed magazine covers, news-related games, apparel, and other merchandise are stocked in the Newseum Store. Public programs and changing exhibits are offered in Arlington and also at the Newseum/NY, a gallery space in the heart of Manhattan. Admission is free of charge at both locations. Contact (703) 284-3544 or (212) 317-7596 or go online at *www.newseum.org*.

in case faucets failed to work. Employers demanded that key management and support staffs work the night of December 31, 1999, or at the very least, remain on call.

Yet as the world celebrated a New Year's Eve like no other—with massive parties, fireworks displays, and galas—it appeared that most of the preplanning had paid off. Y2K-compliant institutions far outnumbered the few that experienced glitches. There was no havoc in the headlines. It was just another new year, only this time ushering in a new century and relegating the 1900s to history.

In honor of the new millennium, OpSail 2000 attracted curious onlookers and sea-loving fans of the tall ships. The official ports for the ships included San Juan, Puerto Rico; Miami, Florida; Hampton Roads, Virginia; Baltimore, Maryland; Philadelphia, Pennsylvania; New York, New York; New London, Connecticut; and Portland, Maine. The official national celebration occurred in New York Harbor during the July 4th weekend.

This was dubbed the "greatest event in maritime history"; the last time the tall ships had assembled together was for the Bicentennial celebration in 1976. Operation Sail was founded by President John F. Kennedy, who said in 1962, "The sight of so many ships gathered from distant corners of the world for Operation Sail should remind us that strong, disciplined, and adventuresome men still can find their way safely across uncertain and stormy seas." Of course, Kennedy, being a naval hero, was a little partial to those who plied the seas!

Capitol Explorations

If you're in Washington, D.C., don't miss visiting the U.S. Capitol. The original structure was designed by Dr. William Thornton, and the cornerstone laid by President George Washington on September 18, 1793. Benjamin Henry Latrobe and Charles Bulfinch, among other architects, directed its early construction. Many changes have occurred over the years, and you can see models and learn more about construction details with the self-guided tours, available seven days a week. And if you'd like to see the House or the Senate in session, do ask your representative or senator for passes to the visitor's gallery. For more information, call (202) 225-6827.

The 2000 Elections

As President Clinton began reflecting on his eight years in office, his wife Hillary Rodham Clinton declared her candidacy for a seat in the U.S. Senate representing the state of New York. Some called her a long shot and a carpetbagger, since she'd established residency with the sole purpose of entering the Senate race. But on November 7, 2000, she prevailed.

The outcome of the presidential contest was less certain. Democratic Vice President Al Gore ran against Republican Texas

Governor George W. Bush, son of the former president. Even before the election, with polls so very close that analysts couldn't make accurate predictions, some were remembering earlier presidential elections such as the 1888 race between Grover Cleveland, who won the popular vote, and Benjamin Harrison, who prevailed in the Electoral College. In order to win the presidency, a candidate must garner at least 270 electoral votes.

No analyst or pundit could have predicted the odd outcome on election night. Television networks were far too quick to call the race. Early in the evening, it appeared Vice President Gore was leading in electoral votes, but this margin later slipped. In the wee hours of the morning, the television networks called George W. Bush the winner, and Gore even telephoned him to concede the race. A short time later, Gore learned that the race was too close to call in the state of Florida. He telephoned Bush again and revoked his concession.

All eyes fell on Florida's twenty-five electoral votes, for they would decide the next president. Never before in American history was an election undecided for days and weeks after voters had gone to the polls. It appeared that Gore had more popular votes and Bush more electoral ones (he had 271 of the 270 required if he carried Florida).

However, the matter grew more complex in the "sunshine state." Everything from absentee ballots and ballot design in certain Florida counties to the way in which the ballots were punched and counted came under the microscope, with each side engaging attorneys to urge or fight a potential recount. Interestingly enough, Jeb Bush, brother of George W. Bush, was Florida's governor. Everyone questioned the media's integrity for predicting results too quickly.

Florida's supreme court as well as the U.S. Supreme Court heard arguments in the matter, which headline after headline dubbed "the Florida recount." There was even talk of amending the Constitution to do away with the Electoral College in future years. But those in favor of keeping it claimed that this system of electing presidents had worked for more than 200 years, and that the Electoral College ensured that less populated states had a voice in an election's ultimate outcome. Without the Electoral College, candi-

Grave Matters

Looking for a famous or historical gravesite? Try these resources. *Who's Buried in Grant's Tomb? A Tour of Presidential Gravesites* by Brian Lamb and the C-SPAN staff is a book providing tombstone locations of many presidents. It also lists presidential libraries and a bit of each president's legacy. It's available by calling (877) ON-C-SPAN or at *www.c-spanstore.com*. In addition, visit *www.findagrave.com*.

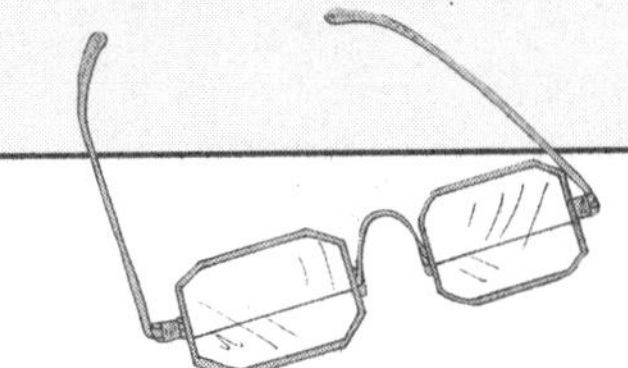

dates would concentrate on the states where the majority of citizens lived, and might forget about campaigning in and addressing the needs of the rest. Still, those who maintain that everyone's vote should count may yet bring forward the idea of amending the U.S. Constitution.

On December 12, 2000—the deadline for Florida to certify its twenty-five electors—the U.S. Supreme Court, in a 5–4 ruling, declared that there could be no further recounting of the disputed Florida votes. This essentially handed the election to George W. Bush. Vice President Al Gore, in an address to the American people, graciously conceded the race while holding firm to his belief that every vote should have been counted. He also pledged his support to the incoming administration.

Appendix I

Presidents and Vice Presidents of the United States

	President	Term	Vice President
1.	George Washington	1789–1797	John Adams
2.	John Adams	1797–1801	Thomas Jefferson
3.	Thomas Jefferson	1801–1809	Aaron Burr; George Clinton
4.	James Madison	1809–1817	George Clinton; Elbridge Gerry
5.	James Monroe	1817–1825	Daniel D. Tompkins
6.	John Quincy Adams	1825–1829	John C. Calhoun
7.	Andrew Jackson	1829–1837	John C. Calhoun; Martin Van Buren
8.	Martin Van Buren	1837–1841	Richard M. Johnson
9.	William Henry Harrison	1841	John Tyler
10.	John Tyler	1841–1845	(no vice president)
11.	James Knox Polk	1845–1849	George M. Dallas
12.	Zachary Taylor	1849–1850	Millard Fillmore
13.	Millard Fillmore	1850–1853	(no vice president)
14.	Franklin Pierce	1853–1857	William R. King
15.	James Buchanan	1857–1861	John C. Breckinridge
16.	Abraham Lincoln	1861–1865	Hannibal Hamlin; Andrew Johnson
17.	Andrew Johnson	1865–1869	(no vice president)
18.	Ulysses S. Grant	1869–1877	Schuyler Colfax; Henry Wilson
19.	Rutherford B. Hayes	1877–1881	William A. Wheeler
20.	James A. Garfield	1881	Chester A. Arthur
21.	Chester A. Arthur	1881–1885	(no vice president)
22.	Grover Cleveland	1885–1889	Thomas A. Hendricks
23.	Benjamin Harrison	1889–1893	Levi P. Morton

	President	Term	Vice President
24.	Grover Cleveland	1893–1897	Adlai E. Stevenson
25.	William McKinley	1897–1901	Garret A. Hobart; Theodore Roosevelt
26.	Theodore Roosevelt	1901–1909	Charles W. Fairbanks
27.	William Howard Taft	1909–1913	James S. Sherman
28.	Woodrow Wilson	1913–1921	Thomas R. Marshall
29.	Warren G. Harding	1921–1923	Calvin Coolidge
30.	Calvin Coolidge	1923–1929	Charles G. Dawes
31.	Herbert C. Hoover	1929–1933	Charles Curtis
32.	Franklin Roosevelt	1933–1945	John Garner; Henry Wallace; Harry Truman
33.	Harry S. Truman	1945–1953	Alben W. Barkley
34.	Dwight Eisenhower	1953–1961	Richard M. Nixon
35.	John F. Kennedy	1961–1963	Lyndon B. Johnson
36.	Lyndon B. Johnson	1963–1969	Hubert H. Humphrey
37.	Richard M. Nixon	1969–1974	Spiro T. Agnew; Gerald R. Ford
38.	Gerald R. Ford	1974–1977	Nelson A. Rockefeller
39.	Jimmy Carter	1977–1981	Walter F. Mondale
40.	Ronald Reagan	1981–1989	George H. W. Bush
41.	George H. W. Bush	1989–1993	Dan Quayle
42.	William Jefferson Clinton	1993–2001	Albert Gore
43.	George W. Bush	2001–	Richard B. Cheney

Appendix II

First Ladies and Official White House Hostesses

Martha Dandridge Custis Washington

Having married a planter, Martha Dandridge Custis was mother to four children, two of whom died in infancy. Widowed at age twenty-five, Martha ran the plantation and eventually caught men's eyes, including George Washingon's. Though they had no children together, Colonel Washington helped raise John Parke and Martha Parke Custis. During the harsh winter at Valley Forge, Martha Washington patched soldiers' clothing and knitted socks. The Revolution won, she recognized their responsibility to the nation, and though she disliked New York and Philadelphia, she graciously relocated to assume official duties as our nation's first lady. The couple retired to Mount Vernon for only a few short years before Washington succumbed to a fatal infection, and his wife passed away a few years later. They're buried next to one another at the Virginia estate.

Abigail Smith Adams

As her husband John joined the American resistance, Abigail tended to their four children, Abigail, John Quincy, Charles, and Thomas, having lost another child in infancy. Mrs. Adams also ran their farm in Braintree (now Quincy), Massachusetts. She wrote to John when he served in both Continental Congresses. Her ideas were well ahead of their time: she urged women's property rights and the rights of slaves. (As wives throughout history can attest, however, Abigail's husband didn't take her advice, either!) John Adams was elected president in 1796, and they became the first couple to inhabit the White House. President Adams asked for her advice on speeches, and she promoted his administration with newspaper editors. When Adams lost reelection, they retired to their farm and are buried together in Massachusetts. She never lived to see her son assume the presidency himself.

Martha Wayles Skelton Jefferson

When she married Thomas Jefferson on New Year's Day 1772, Martha Wayles had an estate of her own near Williamsburg, Virginia. She was said to be beautiful, but no pictures of her have survived. Life together with her husband at Monticello, their mountaintop estate near Charlottesville, was happy, but giving birth to six children strained her health as much as living through six years of the Revolution in which she and the children twice had to flee. Martha died following a lingering illness in 1782, and the bereaved Jefferson never remarried. By the time he ascended to the presidency, he'd been a widower for nineteen years. Needing a hostess, he often asked Dolley Madison, wife of his secretary of state, to preside at dinners, and his daughter Martha Randolph also filled in. Martha's son James Madison Randolph was the first child born in the White House.

Dolley Payne Todd Madison

Congressman James Madison married the young widow, who had one surviving child from her previous marriage. In 1801, the couple moved to Washington, D.C., the new capital, where James became secretary of state, and Dolley threw stylish parties at the White House for the widowed President Thomas Jefferson. She never took much interest in politics, but campaigned for her husband and became fiercely patriotic during the War of 1812. When forced to evacuate, she took time to assemble her husband's papers and historic valuables (including the famous Gilbert Stuart portrait of George Washington that today hangs in the National Portrait Gallery at the Smithsonian). She barely made it out ahead of the British troops, who burned the city. After Madison's death during retirement, she had to sell their Virginia estate to pay off her son's debts. Though poor, Dolley Madison was well respected, and she was awarded a small pension that enabled her to live in Washington, D.C., until her death at age eighty-one.

Elizabeth Kortright Monroe

A bride to James Monroe when she was not quite eighteen years old, Elizabeth had two daughters and a son who died as a baby. She accompanied her husband to France where the French style suited her polished tastes. Our country remained quite popular there, and Mrs. Monroe was dubbed "La Belle Américaine." During the French Revolution, she became a heroine for saving the life of Madame de Lafayette, wife of the Marquis who had aided the United States during the American Revolution. Her simple visit to the prison on execution day spared the Madame's life. In her White House years, Elizabeth imported elegant French furnishings and ended the custom of riding around Washington, D.C., in her carriage to leave a calling card, something congressional wives expected. The nation had grown and so, too, had the first lady's responsibilities. Some snubbed her invitations to the White House as a result. Elizabeth Monroe died in retirement at the couple's Oak Hill, Virginia, estate.

Louisa Johnson Adams

She met the young diplomat in London in 1795, and they were married two years later. Between her living abroad with parents, then her husband's appointment as the U.S. minister to Berlin, Louisa was well traveled and well educated. After moving to the United States, the couple took another appointment in Russia, where Louisa lived unhappily. It's said that John Quincy Adams was a bit cold to his wife, and they quarreled frequently. As the tensions eased, their marriage improved, and in 1824 she helped in her husband's presidential race.

Rachel Donelson Robards Jackson

Having survived a bad first marriage and weathered a divorce, Rachel Robards married Andrew Jackson, who had rented a room in her mother's boardinghouse when they first met. However, there must have been some confusion regarding her divorce decree, because two years later, the Jacksons realized Rachel's divorce was only now final. The couple exchanged vows again. They had no children of their own, but adopted a nephew, naming him Andrew Jackson Jr. While Andrew Sr. traveled, the couple exchanged passionate letters in which Rachel urged him to leave public service. It was devastating when, in the midst of his presidential campaign, his detractors dug up the scandal of her divorce and their marriage, dubbing Rachel an adulteress. (No doubt these were the early roots of tabloid journalism affecting the political scene!) Fortunately, Rachel didn't realize the full extent of the barbs until after the election. Shortly after learning of them, however, she fell ill. She died just days before Christmas 1828. The weeping widower, Andrew Jackson, greeted thousands of mourners at her funeral that Christmas Eve. He long believed that his political enemies killed his wife with their slander.

Hannah Hoes Van Buren

Hannah Hoes and Martin Van Buren grew up as distant cousins in the tiny Dutch village of Kinderhook, New York. They married when she was twenty-three and he twenty-four, and spoke Dutch as well as English in their home. The Van Burens had five sons, one of whom passed away as a baby. Hannah taught street people to read, and before she died of tuberculosis in February 1819, she asked that the money that would ordinarily be spent for her funeral be given to the poor instead. Martin Van Buren never remarried, and when he moved into the White House in 1837, his four grown sons moved in with him. Dolley Madison soon introduced her cousin Angelica to Abraham, the eldest son, who was smitten. They married in 1838, and Angelica served as the president's elegant hostess.

Anna Tuthill Symmes Harrison

Born the year the American Revolution broke out, Anna's mother died shortly after she was born. Years later, disguised as a Redcoat, her father smuggled Anna across British lines to live with her well-to-do grandparents on Long Island. She received an excellent education in New York schools, but left the more refined life for frontier country in North Bend, along the Ohio River, to be with her father.

While visiting her older sister in Kentucky, Anna met Lt. William Henry Harrison, whom she secretly married in 1795. The Harrisons had ten children, one of whom didn't survive. Five were born during Harrison's tenure as governor of the Indiana territory. At the outbreak of the War of 1812, Anna and the children moved back to North Bend, where they remained until her husband was elected president in 1840. She'd fallen ill that winter and didn't accompany him to his inauguration the next spring. As she prepared to join him, Anna received the dreadful news of her husband's death from pneumonia. She lived until 1864 as a devoted mother and grandmother, and was buried next to her husband at North Bend.

Letitia Christian Tyler

Born at her family's plantation near Richmond, Virginia, she grew up a devout Episcopalian. Her engagement to John Tyler lasted five years, during which he wrote her elaborate love letters while he was in law school. The couple had seven children survive to adulthood. Though her wealthy background of social privilege served her husband's political career well, she avoided the public spotlight. She became increasingly religious, shunned the nation's capital for all but one visit (while Tyler was a senator from Virginia), and in 1838 suffered a paralyzing stroke. From then on, her health confined her to home. After John Tyler was sworn in following Harrison's short-lived presidency and death, Mrs. Tyler finally came to Washington, D.C., but never took on the White House hostess duties. Instead her daughter-in-law Priscilla handled the task with poise. Letitia managed the home from the family quarters, but only for a daughter's wedding did she venture downstairs. Letitia Tyler died of another stroke in 1842.

Julia Gardiner Tyler

John Tyler, having mourned the loss of Letitia, fell in love with Julia Gardiner when he met her in Washington, D.C. It wasn't exactly love at first sight for her, however. But when he comforted her upon her father's death in 1844, she too fell in love, and the couple was married that year in New York City. This was the first president to be married while in office, so public excitement ran high. Tyler's sons readily accepted their new stepmother, but his daughters weren't nearly as understanding. Perhaps it was because the new Mrs. Tyler was thirty years younger than her husband. Still, Julia managed to dazzle others with her social grace. In 1845, the Tylers retired to Sherwood Forest, their Virginia plantation. In 1862, Tyler went to Richmond to serve in the Confederate Congress, but soon after that, he died of a stroke. Because of her southern sympathies, Julia Tyler was estranged from her relatives, though she moved back to New York. Impoverished by the depression of the 1870s, Mrs. Tyler applied for a pension as widow of a president, but it wasn't granted until 1880. After living in Virginia for the remainder of her life, she died in 1889 and is buried next to her husband.

Sarah Childress Polk

Always fascinated by politics, Sarah met James Knox Polk, an ambitious young lawyer, in 1821. He proposed to her two years later at the urging of Andrew Jackson, who thought her perfect for him. They married on New Year's Day in 1824. She encouraged him to run for Congress, and moved with excitement to Washington, D.C. Since they had no children, Sarah devoted herself to her husband's political rise by serving as his secretary, campaign manager, and ultimately first lady. On what was supposed to be a trip for rest, Polk caught cholera and died in 1849. Sarah turned their Nashville, Tennessee, mansion into a museum for her late husband. When she died at age eighty-seven, she was buried next to him.

Margaret Mackall Smith Taylor

Margaret met Zachary Taylor when he was a lieutenant home on leave in Tennessee, and they married one year later. The irony of her married life was that having been brought up to be refined and proper, she followed Zachary without complaint from fort to frontier, living in tents and log cabins, encouraging other soldier's wives. She had six children (though two daughters died), and her health suffered. In another irony, the couple's daughter Sarah eloped with Lt. Jefferson Davis (future president of the Confederacy), who served under her father. Zachary Taylor was a Mexican War hero, and he won the White House, which haunted Margaret. She dreaded the public nature of her new role, and so she asked others to perform hostess duties. After laying the cornerstone of the Washington Monument on July 4, 1850, President Taylor fell seriously ill, passing away in office days later. Distraught, Margaret left Washington for her daughter's home in Mississippi and died two years later.

Abigail Powers Fillmore

Left without a father (who died soon after her birth), Abigail was home schooled. When she became a teacher herself, she met Millard Fillmore, two years younger. They respected each other tremendously and were engaged for eight years, through his law education and bar exams. She taught until their son Millard Powers Fillmore was born, making her the first first lady who had held a job before marriage. A daughter Mary Abigail was born, and soon Fillmore went to serve in Congress. He was elected vice president, then sworn in upon Taylor's death. Abigail also disdained the social responsibilities and gladly handed this role over to her daughter, nicknamed "Abby." Loving books as she did, Abigail petitioned her husband and Congress for a library in the Oval Room of the White House. Had Millard Fillmore taken his wife's advice not to sign the Fugitive Slave Act, he might have had a shot at re-election. That cold March day when she watched Franklin Pierce at his inauguration, Abigail caught pneumonia. She died a few weeks later.

Jane Appleton Pierce

At age thirteen, Jane lost her father, and her mother took her to live with wealthy grandparents in New Hampshire. She met Franklin Pierce in 1826 while he was a law student with political ambitions. They were engaged for eight years, and with his subsequent role in Congress, the couple spent much time apart. Their first two children died, and Jane dedicated herself to raising their son Benjamin. When Pierce ran for president, both mother and son lacked enthusiasm for his campaign. In a tragic accident, eleven-year-old Bennie was killed by a train. Mrs. Pierce never quite recovered emotionally from the loss, and she died of tuberculosis in 1863. Jane was buried near Bennie's grave in Concord, New Hampshire.

Harriet Lane Johnston

Born to a prosperous merchant and his wife, Harriet Lane was orphaned at age eleven, and her favorite uncle James Buchanan became her guardian, overseeing her education in Georgetown. He became James Polk's secretary of state and proudly introduced Harriet to Washington society. When James Buchanan traveled to London, Queen Victoria took a liking to his charming niece. With many male eyes cast on her, Harriet remained a level-headed young lady. When her uncle became president in 1857, the only president never to marry, the twenty-six-year-old Harriet moved to the White House to take on the role of official hostess. With sentiment running strong between northern and southern factions, it took all the social aplomb she could muster. She often had to seat enemies apart at important dinners. But as his term ended, James Buchanan retired thankfully to his estate near Lancaster, Pennsylvania. As she approached age thirty-six, Harriet married Baltimore banker Henry Elliott Johnston.

Mary Todd Lincoln

Mary Todd's mother passed away when Mary was six. Mary was raised by her father and stepmother in Kentucky, where she attended fine schools. She lived for a while with her married sister in Springfield, Illinois. There, at a dance, Mary met the tall, gangly-looking Abraham Lincoln. Though her family didn't deem Lincoln worthy of their daughter, the couple was powerfully attracted to one another. Even then, the idea that opposites attracted proved to be very real. The two dated several years before tying the knot in 1842. They settled in Springfield for Abe to practice law, and they had four sons. Mary was always lively but sometimes prone to irrational fears and bursts of anger.

She encouraged her husband to run for Congress and weathered his unsuccessful bids for the Senate. Finally, in 1860, with the country on the verge of civil war, Lincoln won the presidency. Mary was ridiculed for refurbishing the mansion and because her half-brothers fought for the Confederacy. When her eleven-year-old son Willie died of typhoid fever in 1862, an inconsolable Mary went insane. She feared son Robert would die in the war, but he was given a secure post. Just when the war was won and the family's luck seemed to improve, Mary watched as her husband was felled by an assassin's bullet. He was carried out of Ford's Theatre to a nearby home, where he died the next day. Too distraught to attend his funeral, she lay in bed for weeks. She feared poverty, as her debts were substantial. When son Tad died at eighteen of tuberculosis, her mental health faltered further, to the point that her remaining son Robert committed her to a hospital in 1875 (though she managed to get herself released). In 1882, she died at her sister's house in Springfield, Illinois, and is buried next to Lincoln in the Oak Ridge Cemetery.

Eliza McCardle Johnson

An only child brought up by her mother after her father's passing, Eliza met Andrew Johnson when he first came to Greeneville, Tennessee, as a struggling tailor's apprentice. They must have each been smitten, as they married in no time at all. Interestingly enough, Eliza taught Andrew how to read and tutored the future president in math as well. They had five children. With her encouragement, Andrew ran for mayor, then a U.S. Senate seat. When Jefferson Davis ordered Union supporters out of Confederate Greeneville, Eliza, already sick with tuberculosis, worsened. Her husband assumed the presidency upon Lincoln's death. She quietly lived at the White House, but her daughter, Martha Johnson Patterson, served as hostess. Having stood by her husband during his Senate impeachment trial, she reportedly exclaimed, "I knew it!" upon hearing of his acquittal. The Johnsons moved to Greeneville following his presidency, but retirement was short-lived, as Andrew Johnson was elected to the Senate and returned to Washington, overcoming the disgrace of impeachment. Sadly, he died of a stroke the following year, and Eliza survived him by about six months, finally succumbing to tuberculosis.

Julia Dent Grant

Born in St. Louis, the fun-loving Julia attended boarding school, where her personality attracted the attention of her brother's West Point classmate, Ulysses S. Grant. Neither the Dent family nor the Grants approved of the marriage; her parents thought he was too poor, and her family owned slaves. Despite these objections, the couple married in 1848 after a four-year engagement. The Grants didn't attend the wedding but grew to accept their daughter-in-law, whose position on slavery differed from her father's. Julia followed her new husband to military posts and lived with her family while he served out West. They had four children, survived business failures, and made it through his tenure commanding the Union Army. She was much praised as first lady, even hosting a White House wedding for their daughter, Nellie. Mrs. Grant was disappointed when Ulysses opted not to seek a third term, but a world tour mended that in 1877. They lived quietly until financial problems worsened and her husband was diagnosed with throat cancer. He died in July 1885, and Julia was overcome with sorrow. Ironically, though, the former general and Civil War hero had penned a bestselling book, which left her financially secure. Julia settled in Washington, D.C., with her children and grandchildren, writing her own memoirs until her death in 1902. The Grants are buried together in an imposing mausoleum in New York City's Upper West Side.

Lucy Ware Webb Hayes

Though her father died when she was two, Lucy received a fine education and graduated from the Wesleyan Female College in Cincinnati, Ohio. While a student, she met Rutherford B. Hayes, and when he moved to Cincinnati, they spent more time together. On December 30, 1852, they married. Prior to becoming a bride, Lucy was all for women's rights, but after their nuptials, marriage moderated her view to suit his, that hearth and home were the correct responsibilities for a wife. However, her determined antislavery sentiment was strong enough to sway her husband's position. Lucy bore eight children, though three died in infancy. During the Civil War, she visited her husband and the soldiers in his command to tend the sick and dying. When she was White House hostess, some complained about the lack of alcohol, but her stance made her a heroine of the Women's Christian Temperance Union. However, she disappointed Susan B. Anthony and Elizabeth Cady Stanton by not supporting a bill allowing female attorneys to appear before the U.S. Supreme Court. This surprised them because she was the first college graduate to serve as first lady. In 1881, the Hayses retired to Ohio for church activities, travel, and grandchildren. Eight years later, Lucy died of a stroke.

Lucretia Rudolph Garfield

James Garfield attended school with Lucretia, and as they recognized their different traits early, they weren't as sure as some couples that opposites attracted. He was social while she more reserved. They were both members of the Disciples of Christ Church, and they shared an enjoyment of lectures and concerts. In 1858 they married, symbolically committing to their love, though during his years of military service away from home they might have doubted each other's devotion. At times their relationship seems tested and uncertain. Once their separation ended, Garfield was elected to Congress, and they were busy with five children (three others did not survive). Like Mrs. Hayes, she changed her views on women's equality after marriage, no longer favoring a woman's right to vote. She was elated to see her husband achieve high office, but a few weeks after his inauguration, she fell ill with malaria. As she recuperated at a resort in July 1881, she learned that an assassin (Charles Guiteau) had shot her husband. Rushing home, she tried to nurse him back to health, but President Garfield died that September. Lucretia retired to preserve the president's records and watch her grandchildren. In 1918, she passed away in California, but is buried with her husband in Cleveland, Ohio.

Ellen Lewis Herndon Arthur

Ellen Herndon was born into a southern family where her father was a naval officer. "Nell," as they called her, moved with them to Washington, D.C., where her father helped to establish the Naval Observatory. When she was in New York in 1856, Nell met a tall lawyer named Chester Arthur, after an introduction from her cousin. They fell in love, and when Nell's father passed away in 1857, Chester Arthur helped the family through their crisis and in particular with her mother's financial affairs. In October 1859, the couple was married in Calvary Episcopal Church in New York City. As in many families, relations were strained during the Civil War: the Herndons supported the Confederate cause, while Arthur sympathized with the Union and served in the New York militia. But he helped his wife's family whenever possible. After the war, Arthur's law practice thrived, and in President Grant's administration, he was the collector of the port of New York. With their two children, they lived lavishly. But during the Hayes administration, Arthur was accused of corruption and relieved of his post, though he soon recovered politically. Ten months before Chester Arthur was elected vice president in November 1880, his wife caught pneumonia, and she died in January 1881 at the age of forty-two. It's said he missed her so much that he had flowers placed daily next to her photograph. He assumed the presidency upon Garfield's death, and despite his mourning for Nell, he entertained with elegance: his youngest sister Mary McElroy served as his hostess during his White House tenure. By the time he left office, he, too, was seriously ill (with a kidney ailment). Chester Arthur died in November 1886 in New York City and is buried next to his beloved wife in Albany, New York.

Frances Folsom Cleveland

Frances Folsom had known Grover Cleveland, her father's law partner, since her childhood. When Frances was only eleven, her father died, leaving Cleveland the administrator of his estate and the unofficial guardian to Frances. As she went off to college, Cleveland wrote to her and sent her flowers, and they fell in love. However, he waited to propose until after she finished her schooling and he was president. Many suspected that the president was planning to be married, but most figured that the bride-to-be was his partner's widow, not the daughter! Cleveland has the distinction of being the only president to be married in the White House. Only a few guests, mostly his cabinet members, were in attendance.

Frances Cleveland, at twenty-one, was the youngest first lady. The couple had five children, including the first child born to a president in the White House (Thomas Jefferson's grandson was the first born in the mansion). The Baby Ruth candy bar is reportedly named after one of the Cleveland daughters. In 1897, when Cleveland's second term in office was up, the couple retired to Princeton, New Jersey, where he became a trustee at the university. But then his health failed him, landing him in bed for weeks at a time with rheumatism. In 1904, their twelve-year-old daughter Ruth died of diphtheria, and then, four years later, the former president died of a heart attack. Having stayed on in Princeton, Mrs. Cleveland married Thomas J. Preston Jr., a professor of archeology, five years later. At the age of eighty-three, she passed away in her sleep and is buried next to President Cleveland in Princeton.

Caroline Scott Harrison

A well-educated, very talented young lady, Caroline (Carrie) Lavinia Scott met Ben Harrison when she was seventeen. Harrison was a student of her father, a Presbyterian minister. Secretly engaged at first, they married in October 1853, sooner than each had anticipated. To save money, they lived on her father's farm while Ben finished his law studies in Oxford, Ohio. Moving on to Indianapolis, Indiana,

Ben Harrison built a law practice while Carrie tended to their two children. During the Civil War, the couple was separated while he served in the Union Army. In 1881, Harrison began serving as a U.S. senator. When her husband was inaugurated as president in 1889, Mrs. Harrison was excited about her new role. She wanted to enlarge the White House a bit, but settled for some improvements authorized by Congress. Still, the Harrisons shunned electric lights, a little wary of the new invention. Carrie helped found the Daughters of the American Revolution (DAR), established the White House china collection, and put up the first White House Christmas tree. During her husband's re-election campaign in 1892, she fell ill with tuberculosis. Caroline Harrison died in October 1892 at sixty years of age.

Ida Saxton McKinley

Born into a well-to-do banking family, Ida Saxton went to fine schools and toured Europe when finished with her formal education. She began working as a cashier at her father's bank, and then met William McKinley, a young lawyer. It didn't take long for them to fall in love, and when she was twenty-three (and he twenty-seven), they were married in Canton, Ohio, in January 1871. Ida's father had purchased a home for them, and on Christmas Day that year, their first daughter Katie was born. The couple lived quite happily until they lost Ida's mother in 1873. A few months later, they mourned the passing of their new baby. From this point on, Ida's health went downhill, with headaches, epileptic seizures, and phlebitis that partially crippled her. Daughter Katie died of typhoid fever in 1876 when she was only four years old. With all the personal tragedy and turmoil, McKinley's election to Congress that same year was probably a blessing, for he moved Ida to Washington, where he spent considerable time with her, taking carriage drives and attending the theater and dinners. When he was elected governor of Ohio in 1892, they moved once more, often waving to one another during the day—she from the governor's residence and he from the office across the street. Ida was happy to see William sworn in as president in 1897 and determined, despite her frail health, to contribute something as first lady, even if that meant greeting guests seated on a chair.

Following McKinley's re-election, they had traveled to the Pan-American Exposition in Buffalo, New York. While there, on September 6, 1901, an anarchist named Leon Czolgosz shot and mortally wounded President McKinley. He lingered for several days, succumbing to an infection on September 14. After his death, Ida returned to Canton, where her own health steadily worsened. Yet she visited her husband's grave every day. At the age of fifty-nine, Ida passed on herself and is buried next to William and their daughters.

Edith Carow Roosevelt

Edith Carow grew up in high society. Their home in New York City was next to the Roosevelts', where Edith got to know Theodore and his sisters. She spent time with him at the Roosevelt summer home on Long Island, and the two shared similar interests in nature and reading. When he left for

Harvard in 1876, they were sweethearts, but then broke up. In 1880, Theodore married a Boston girl named Alice Hathaway Lee. Alice, however, died in 1884, shortly after their daughter Alice was born. That next year, Theodore and Edith met again and fell back in love. They were married in December 1886 in London, where her family was then living, and set up residence on Long Island. Besides his daughter Alice, they had five children together. In 1900, Theodore was governor of New York. Edith urged him not to run for vice president with William McKinley, but he did so. The president's untimely death made Roosevelt president. As first lady, Edith managed a hectic schedule of teas, receptions, and dinners, along with Alice's wedding and their daughter Ethel's social debut. She also supervised the addition of the East and West Wings. The couple was happy to retire to Long Island, and they enjoyed life until their son Quentin was killed during World War I in 1918. Her husband's health failed, leading to his death that next year. Edith kept busy in retirement supporting conservative causes, and when her husband's cousin Franklin ran for president, she did not lend her support. Edith passed away in 1948 at the age of eighty-seven and is buried next to her late husband.

Helen Herron Taft

Helen Herron's father, Judge John W. Herron, was a law partner of Rutherford B. Hayes. With these connections, Helen was fascinated by politics from an early age, visiting the White House as a teenager and deciding she'd like to live there herself some day. Nellie, as she was called, graduated from the Cincinnati College of Music, attended Miami University, and later taught school. It was at a bob-sledding party that Nellie met Will Taft, a young lawyer. He liked her intelligence and her driven nature. Following a lengthy courtship, they became engaged, and they married in June 1886. They settled in Cincinnati, where Taft set up a law practice, and they had three children.

In January 1900, President McKinley appointed William Taft governor-general of the Philippine Islands. Clearly, Mrs. Taft viewed this as a tremendous opportunity to advance her husband's political career. When Theodore Roosevelt succeeded McKinley, he offered Taft a Supreme Court appointment, a lifetime commitment. This had been Taft's dream, but his wife urged him to hold out for another appointment. Thus, in 1904, Taft became secretary of war. In Washington, she cultivated numerous contacts in hopes of winning her husband the Republican nomination for president in 1908. It would appear that her driven nature led to success. As William Howard Taft was inaugurated president, Helen basked in the glory of the moment. However, she suffered a stroke in May, which left her unable to walk normally for nearly a year. Driven again, she recovered. As first lady, her most enduring achievement was the planting of three thousand cherry trees in Washington. In March 1913, they left the White House for Connecticut. The former president felt relief while his wife was sorry to leave.

Taft's lifelong dream, however, came to pass, as President Warren Harding appointed him to the Supreme Court in 1921. Mrs. Taft was now thrilled with the prospect, for it took her back to Washington. In 1930, William Taft died of heart disease, and his widow continued to live in the city she loved. Their son Robert had become a U.S. senator, their daughter Helen the dean of Bryn Mawr College, and their son Charles a Cincinnati civic leader. Helen died in May 1943 at age eighty-one. She's buried beside her husband at Arlington National Cemetery.

Ellen Axson Wilson

Born into the family of a Presbyterian minister, Ellen was well studied in the arts—music, literature, and painting. While studying in Rome in the spring of 1883, she met Woodrow Wilson, a lawyer who was there visiting relatives. By September, they were engaged. They married two years later, following his graduate schooling and her study of painting in New York City. The newlyweds moved to Pennsylvania, where Woodrow taught at Bryn Mawr College. Then the family moved to other universities, including Wesleyan in Connecticut and Princeton in New Jersey. Ellen proofread her husband's articles and books, lending her intelligent insights whenever possible. She made do on a professor's paltry salary and raised their three daughters. After Wilson became governor of New Jersey in 1911, he contemplated a run for president in 1912. Again, Ellen threw her support behind him, and he won, representing the Democratic Party. Although she didn't care for the trappings of being first lady, she entertained with grace and style. She supported improved working conditions for federal government workers and the installation of restrooms for women. In 1914, Mrs. Wilson fell ill with Bright's disease, then a fatal kidney ailment. She died later that year and was buried with her parents in Georgia.

Edith Bolling Galt Wilson

While still mourning Ellen's passing, President Woodrow Wilson quite surprisingly met Edith Galt, a widow, who was visiting the White House to see her friend, Wilson's cousin Helen Woodrow Bones. They were immediately drawn to one another, and within a few months they were engaged. It had been only one year since his first wife's death, and Wilson's advisors cautioned him about the damage romantic involvement this soon could cause to his political career. In spite of these deterrents, the couple was married in December 1915 in a small, private ceremony. She was forty-three years; he was fifty-eight. Like Ellen, she supported Woodrow in everything, even running their financial affairs. As World War I was ending in a peace treaty, Edith Wilson accompanied the president to Paris to work out the details, but she feared he was pushing himself far too hard. Back in the United States in the summer of 1919, he worked tirelessly to establish the League of Nations, but in October, he suffered a stroke that partly paralyzed him. Many, including Mrs. Wilson, felt the president should resign, but the doctors persuaded Edith to allow no one other than herself to see the president. She reviewed all official papers and conveyed his decisions to others. She adamantly denied that she made any government decisions herself (an allegation that had given rise to the term "petticoat government").

When the president finally recovered enough to appear in public, he still wasn't functioning fully. In March 1921, the couple retired to their Washington residence, where he died in February 1924. Living in Washington, Edith remained active in the Democratic Party, supported Franklin Roosevelt's campaign, and published her own account of the Wilson administration with *My Memoir*. When the United States joined the United Nations in 1945, Edith rejoiced that Woodrow's dream was still alive. Her last public appearance was riding in John F. Kennedy's inaugural parade, but she died later that year at the age of eighty-nine. She and her late husband are buried side by side at Washington's National Cathedral.

Florence Kling De Wolfe Harding

Born in Marion, Ohio, Florence Kling studied music at the Cincinnati Conservatory of Music. Though strong-willed and very intelligent, she eloped at nineteen with Henry De Wolfe, a coal dealer's son. The marriage didn't last: Henry deserted her and their baby. She returned to Marion, where she supported herself and her son Marshall by giving piano lessons. She divorced De Wolfe and decided that her parents could better raise Marshall. In 1890, Florence met Warren Harding, then owner of the Marion newspaper. Though her father was against the match, they married in July 1891, when she was thirty and he twenty-five. She began to help with the newspaper and traveled often with her husband. When he began to rise in politics, Florence supported him and was delighted at his move from state senator to U.S. senator in 1914. Her Washington life was fun, and when the Republicans wanted to nominate her husband in 1920, she gave him the final push to say yes. Harding won the election, and Florence stepped into her role as first lady determined to make an impression, despite some health concerns that might have otherwise slowed her down. She particularly enjoyed throwing garden parties for World War I veterans, and it's said she poured her husband's drinks at his private poker parties for years (even in the era of Prohibition). But when the Teapot Dome scandal took hold, the president became depressed and his first lady rightfully anxious. To give themselves a change of scenery and much-needed rest, the Hardings set off on a West Coast and Alaska trip, but en route the president suffered a heart attack. On August 2, 1923, he died in San Francisco of a stroke. Without her husband, Florence found life difficult. She returned to Marion, Ohio, and in November 1924, she succumbed to the kidney ailments that had plagued her.

Grace Goodhue Coolidge

Burlington, Vermont, was Grace Goodhue's first home. Educated at the University of Vermont, she moved in 1902 to Northampton, Massachusetts, to teach at a school for the deaf. Her first glimpse of the man who would become her husband—Calvin Coolidge—was through a window as she caught him shaving. Hearing her laugh, he was determined to meet her. Once again, the opposites theory held, as Grace was perky and very sociable while Calvin remained somewhat stern and silent. Still, they hit it off: they married in October 1905 at her parents' Burlington home. They made their first home in Northampton, where Calvin was elected mayor in 1910. Grace raised their two boys, and she weathered Calvin's work in Boston fairly well, since he served both as lieutenant governor and governor of Massachusetts. Home on weekends, Coolidge used his position as head of household to tell Grace what to do and to complain a lot. He was just plain picky at times. When Calvin became vice president in 1921, the family moved to Washington, where she immediately fit in. Upon Harding's death in 1923, Coolidge was sworn in as president. Grace wasn't initially enthusiastic about being thrust into the very public role of first lady, but she entertained with genuine friendliness. Her darkest moment had to have been the death in 1924 of their son Calvin Jr., from blood poisoning. In 1928, President Coolidge opted not to run for re-election, and they returned to Northampton, where she worked for the Red Cross and he served as a trustee at the school for the deaf (where Mrs. Coolidge had taught many years before). In January 1933, he died suddenly of a blood clot in the heart. Grace continued with life, traveling and spending time with her surviving son John and his family. During World War II, she helped to bring refugee children to the United States. A heart attack finally claimed her in July 1957, and she's buried next to her husband in Plymouth, Vermont.

Lou Henry Hoover

Born in Iowa, Lou Henry and her family moved to California when she was ten years old. At Stanford University in Palo Alto, Lou was the only female geology major, and while there she met Herbert Hoover in the lab. They had much in common, including their Iowa roots and their moves to the west coast. Determined to finish her studies, Lou postponed getting married while Herbert worked as a mining engineer in Australia. In February 1899, they married at her parents' home in Monterey, honeymooned on a boat to China, and reached the continent, where Herbert began a new mining job. Lou quickly learned to speak and understand Chinese. She even trekked to remote mining sites with her husband when necessary. But in June 1900, the Boxer Rebellion broke out in China against foreigners. The next year, Hoover joined a British mining firm, and for the next several years, the Hoovers and their two sons traveled all over the world. Through his business successes, Hoover became a millionaire.

During World War I, President Wilson appointed Hoover as food administrator, and they returned to the United States. After her husband won the presidency by a wide margin in 1928, Lou moved proudly into the White House. Any happiness over their achievements was short-lived, however: the stock market crash signaled the onset of the Great Depression. Although the Hoovers cut back on their lavish lifestyle, many blamed Hoover for the economic woes. It was a bittersweet moment when they left the White House after the 1932 election, but they enjoyed their retirement in California. When World War II erupted, the couple became active in humanitarian projects, but in January 1944, Mrs. Hoover died suddenly of a heart attack.

Anna Eleanor Roosevelt Roosevelt

Born to Anna Hall and Elliott Roosevelt in New York City, Eleanor had a society-conscious mother who, it's said, was disappointed in her daughter's rather homely appearance. Eleanor adored her father, though he was an alcoholic who spent much time away from home. By the time Eleanor turned ten, both her parents had died, and she lived with her strict Grandmother Hall. At fifteen, Eleanor left the States for London to attend school. There she gained much confidence. Though she dreaded her social debut at age eighteen, she caught the attention of her charming distant cousin Franklin Delano Roosevelt. Eleanor gave him a tour of the tenements where she taught on the Lower East Side of Manhattan. Much to their surprise, they fell in love, and they married in New York in March 1905. The young bride had mother-in-law woes that surpassed what many couples endured. Sara Delano decided where they would live and influenced how their six children would be raised. Eleanor was unhappy with this, but good luck came their way when Franklin won a seat in the state senate and introduced Eleanor to politics.

President Wilson appointed Franklin his assistant secretary of the Navy in 1913, and the family moved to Washington, D.C. This began Franklin's serious political ambitions. When he was stricken with polio in 1921 and paralyzed, Eleanor not only cared for Franklin, but encouraged him to continue his political aspirations. In 1928, she helped him campaign for governor of New York. Once he was elected, Eleanor became essential as his eyes and ears, since the governor was restricted in terms of travel. Eleanor's conviction that he could lead the country out of the Great Depression convinced him to run for president in 1932. He won. As first lady, Eleanor traveled to some of the country's most impoverished areas, held weekly press conferences, and wrote magazine and newspaper columns as well as books. Mrs. Roosevelt also worked for the rights of African-Americans and raised morale with her visits to the troops in World War II.

In 1945, having won his four contests for high office, Franklin Roosevelt died suddenly of a cerebral hemorrhage. President Truman sent Eleanor to the newly created United Nations, and she kept speaking out for Democratic ideals. In November 1962, at seventy-eight, Eleanor Roosevelt died of aplastic anemia. She's buried in Hyde Park, New York, beside her husband. History would record that people either fervently admired or publicly chided Eleanor as first lady.

Elizabeth Virginia Wallace Truman

Although her name at birth was Elizabeth Virginia Wallace, folks knew her best as Bess, an athletic girl fond of playing baseball and tennis. A tomboy! Tragedy struck fairly early, as Bess's father, heavily in debt and fond of alcohol, killed himself. It was a loss whose echoes would linger. Bess, her mother, and three brothers lived with her well-off grandparents, the Gateses, in Independence, Missouri. Bess met Harry Truman in Sunday school, and they continued as classmates throughout high school. While Bess left to finish her education in Kansas City, Harry was too poor to attend college. So he left Independence to help on his family's farm. When he returned to visit in 1910, he met up with Bess, and courtship began. In no rush to marry, Bess kept in touch with Harry, and after he returned from fighting in World War I, they finally married in June 1919. After their honeymoon, they moved into the Gates's mansion with Bess's mother.

As Harry began his political rise, Bess was moderate in her moves to support his efforts. She'd appear publicly, but decided against granting interviews or giving speeches herself, and generally chose to cast off the public spotlight. In private, however, she was never shy about offering her thoughts to Harry.

The Trumans, along with their daughter Margaret (born in 1924), moved to Washington, D.C., after Harry's election to the U.S. Senate. Bess worked in Harry's office helping with a variety of tasks. When in 1944 FDR asked Harry to become his running mate, he at first refused. Bess was afraid that the campaign would force her to relive her father's suicide, if that was uncovered. But the more Harry thought about the decision, the more he leaned toward running. And he did.

Roosevelt's health declined shortly after his fourth-term re-election, and when he died in office, Truman was sworn in on April 12, 1945, with Bess beside him. She began to offer her opinions to her husband, sometimes sitting in on sessions with his advisors. The Truman presidency tackled the end of World War II, the Korean War, McCarthyism, and more. Bess talked Harry out of running for a third term. The thought of returning to Independence was indeed tempting. After Harry's death in 1972, Bess lived quietly, following her passions of baseball, reading, and keeping in close contact with her daughter Margaret. In 1982, she died of heart failure and was buried beside her beloved husband in Independence, Missouri, in the courtyard of the Harry S. Truman Library.

Mamie Geneva Doud Eisenhower

Mamie was born in Iowa, where her father was successful in business. He moved the family to Denver, Colorado, where she grew up with servants, finishing school, and vacations in other states. In October 1915 at Fort Sam Houston near San Antonio, Texas, Mamie met the young Second Lieutenant Dwight Eisenhower, nicknamed Ike. They began courting steadily and were married at her Denver home in July 1916. After honeymooning, they moved to military housing at Fort Sam Houston. Weeks later, Mamie would learn an enduring dictate in their marriage. "My country comes first and always will," Ike explained. Though the message fell on her as something of a shock, Mamie had little choice but to accept it. She believed in her heart that Ike was destined to rise within the military. So they moved from one post to another—twenty-seven times in thirty-seven years. She handled their finances, coached her husband on social matters, threw parties, and raised their children. Son Doud died at the age of three from scarlet fever, and his death devastated them. After they learned to live with the loss, son John Sheldon Doud was born at the base in the Panama Canal Zone.

The Eisenhowers served in the Philippines, and on December 7, back in Texas, they learned the news that the Japanese had bombed Pearl Harbor. Her husband's tenure overseas left the couple writing letters. Mamie volunteered while he commanded the Allied Forces. She even endured the ridicule of being dubbed drunk, when in reality she suffered from an inner ear disorder.

Now a war hero of international fame, Eisenhower looked to the future, and in 1952 he was perfectly poised to run for the presidency. As first lady, Mamie enjoyed her hostess duties, although years as a military wife must have rubbed off on her. The White House staff reported that she ran a pretty tight regime. In spite of his 1955 heart attack, the president ran for re-election and won easily. But when he suffered a stroke in 1957, Mrs. Eisenhower worried further. Good health returned, and the couple retired to their estate in Gettysburg, Pennsylvania—their first permanent home after all the years living with the military. Three years after they celebrated their fiftieth wedding anniversary, the former president had another heart attack. He died in March 1969, with Mamie by his side. She busied herself attending memorials to honor her late husband until her death from a stroke in 1979.

Jacqueline Bouvier Kennedy Onassis

Wealthy, sophisticated, and born with strikingly good looks, Jacqueline Bouvier still had her struggles. When she was eight, her parents—John "Black Jack" Bouvier and Janet Lee—separated, and in 1942, her mother married Hugh D. Auchincloss, another wealthy stockbroker like her father. Jackie attended the very finest of schools, from Miss Porter's School in Farmington, Connecticut, to Vassar College, studying art history at the Sorbonne in Paris, then finally finishing her degree at George Washington University. In 1952, she began working for the *Washington Times-Herald* as an inquiring photographer tracking down Washington's notables. One of those notables was a dashing young senator from an ambitious Bostonian family—John F. Kennedy.

The couple dated, fell in love, and married in September 1953. Kennedy's family gave their blessing to the union, as Jackie's sense of style, culture, and good looks were certain assets for Jack's future political aspirations. Their reception in Newport, Rhode Island, attracted great press coverage and more than 1,700 guests. After a honeymoon to Acapulco, Mexico, the Kennedys settled in Georgetown.

From the start, health concerns plagued the young couple. His war injury caused back problems. In 1954, he barely made it through spinal surgery, and Jackie helped to nurse him back to health. She suffered a miscarriage, but in 1956, gave birth to daughter Caroline. Jack's father had groomed first son Joseph P. Kennedy Jr., for a presidential run, but those hopes were dashed when he was killed during World War II. Thus, the family torch was passed to Jack, who was elected in 1960 as the first Roman Catholic president. Just weeks after his election, the couple's son, John F. Kennedy Jr., was born.

Mrs. Kennedy brought a sense of style to the presidential mansion. Not only did she supervise the restoration of the White House interior, but she also invited talented musicians and artists to attend official functions. As first lady, she conceived the idea of an official illustrated guidebook for visitors to the White House. Since its debut in 1962, the guidebook has been revised approximately twenty times.

The Kennedy marriage had its problems—her extravagant and expensive taste and his dallying with other women. In August 1963, the death of their newborn son Patrick brought the couple closer. In an effort to help with re-election, she accompanied him to Dallas, Texas, where she was sitting beside her husband when he was struck by an assassin's bullets. Stoic throughout the horrendous weekend of national mourning, she orchestrated his state funeral and saw to the birthday celebrations of her children, held on the heels of their father's death. Mrs. Kennedy granted few interviews, but in one, she suggested that the Kennedy era resembled Camelot. The name stuck.

After leaving the White House, Mrs. Kennedy, Caroline, and John were pursued relentlessly by photographers. It was in her quest for greater privacy and anonymity that she left Georgetown for the urban oasis of Manhattan. When her brother-in-law Robert was assassinated, it awakened fears that her children might be targets. That year, she married Greek shipping magnate Aristotle Onassis. She was ridiculed for her decision, but this provided her a bit of refuge, and some happiness in which to escape with John and Caroline, whom she was determined to raise out of the spotlight and to give as normal a childhood as possible. She's quoted as saying, "If you bungle raising your children, I don't think whatever else you do matters very much."

In the 1970s, still doggedly pursued, she was dubbed Jackie O. Following her second husband's death, Jackie chose to work part-time as a book editor to make a contribution and set an example for her children. It was doubtful that she needed the income. Her work in publishing was highly regarded, and she was also instrumental in the creation of the late president's library in Boston. As she became grandmother to Caroline's three children (who called her Grand Jackie), she'd take them to Central Park or Martha's Vineyard, sometimes with her devoted companion, whom she never married. But in early 1994, she was diagnosed with non-Hodgkins lymphoma, and her health deteriorated. Jackie died months later in her New York apartment, with her children by her side. After a private memorial service in Manhattan, her body was flown to Washington for interment. She is buried beside the late president at Arlington National Cemetery, where the couple's two deceased infants rest in peace with them. Sadly, her son John Jr. was killed flying his airplane in 1999, leaving daughter Caroline the sole survivor of Camelot.

Claudia Taylor Johnson

Claudia Alta Taylor was nicknamed "Lady Bird" at a young age. She lived in Texas, and sadly lost her mother, who died of a bad fall when Lady Bird was five. With the help of an aunt, her father raised her and taught his daughter the business aspects of his general store. In 1934, she met Lyndon Baines Johnson, who was working in the office of a congressman. Lyndon must have been smitten, as he asked Lady Bird to marry him the day after their first date! She didn't say yes immediately, but on November 17 of that year, they tied the knot in San Antonio. It's said Johnson was a bit demanding, but nonetheless, his wife was excited about politics. With her sharp business sense, she handled the finances. She invested her inheritance in his bid for Congress (which proved to be a successful investment!), and during his absence in World War II, she purchased an Austin radio station, developing it into a thriving business. All this while raising their two daughters—Lynda Bird and Luci Baines.

In 1948, Lyndon ran for the U.S. Senate and went on to become the majority leader, the youngest in the Senate's history. When John F. Kennedy went after the presidency in 1960, he and his advisors thought Lyndon Johnson might secure southern votes, and Johnson was chosen as the vice-presidential running mate. On November 22, 1963, the Johnsons rode in the fateful Dallas motorcade when Kennedy was shot and killed. A Texas judge swore in the new president aboard *Air Force One*. The historic photograph shows him flanked by Mrs. Johnson and Mrs. Kennedy.

As first lady, Mrs. Johnson entertained with ease and urged the president to appoint more women to higher governmental posts. After he won re-election on his own, she persuaded Congress to pass the Highway Beautification Act and encouraged conservation groups in addition to promoting Head Start, a federal program for disadvantaged young children.

When the Vietnam War took hold of the Johnson administration, Mrs. Johnson advised the president, with others, against running again. In 1969, they retired to the LBJ Ranch in Texas to enjoy their daughters and grandchildren. Lyndon Johnson died of a heart attack in January 1973. Lady Bird has served on many advisory boards, and she campaigned for her son-in-law Charles S. Robb (Lynda's husband) for the post of lieutenant governor of Virginia in 1976. She also supported the Equal Rights Amendment, founded the National Wildflower Research Center in 1982, and attended the 200th anniversary celebration of the White House, along with other former first ladies, in 2000.

Patricia Ryan Nixon

Thelma Catherine Ryan changed her legal name to Patricia, perhaps because her father used to call her his "St. Patrick's Day babe." Soon after her birth, the family had moved from Nevada to California. When Pat was thirteen, her mother died, and for several years she kept house for her father and brothers. Then at seventeen, she lost her father, who died of miner's lung disease. A hard worker, Pat worked her way through the University of Southern California cleaning offices and playing bit parts in movies. Upon graduating with honors in 1938, she taught typing at Whittier High School. That same year, she met Richard Nixon, a young lawyer. Two years later, they were married in a Quaker service in Riverside, California.

The Nixons settled in Whittier, and she continued to teach until World War II, when she worked for the Office of Price Administration (while her husband served in the Navy). Upon his return, he ran for a seat in Congress in 1946, the same year that their first daughter Patricia (Tricia) was born. Upon election, they moved to Washington, D.C., where their second daughter Julie was born in 1948.

In 1952, now-Senator Richard Nixon ran for vice president with Dwight Eisenhower. Pat traveled with Nixon on trips abroad. Although she was disappointed that he lost the 1960 election against Kennedy, she returned to private life quite happily. When Nixon ran for governor of California in 1962, she was not thrilled at the prospect. Nonetheless, she helped him. Nixon lost that election as well, and had a reprieve from politics until his comeback in the 1968 presidential race. As first lady, Mrs. Nixon continued with White House restoration, and in June 1971, she orchestrated Tricia's wedding to Edward Cox in the White House Rose Garden (daughter Julie married David Eisenhower, Ike's grandson, in 1968).

Soon the Watergate scandal erupted, and the House Judiciary Committee recommended articles of impeachment against her husband. Pat, along with her daughters, believed in his innocence and wanted him to fight the charges. Stoically, she stood on the dais the morning he spoke to White House staff and a television audience before departing for California. He'd announced his resignation the night before. The couple lived in seclusion in San Clemente, where her husband wrote books. Pat suffered a stroke, which partly paralyzed her, and soon the Nixons moved to New Jersey to be closer to their grandchildren. In June 1993, Pat Nixon died of lung cancer, and with his daughters, the tearful former president laid his wife to rest at the Richard Nixon Library and Birthplace in Yorba Linda, California. The next year, he passed away and was buried there as well.

Elizabeth Bloomer Warren Ford

Although born in Chicago, Elizabeth Anne (Betty) grew up in Grand Rapids, Michigan. She took ballet lessons and dreamed of becoming a professional dancer. Her father passed away when Betty was sixteen, and she helped to support the family, taking modeling jobs and teaching dance. After high school, she studied dance in Vermont and again in New York with the famous dancer Martha Graham.

Returning to Grand Rapids, Betty taught dance lessons and dance therapy while serving as a fashion coordinator for a department store. In 1942, she married William Warren, an insurance salesman, but they divorced five years later. That same year, she met Gerald (Jerry) Ford, a former college football star turned lawyer in Grand Rapids. Not even a year later, they were engaged, and she soon began work for his first congressional campaign. In October 1948, they married, and after his election to Congress they took up residence in Washington.

Ford served many terms in Congress and worked his way to minority leader in the U.S. House of Representatives. But that left Betty alone to raise their four children—Michael, John, Steven, and Susan. Betty suffered from chronic pain because of a pinched nerve as well as arthritis, and she became dependent on medication. In October 1973, President Nixon appointed Ford his vice president after scandal forced Spiro Agnew out of office. Then when Watergate forced Nixon to resign, Ford was sworn in at noon on August 9, 1974. Suddenly thrust into roles they had never campaigned for, the Fords helped heal the nation. Mrs. Ford favored the

Equal Rights Amendment, and when she battled breast cancer, the country rallied around. Most appreciated her talking about her trauma. No doubt she saved countless lives as millions of other women learned about the disease.

Betty was thoroughly disappointed when her husband lost re-election, although the pardon he'd given his predecessor, a weak economy, and other factors contributed to his defeat. They retired to Palm Springs, California, and Betty sank into depression, complicated by her addiction to prescription painkillers and dependence on alcohol. Her family bravely confronted her, and she sought rehabilitation. Following her recovery, Betty Ford spoke out as openly about this as she had about her cancer, and she went on to create the Betty Ford Center for Drug and Alcohol Rehabilitation in Rancho Mirage, California. Today, the Center treats many others, including notables and celebrities. In 1987, she published *Betty: A Glad Awakening*.

Rosalynn Smith Carter

Brought up by loving but strict parents, Rosalynn Smith dreamed of seeing the world beyond Georgia. Little did she know the opportunities she'd have in store for her! But first came some struggle, as her father passed on when Rosalynn was thirteen, and the family went through financially tough times. She helped her widowed mother in her dressmaking business.

Valedictorian at her high school, Rosalynn and her mother found enough money for her to attend Georgia Southwestern, a junior college in Americus. In 1945, she met and began dating Jimmy Carter, who lived in Plains. Rosalynn already knew his sister Ruth, and seemed slightly awed by this student at the U.S. Naval Academy at Annapolis. They wrote to each other every day while they finished their education, and they were married in July 1946 in the Plains Methodist Church, when she was eighteen.

Jimmy served in the Navy for the next seven years, and their moves from one naval base to another helped fulfill Rosalynn's earlier yen for travel. During this time their three sons—John William (Jack), James Earl (Chip), and Jeffrey—were born in different cities. In 1953, Carter left the Navy, returning to Plains to run the family peanut business. And when Jimmy ran for the state Senate in 1962, Rosalynn managed the business while he was away. Their daughter Amy was born in 1967, and three years later, Jimmy was elected governor. Rosalynn learned to speak before large crowds and worked diligently to improve conditions for mentally retarded children. When Jimmy decided to run for president as a Washington outsider, she toured the country campaigning for him.

After watching Jimmy take the oath of office, Rosalynn walked hand in hand with him down Pennsylvania Avenue to the White House. Rosalynn sat in on cabinet meetings and traveled even farther as his representative. She was the first first lady since Eleanor Roosevelt to testify before Congress, on behalf of mental health programs. She also gave a voice to the concerns of women and the elderly. In the 1980 election campaign, her husband chose to stay behind in Washington because the Iranian hostages were held captive. Rosalynn did most of his campaigning for a re-election he ultimately lost.

Back in Plains, the Carters found a new focus building houses for the needy with Habitat for Humanity, and they each wrote bestselling books. Mrs. Carter continues to support mental health programs and awareness.

NANCY DAVIS REAGAN

First named Anne Frances as a baby, she was always called Nancy. Her parents separated when she was two years old, and her mother returned to the stage as an actress while Nancy lived with an aunt and uncle. When she was seven, her mother married a neurosurgeon, Dr. Loyal Davis of Chicago, and to Nancy's delight, they moved her to be with them. From that point on, she looked on Dr. Davis as her father.

Nancy had an active youth, meeting celebrities who were acquaintances of her parents, attending parties and dance classes, and making her social debut in December 1939. She graduated from Smith College in Massachusetts, where she majored in drama, and she worked in theater in New York. By the spring of 1949, she made it to Hollywood for a screen test and began a career in films.

That fall, she asked friends to introduce her to Ronald Reagan, also an actor. Nancy thought he was rather handsome, and he had just separated from his wife. In March 1952, they were married in the San Fernando Valley. She made several movies, including *Hellcats of the Navy* in 1957 with her husband. When motherhood entered her life with Patricia and Ronald, their children, she relinquished her Hollywood stardom for more homey pursuits. Nancy had never given politics much thought until her husband ran for governor of California in 1966. She campaigned for him, and his bid was successful. As the state's first lady, Mrs. Reagan wore stylish attire and continued her social pursuits.

Reagan talked about old-fashioned ideals, and his message appealed to voters after years of scandal and problems in the country. Thus, he was tapped as the Republican nominee in 1980 after losing the party's nomination to Ford in 1976, and he was sworn in in January 1981. Just two months into his presidency, it nearly came to a tragic end. An assailant shot Ronald Reagan outside a Washington hotel. A terrified Nancy Reagan rushed to the president's side, monitored his medical care, and emphasized his recovery with the waiting public.

Although Ronnie (as she playfully called him) was well liked, Nancy was criticized for her lavish lifestyle and spending. While Reagan cut programs for the poor, Nancy ordered new White House china at a cost of $200,000. To improve her image, she began working again with the Foster Grandparent Program, where she'd once been active as California's first lady. On a national level, she also instituted an antidrug program called "Just Say No."

After two terms in office, the Reagans retired to their Santa Barbara ranch and she penned her memoirs, *My Turn*, published in 1989. With her encouragement, former president Reagan announced to the public his diagnosis with Alzheimer's disease. Her husband's condition steadily degenerated. The former president has not been seen in public, and Nancy has limited her appearances to care for him.

Barbara Pierce Bush

Barbara was born in New York City, where her father Marvin was president of the McCall Corporation. She lived in the suburb of Rye, New York, but attended high school in Charleston, South Carolina. During her Christmas vacation in 1941, Barbara went to a dance and met George Bush, a senior at Phillips Academy in Andover, Massachusetts. Two years later, before she entered Smith College, they became engaged. Her concerns were obviously with him as he fought in the Navy during World War II. Thinking of nothing else but George, she dropped out of Smith during her sophomore year and married him during his leave in January 1945. Barbara was nineteen.

After the war, George finished his education at Yale, and they moved to Texas so that he could work in the oil business. The couple had six children—George W., Robin, John (Jeb), Neil, Marvin, and Dorothy. In 1953, their daughter Robin died of leukemia. Within the next ten years, George would become active in the Texas Republican Party, and in 1966, he won a seat in Congress. His rise in politics continued throughout the 1970s with various appointments, including U.S. ambassador to the United Nations, national chairman of his party, then U.S. envoy to China in 1974. The next year, he returned to the States to head the Central Intelligence Agency (CIA). In 1980, Ronald Reagan tapped Bush to become his running mate, and the next eight years were also spent in Washington.

Barbara appeared grandmotherly and would always be remembered for her signature white pearls. As first lady, she spoke out in favor of literacy campaigns, and although she never disagreed in public with her husband's political positions, she is said to have privately expressed her opinions that were sometimes much more liberal than his. During her White House years, she also penned a book about their dog Millie.

In 1994, in retirement, Barbara Bush wrote her autobiography, *Barbara Bush: A Memoir*, another bestseller. As her son George W. Bush, the governor of Texas, ran for the presidency in 2000, she threw her support behind his candidacy.

Hillary Rodham Clinton

Hillary Diane Rodham was born in October 1947 in Chicago, Illinois. She and her two younger brothers grew up in the middle-class suburb of Park Ridge, and Hillary excelled in school as well as in student leadership. She was active with her Methodist youth group, where she took an interest in migrant workers and inner-city struggles. When Hillary heard Dr. Martin Luther King Jr. speak in Chicago in 1962, she was deeply moved. Graduating with honors from Wellesley College in Massachusetts in 1969, she set her sights on a legal career, and despite the male-dominated profession at the time, she enrolled in Yale University.

While at the law library, she met another student, Bill Clinton from Arkansas. Bill was bright, energetic, and devoted to public service. He was attracted to her mind and her unusual confidence. Hillary worked following her graduation as an attorney for the Children's Defense Fund, and from the end of 1973 to August 1974, she worked for the House Judiciary Committee, evaluating impeachment evidence against then-President Richard M. Nixon. Following Nixon's resignation, Hillary Rodham had her pick of any number of high-paying positions in law firms. Instead, she moved with Bill Clinton to Arkansas. They were married in October 1975 near the University of Arkansas at Fayetteville, where she taught law. She kept her maiden name. In 1976, when he was elected attorney general for the state, they moved to Little Rock, where she joined the Rose Law Firm.

Two years later, Bill Clinton was elected governor, and their daughter Chelsea was born two years after that in February 1980. In November, Bill lost his re-election bid. Hillary attributed the loss to her role as an independent, career-minded governor's wife. So, she took a leave of absence from the law firm and announced that she was changing her name to Clinton. Whether these measures helped him win re-election in 1982 is uncertain, but they were back in the Arkansas governor's mansion, where Bill governed for ten years. She resumed her law career and always took on the causes of children and families.

In 1991, the Clintons decided that Bill should run for the presidency. However, during his campaign, when she alluded to her future involvement in the administration, some felt she was too assertive and had her own agenda. She was indeed a striking contrast to the grandmotherly Barbara Bush.

Working as a team, the couple achieved their political goals, and Hillary planned to take on a somewhat dual role as first lady and policy wonk. When the president appointed her to head his Task Force on National Health Care Reform, she took on the challenge with gusto, but her detractors ridiculed her. Many special interest groups resisted change in health care, and the massive initiatives the Clintons would have liked to achieve failed.

Hillary Clinton next opted for a lower profile as first lady, writing the bestselling *It Takes A Village* and continuing to speak out on children's issues, education, and health care. When her husband openly admitted his involvement with another woman (after she'd endured campaign rumors), she handled the disgrace with public humility, claiming they were a team and would work through their marital problems. But those close to Mrs. Clinton suspected she had further ambitions. Indeed, she announced her own candidacy for a Senate seat representing the state of New York. After establishing residence in Westchester County, Mrs. Clinton campaigned throughout the state, capitalizing on her single-name introduction as Hillary. Her formidable opponent was New York City Mayor Rudolph Giuliani, who had made such a difference in his city. But he was forced to bow out of the Senate race because of his health and his own marital problems. Never taking victory for granted, and despite opposition from Rep. Rick Lazio, Hillary Rodham Clinton was elected to the U.S. Senate on Election Day, November 7, 2000. That makes her the first first lady to seek and win political office, and it also made her husband, President Bill Clinton, a Senate spouse. Rumors have it that Mrs. Clinton might like to return to the White House someday—only as president, not first lady!

Laura Welch Bush

Growing up in the small oil town of Midland, Texas, during the 1950s, Laura had a fairly calm adolescence, grabbing a burger with friends, and always loving to read. In 1964, she went off to Southern Methodist University to study education, and it was during her first teaching job at a predominantly black elementary school in Houston that the country's racial divide struck her. Determined to help the cause of literacy, she headed back to the classroom to obtain her graduate degree in library science from the University of Texas. While a graduate student, her longtime friend Jan tried desperately to fix her up with the young George W. Bush, but Laura hesitated. Finally, three years later on a trip back home to Midland, she relented and met him at her friend's house, hoping she would like the barbecue a lot better than she liked politics. To everyone's surprise, perhaps even their own, the two married three months later.

After they spent their honeymoon canvassing parts of west Texas for George W.'s unsuccessful congressional bid, they settled down to have a family. After years of trying to conceive, they had decided to adopt when Laura discovered that she was carrying twins—their daughters Jenna and Barbara.

As George's father's career led to the White House, George W. got out of the oil business and became a managing partner in the Texas Rangers baseball team. Although her husband reportedly overindulged in alcohol over the years, she encouraged him to kick the habit. And when he decided to challenge incumbent governor Ann Richards in 1994, Laura was less than enthusiastic. Over the years as the first lady of Texas, however, she learned to campaign and to address the crowds. Of course, she used her position to champion her favorite cause (and every other librarian's)—literacy and the love of reading. No doubt this will be a primary focus for her during her White House years, as it was for her mother-in-law Barbara years ago.

Appendix III

The Presidential Libraries

Presidential libraries and museums are uniquely American institutions. In excess of 1.5 million visitors tour them annually. It's interesting to learn how these buildings and collections that pay homage to a particular person and era of American history came to be.

Most presidential libraries and museums are privately planned, funded, and constructed before being turned over to the federal government. Today, the National Archives and Records Administration's (NARA) Office of Presidential Libraries is responsible for administering these repositories of presidential history (all but the Hayes library and the Nixon library, which is privately operated). Indeed, there never used to be a set tradition that preserved a president's papers and artifacts. Some of the material from earlier chief executives was destroyed, damaged, lost, or otherwise dispersed by a president's heirs. Material prior to Herbert Hoover's administration is scattered through historical societies, private collections, and in part within the Library of Congress. The Rutherford B. Hayes Presidential Center was the first institution of its kind, and Franklin D. Roosevelt used that model in creating his own library, turning material over in 1939 for that work to begin.

Few might realize that President Franklin Roosevelt introduced the system of archiving that most former presidents follow today, with the building eventually deeded over and maintained by the federal government. Using this model, Congress passed the Presidential Libraries Act in 1955, whereby the National Archives has the authority to accept papers, artifacts, land, and buildings to establish a presidential library. Following the Watergate controversy, in which the Nixon administration guarded historical materials, Congress took possession of certain Nixon records with the Presidential Recordings and Materials Preservation Act of 1974. The Presidential Records Act of 1978 established that presidential records that document the constitutional, statutory, and ceremonial duties of the president are government property. Further, the Presidential Libraries Act of 1986 made significant changes to these libraries, requiring private endowments linked to the size of the facility in order to offset a portion of the maintenance costs.

This act also mandated that the National Archives preserve, process, and prepare presidential papers and material for public exploration at the offices in College Park, Maryland (just outside Washington, D.C.). When a president leaves office and until a library is built and transferred to the government, the NARA establishes a presidential project to begin collections.

Today, there are ten presidential libraries, the Nixon Presidential Materials Staff (separate from his private library), and the project established for President Bill Clinton until his library is constructed.

The following describes presidential libraries in brief detail and gives the contact information you would need to visit and explore a bit of American history on your own. For more detail, read *Presidential Libraries and Museums: An Illustrated Guide* by Pat Hyland (Congressional Quarterly Inc., 1995).

Rutherford B. Hayes Presidential Center

Opened May 30, 1916 in Fremont, Ohio, the Rutherford B. Hayes Presidential Center was founded by President Hayes's son Webb C. Hayes and the Ohio Historical Society. This tribute was the first of its kind. In 1982, it was expanded and given its present name. The museum and library are housed in a two-story building of classical proportions. President and Mrs. Hayes's thirty-three-room mansion was opened to the public in 1966. The meeting center was once a nineteenth-century Victorian building. As you'll find at many other libraries and museums, the former president and his beloved wife are also buried on the grounds. The library takes you through Hayes's career prior to the presidency, his administration and family life, and his devotion to ending Reconstruction and preserving nationalism. Other exhibits feature military equipment, including weapons General Hayes used during the Civil War. You can reach the Hayes Presidential Center by calling (419) 332-2081. It's located at Spiegel Grove, 1337 Hayes Avenue, Fremont, Ohio 43420.

Herbert Hoover Presidential Library

Presidential libraries aren't necessarily constructed and dedicated in the same order as the presidential roster. That was certainly the case with this library, as those for Roosevelt, Truman, and Eisenhower were already established by the time this library was dedicated on August 10, 1962. The exhibits tell how President Harry Truman called upon Hoover to head two post–World War II global relief missions that kept people from starving, and how this work was similar to Hoover's efforts following World War I. At the dedication ceremony, Hoover explained why his library is located in West Branch: because, although he took few, if any, material assets from the town, what he did carry with him he considered far more precious—religious faith, warm childhood recollections, and the family disciplines of hard work. Galleries explore his White House years and his retirement to New York's elegant Waldorf

Towers, where he wrote books and articles and supported many other causes. Other aspects to the complex include the birthplace cottage, the blacksmith shop, the Friends meeting house, a one-story schoolhouse, and the gravesites of Herbert and Lou Henry Hoover. For more information, call the library at (319) 643-5301. The National Park Service Visitor Center is on Parkside Drive and Main Street, not far from Interstate 80, in West Branch, Iowa.

The Franklin D. Roosevelt Library and Museum

Because FDR was elected to an unprecedented four terms, this library has a lot to offer, from his boyhood memories to a view of the Oval Office desk as it must have been during his twelve years as president. Of course, much of Roosevelt's New Deal is explored in exhibits covering his now-famous first 100 days in office, characterized by more than a dozen actions that set the country on a recovery path. Wartime efforts for achieving peace are chronicled, and so, too, are the more personal sides to Roosevelt, including fireside chats and his dog Fala. In the Eleanor Roosevelt Gallery, added to the original library in 1972, you'll learn about her dedication to FDR's political career after his bout with polio, her tough stands on issues, and her service as a United Nations delegate. Just behind the library and museum is the Franklin D. Roosevelt National Historic Site, the lifelong home of the thirty-second president. The Roosevelt library is approximately two hours from New York City, located at 511 Albany Post Road, Hyde Park, New York 12538. Call (914) 229-9115 for more information.

The Harry S. Truman Library

When the town of Independence, where Truman lived before and after his presidency, offered to donate land for his library, work began on the site in 1955. Local architect Alonzo H. Gentry, with the assistance of Edward Neild, completed the building in two years. The style is somewhat modern, yet the square entrance columns give it a classic Egyptian look. There are video presentations, the table and chair the president used to sign the Truman Doctrine, and the Steinway piano he often played. Photographs are prominent, including the famously inaccurate headline "Dewey Defeats Truman." The Truman Library is approximately ten miles east of downtown Kansas City on U.S. Highway 24 and Delaware, Independence, Missouri 64050. Call (816) 833-1225 or (816) 833-1400 for prerecorded information.

The Eisenhower Center

If you ever wondered about the origins of Eisenhower's nickname "Ike," you'll find the answer here in a complex of five buildings. Dedicated May 1, 1962, the center includes a library, visitor center, the family home (on its original site), a museum, and the place of meditation (the final resting place for Dwight, Mamie, and Doud Eisenhower). You can't miss the eleven-foot statue of Eisenhower, *The Soldier,* which was a gift from Harry Darby, a former U.S. senator representing Kansas. It rests on a five-sided pedestal of Georgia granite. One of the exhibits includes the D-day planning table, a mahogany Sheraton pedestal table with twelve Chippendale chairs, from which General Eisenhower gave orders to launch the massive Allied invasion of Normandy that brought freedom to Europe and peace to the United States as well. To reach the Eisenhower Center, call (913) 263-4751. It's located two miles south of the Abilene exit off Interstate 70 on Kansas Highway 15 (also called Buckeye Avenue).

The John F. Kennedy Library and Museum

Located at Columbia Point with a beautiful view toward Boston Harbor, made complete by his sloop *Victura* cradled on the lawn outside, this museum was designed by architect I. M. Pei and was dedicated on October 20, 1979. It underwent a redesign in 1993. Begin your tour with a film in which JFK himself narrates the story of his early life, then step back in time as the library recreates the Kennedy presidency. The 1960 campaign leads up to the Kennedy–Nixon debates, where you'll find a reproduction of the Chicago television studio where they actually took place. Election results were so close that Kennedy retired for the night, as many Americans did, not knowing the outcome. He was the first Catholic president, and the youngest man ever elected to the job. His inaugural address won't disappoint you, no matter how many times you've heard it.

A symbolic portal welcomes you to the White House corridor, where you'll find presidential gifts from world leaders. Of course, you can learn more about the space program, the Cuban Missile Crisis, and the Peace Corps, and you'll see the Oval Office as it appeared in June 1963 with JFK's desk, rocking chair, and globe. After such splendor, pass through a dark corridor where Walter Cronkite tells a stunned nation, through his own visible emotion, that the thirty-fifth president is now dead. When the museum received many historical artifacts from the estate of Jacqueline Kennedy Onassis, it expanded in 1997 with a stronger presence by the former first lady. Each year, the Kennedy Library Foundation presents the John F. Kennedy Profile in Courage Award to an individual who exemplifies political courage as Kennedy defined it in his Pulitzer Prize–winning book of the same title. The Kennedy Library is adjacent to the University of Massachusetts/Boston Harbor Campus. For more information, call (617) 929-4523. The John F. Kennedy National Historic Site (JFK's Brookline birthplace) is administered by the National Park Service. Call (617) 566-7937.

The Lyndon Baines Johnson Library

Dedicated May 22, 1971, this was the first presidential library to be placed on a college campus. This one sits at the University of Texas at Austin. In conjunction with the library is a graduate school of public affairs. The eight-story structure overlooks the campus. When you enter the modern building, notice the travertine marble throughout the structure. In the Orientation Theater, see the documentary film on LBJ's life and career. Don't miss the bronze busts of LBJ and Lady Bird Johnson, works designed by sculptor Robert Berks. There are letters to Mrs. Johnson from White House residents from Jackie Kennedy to Bill Clinton. One exhibit chronicles that fateful motorcade in Dallas where Johnson took the oath of office aboard *Air Force One*, following Kennedy's assassination. Suddenly your thoughts arrive at Andrews Air Force Base, just as Johnson did, addressing a shaken nation. Reflecting happier times, you'll see the family album with photographs of Lynda and Luci and their families. You'll learn about LBJ's vision for a Great Society, and even a little about the culture of the 1960s. Find the Johnson Library at 2313 Red River Street, Austin, Texas 78705, or call (512) 482-5279.

The Richard Nixon Library and Birthplace

Dedicated on July 19, 1990 in Yorba Linda, California, this is the only one of the presidential libraries to be totally operated with private funds. The complex spans nine acres on which Nixon's parents worked when it was a citrus grove. Designed by Langdon Wilson Architecture and Planning in Newport Beach, California, the library has an atmosphere that is traditional rather than monumental. A fountain greets you out front. Visitors are reminded of Nixon's Quaker heritage by the high-peaked ceiling reminiscent of Quaker meeting halls. Exhibits chronicle Nixon's early life, his marriage to Pat, and the young Nixon family with their daughters. Since Nixon became vice president when television was taking hold, you can see five minutes of his black-and-white televised address to the nation on September 23, 1952, with his famous rebuttal to charges that he kept a secret slush fund while a senator. It became known as the Checkers speech. The years from his 1960 presidential race to resuming his law practice upon that election's loss and then to his comeback in the 1968 campaign are all outlined. The presidential focus features foreign affairs, where the president was particularly skilled, including a photo of this first American president to travel to Communist China. Discover Pat Nixon's life and travels as first lady as well as the dresses from their daughters' weddings. A long, darkened corridor titled "Watergate: The Final Campaign" ends with the former president waving goodbye on August 9, 1974. Read a transcript or listen to the recorded conversation Nixon had with his chief of staff Bob Haldeman—a conversation known as the smoking gun. Nixon's post-presidential work is also recounted. Exiting, you enter the formal garden surrounding the reflecting pool. From here it's a short walk to Nixon's birthplace (a modest farmhouse), and along the path you'll discover the simply marked burial site of Richard and Pat Nixon. The address of the Nixon Library is 18001 Yorba Linda Boulevard, Yorba Linda, California 92686. Call (714) 993-3393 for more information.

The Gerald R. Ford Library

This president's archives are located on the campus of his alma mater, the University of Michigan, and Ford's museum sits within his old congressional district that he served for twenty-five years. The complex is built along the west bank of the Grand River. It's a sleek architectural design by Marvin De Winter Associates, made even more impressive by the fountain and reflecting pool. Learn about Ford's life of public service. What surprises the average visitor is the fact that Gerald Ford wasn't born with that name, but the name of Leslie L. King Jr. After his mother fled an abusive marriage, taking her son with her, she met and married Gerald R. Ford, and at the age of twenty-two, Leslie King Jr., changed his name to Gerald R. Ford Jr., in honor of the father who raised him. You'll see a copy of the Twenty-fifth Amendment to the Constitution, which states that whenever there is a vacancy in the office of vice president, the president shall nominate a vice president who shall take office upon confirmation by both Houses of Congress. Tally sheets document Ford's confirmation, and another exhibit profiles the man who became Ford's vice president—Nelson Rockefeller. Letters regarding Ford's pardon to President Nixon are displayed, and the campaign against the relatively unknown Jimmy Carter shows up as well. You can find the Ford Library at 303 Pearl Street, N.W., Grand Rapids, Michigan 49504, or call (616) 451-9263.

The Carter Presidential Center

In their book *Everything to Gain*, the Carters describe finding the perfect site for their library in the heart of Atlanta, with an impressive view of the Atlanta skyline. In architectural terms, it's understated, with two small lakes separating the high-traffic library and the remaining buildings. In the exhibit honoring the century's presidents, the description above Jimmy Carter's name reads "peacemaker/protector of human rights." Historic photos such as the one of Carter shaking hands with Egyptian President Anwar Sadat and Israeli Prime Minister Menachem Begin are proud reminders of his strides in foreign relations. An interactive town meeting area is set up where, in recordings, Carter answers typical questions. Rosalynn Carter is revealed more as the president's partner, showing her as a mental health advocate with an impressive record. The Carter Center is about fifteen miles from Atlanta's Hartsfield International Airport and only three miles from downtown Atlanta, located at One Copenhill Avenue, Atlanta, Georgia 30307. You can call (404) 331-0296.

The Ronald Reagan Library

The president's library was dedicated November 4, 1991, in Simi Valley, California. Presidents Ford, Nixon, Bush, Reagan, and Carter stood in a replica of the Oval Office to have their photo taken during the dedication of Ronald Reagan's library, which is set in the rugged Western landscape that both Ronald and Nancy Reagan loved. It's a rambling Spanish-mission-style building designed by the architectural firm of Stubbins Associates using redwood and adobe tile. View a documentary film on Reagan's life leading up to his job as commander in chief. Those early years include his Hollywood Wall, as the former president made fifty-three films in his prior career. In this part of the museum, you'll find the only picture of Reagan's first wife, actress Jane Wyman. His movie career interrupted by World War II, Reagan also served as the public relations speaker for General Electric Company, largely in the 1950s. His political life includes serving as president of the Screen Actors Guild, supporting Barry Goldwater's unsuccessful presidential bid in 1964, and then making it to the governor's mansion in California. In the section covering Reagan as president, exhibits range from prosperity to peace and freedom, the end of the

Cold War, and life in the White House. In the first lady's gallery, the spotlight shines on his wife, with the video *Nancy Reagan: A Personal Portrait.* As you return to the lobby, notice the authentic section of the Berlin Wall with a marker bearing Reagan's words " . . . to every person trapped in tyranny . . . our message must be: Your struggle is our struggle, your dream is our dream, and someday you, too, will be free." The library is located at 40 Presidential Drive, Simi Valley, California 93065; you can also call (805) 522-8444.

The George Bush Presidential Library and Museum

This 69,000-square-foot complex, made of limestone and granite and dedicated on Noverber 6, 1997, is located on a ninety-acre site on the West Campus of Texas A&M University. It sits on a plaza adjoining the Presidential Conference Center and the Texas A&M Academic Center. It was the tenth presidential library operated by the National Archives, and when it opened, Presidents Ford, Carter, Bush, and Clinton were together along with the first ladies (including Nancy Reagan, who represented her husband). Inside, visitors will find a World War II Avenger Bomber along with other memorabilia pertaining to Bush's service during the war. There are replicas of the office the former president used at Camp David and in *Air Force One*. The museum collection also contains approximately 60,000 historical objects, ranging from gifts from heads of state or ordinary Americans to personally used items; thousands of hours of audio recordings and videotape; and approximately 1 million photographs. One unique feature of this library is the classroom to be used by student groups as a computer learning lab or as a traditional classroom—the first of its kind in the presidential library network. Also on the university campus is the Bush School of Government and Public Service. For more information, call (979) 260-9554. The library is located at 1000 George Bush Drive West, College Station, Texas 77845.

The William J. Clinton Presidential Center

At press time, plans for President Bill Clinton's library were just beginning to take shape. However, we do know that it will be in Clinton's home state of Arkansas on the banks of the Arkansas River, surrounded by parkland. Clinton, who reportedly has visited seven of the ten presidential libraries, said, "I hope that it will not only allow people to see these remarkable eight years, but will help to empower people and give them the confidence that they can build America's greatest days in the new century." It's expected that the estimated $100 million endeavor will be the largest construction project in Little Rock history, but that it will contribute a substantial amount of revenue to the city as well.

INDEX

Page numbers in italics refer to illustrations.

About the Author

Loriann Hoff Oberlin is a freelance writer and author of numerous books, including *Surviving Separation and Divorce: A Woman's Guide to Making It Through the First Year*, *Working at Home While the Kids Are There, Too*, and *Writing For Money*. She also served as a coauthor on the *Insider's Guide to Pittsburgh* and *The Angry Child* (written with Dr. Tim Murphy).